Laogai—The Chinese Gulag

Laogai—The Chinese Gulag

Hongda Harry Wu

Translated by Ted Slingerland

Foreword by Fang Lizhi

Westview Press

BOULDER • SAN FRANCISCO • OXFORD

Published in 1992 in the United States of America by Westview Press, Inc., 5500 Central Avenue, Boulder, Colorado 80301, and in the United Kingdom by Westview Press, 36 Lonsdale Road, Summertown, Oxford OX2 7EW

Library of Congress Cataloging-in-Publication Data
Wu, Hongda Harry.
    Laogai, the Chinese Gulag / cHongda Harry Wu; translated by Ted Slingerland; foreword by Fang Lizhi.
        p. cm.
    Includes bibliographical references and index.
    ISBN 0-8133-8154-1. ISBN 0-8133-1769-X (pb.)
    1. Concentration camps—China. 2. Political prisoners—China.
3. Forced labor—China. I. Slingerland, Ted. II. Title.
HV8964.C5W8 1992
365'.45'0951—dc20   91-27452
                                                                              CIP

Printed and bound in the United States of America

The paper used in this publication meets the requirements of the American National Standard for Permanence of Paper for Printed Library Materials Z39.48-1984.

10   9   8   7   6   5   4   3

Contents

Illustrations

Foreword

In the past forty years under the Communist regime in China, the term *human rights* has rarely been seen in public because it was classified into the category of anti-Communist ideas and was forbidden to be mentioned. This led to the creation of the long-standing impression that no records of violations of human rights had been found in China.

Obviously, this situation itself is evidence to show how serious is the human rights record in China. No record is the worst record. For instance, in the 1957 anti-rightist campaign probably as many as 500,000 persons were punished in one way or another; some lost their jobs, some were sent to labor reform camps. Many of them died or disappeared under the punishments without a trace of when, where, and how these persons had been treated.

In the past decade, under Deng Xiaoping's reform, the Chinese authorities wanted to show to the world that there were no human rights problems in China. However, the authorities had made no change in their policies forbidding outsiders to look up human rights records in China. In 1986 two of my colleagues and I made plans to organize an academic conference on the thirtieth anniversary of the Anti-Rightist Movement. The aim was to look back at the Anti-Rightist Movement from a perspective of thirty years and to establish a record of the true history of this period. Our plan was promptly suppressed by the authorities. In mid-December 1986, we sent out our first announcement of the conference. The authorities acted quickly. Two weeks later there was no alternative except for us to announce that the conference could not be held. This showed that, even for events of human rights violations that had taken place thirty years earlier, the Communist authorities remained unwilling to allow the slightest opening of the records to the public. This is one of the aspects of Deng's so-called openness.

Therefore, one of the tasks of protesting human rights in China is to unmask the real records in the past four decades and in present days. The 1989 Beijing massacre is, in fact, only the tip of the iceberg and does not reveal the scale of the violations of human rights in China.

I greatly appreciate Professor Hongda Harry Wu's writing this book on the Chinese Gulag. As he mentions, the number of labor reform camps now known in China is 990. No detailed information of the population of such camps is available. But several camps, such as Qinghe Farm of Beijing, Koryile Labor Reform Detachment of Xinjiang, and No. 2 Labor Reform Detachment of Qinghai, have populations ranging from 50,000 to 80,000 of which about 10 percent are counter-revolutionary prisoners, the synonym of *political prisoners* in Chinese. Because the concept of human rights is no different in the East than in the West, the principle of human rights befits the East as well as the West. I am sure that this book will lead more people all over the world to concern themselves with human rights in China under the spirit of the universality of human rights.

Fang Lizhi

Preface and Acknowledgments

The grandfather of Communist theory, Karl Marx, in *The Communist Manifesto* (published in 1848) said that "A spectre is haunting Europe—the spectre of Communism." Sixty-nine years later this "spectre" came to earth in Russia, and another thirty-two years after that it appeared in China. During the middle of the twentieth century, communism spread to encompass much of the world. Marx's prophecy, it seemed, had been fulfilled.

However, as the end of the twentieth century approaches, it has recently become apparent that the days of this spectre's sojourn upon earth are numbered.

When communism arrived in China, it merged with an already deeply entrenched feudalism, producing a new hybrid. This hybrid form of communism, in comparison with standard Marxism or Leninism-Stalinism, contains even more inconsistencies, is even more ruthless in outlook, and presents a significantly greater danger.

This Chinese hybrid seems as if it will linger as the last strain of communism left in the world. One of the most frightening aspects of this last example of communism is its use of a system designed to physically and spiritually destroy human beings—a system deceptively packaged in seemingly innocuous governmental policies.

As a survivor of nineteen years of imprisonment in a labor reform camp, or *laogaidui,* I feel that the investigation of the subject of labor reform camps in the People's Republic of China is both a personal responsibility and a matter that cannot be ignored by civilized society.

In 1933, Nazi Germany established its first concentration camps. Although the actual total number of prisoners in Nazi concentration camps will probably never be known with exactitude, Eugen Kogon's estimate of 2,151,200 is considered the most reliable.[1] To this figure must be added approximately 4 million Jews murdered in the six Nazi *Vernichtungslagern* (extermination camps), 220,000 Gypsies, and about 6 million Soviet Prisoners of War (POWs) also incarcerated in concentration camps. None of the first two of these categories of prisoners, it might be added, were ever registered, so the exact figures are not firmly known. In all, Kogon lists 7,820,000, of whom no more than 700,000 survived.[2] The survival rate of Soviet POWs was also very small. However, many Soviet POWs joined the Nazis, becoming HIWIS (*Hilfs-willinge,* i.e., volunteers). Moreover, the figures cited here relate only to concentration camps established after 1934 under the authority of the Schutzstaffel (the SS). An unknown number of "wild camps"—with an estimated 27,000 prisoners—were created and disbanded under the authority of the Sturmabteilung (the SA) in 1933.

Also clouding estimates of camp population is the fact that an inmate could be released from the German camps until 1936; in fact, 75 percent of those held in 1933 were released by January 1936. Thereafter, inmate release—except under exceptional circumstances—was not permitted. Jewish men incarcerated after *Kristallnacht* (November 9–10, 1938), for example, could be released only if their family could prove to the local Gestapo that they would be emigrating shortly.[3] In sum, a minimum of 7 million inmates (including 4 million Jews sent directly to extermination camps) and another 6 million Soviet POWs perished in the Nazi camps between 1933 and 1945.

The first gulags in the Soviet Union were established under Lenin in the period between 1917 and 1921.[4] Stalin built on the Leninist camps, developing them into a full-scale concentration camp system on the Nazi model. There was, however, one difference, insofar as no extermination camps per se were ever built in the Soviet Union. There is no generally agreed upon figure for the number of victims of the Leninist/Stalinist camps, although Robert Conquest has estimated a total of 10 million victims during the Stalinist terror of the late 1930s.[5] Of course, not all of these victims died in Soviet camps. As with the Nazi concentration camps, there are a large number of reports, novels, and other material documenting the Soviet labor camps, one of the most powerful of which is the Nobel prize–winning *The Gulag Archipelago* by Aleksandr Solzhenitsyn. Hence the word *gulag* has become synonymous with the Soviet labor camps, which still exist today, albeit reduced in scope.[6]

In order to uphold its rule and to suppress its people, every dictatorship must be accompanied by a prison system, whether it be a concentration camp (in which the death of the prisoner is the ultimate goal) or a labor camp (in which the prisoner's work is exploited for economic gain). The Chinese Communist labor reform camps (*laogaidui*) have been in existence for over forty years, and in every respect—in terms of scope, cruelty, and the number of people imprisoned—they rival the Nazi and Soviet systems.

However, the world knows very little about the reality of the Chinese labor reform camps. The reasons for this are numerous and complex:

cultural and political differences between East and West, the West's concern for its strategic interests, and the success of long-term political propaganda and secrecy by the Chinese Communist Party.

Indeed, several difficulties are encountered in researching the Chinese Communist labor camps. For one thing, it has been over forty years since the founding of the People's Republic of China, but the basic laws essential to legitimize a nation have never been completely formulated. Take, for example, the Constitution, of which there have been four versions in forty years. The Constitution has not only lost its authority and integrity due to these constant revisions, it has also never, in the actual political and social life of mainland China, achieved any real respect. Guiding principles and policies of the Chinese Communist Party serve in place of law. These are spread by means of numerous "documents" that come from every branch of the Chinese Communist Party and even include "instructions" and "spiritual talks" by every level of party leader from Mao Zedong down. As a popular saying in mainland China has it, "policy is better than law, and leadership is better than policy."

For the past forty years, there has been virtually no law to abide by in mainland China. Only in 1980, after the People's Republic of China had been in existence for thirty-two years, was a criminal code established. In the early 1960s, Mao Zedong announced that China must establish a criminal code and so brought together specialists who, depending heavily upon the Soviet model, compiled the Criminal Code Draft, which was revised over thirty times. At no point, however, was this code formally approved by the supreme judicial organization— National People's Congress—or made public. Only in 1980, under the direction of Deng Xiaoping's Four Basic Principles, was a criminal code disseminated.

A second difficulty is that "convicted labor reform" (*laogai*, or labor reform accompanied by arrest and conviction) has been the subject of thirty-six documents at the central level of authority since 1949, according to Chinese Communist Party sources. Four of these documents (11 percent) have been approved by the National People's Congress. The other thirty-two documents are all regulations and notices from Public Security and other administrative departments.[7] Furthermore, for the practice of reeducation through labor (*laojiao*), only two documents have the status of law: Resolutions Concerning Reeducation Through Labor, approved in 1957 by the National People's Congress, and Supplementary Regulations of 1979.

However, when the organs for reeducation through labor in each locality now examine and approve cases, they no longer rely on these two documents but operate under the provisions of Experimental Methods in Reeducation Through Labor, formulated in 1982 by the Public Security Bureau (and labeled as an internal document of the central authorities). This document has never been examined or approved by the National People's Congress, nor has it been publicized. This kind of "internal document," especially when formulated by Public Security and other security departments, is always handled as a special classified document. Anyone discovered leaking these documents may be convicted as a counter-revolutionary who has "stolen and sold state secrets."

Yet a third difficulty is that the labor reform system is off limits in mainland China. Over the past forty years, no national or local newspaper, magazine, or government document has reported on the number of camps, the number of prisoners, the general scope of labor reform; or the number, categories, and nature of the production from prison labor; or on the daily life of the prisoners. What does appear in the press are laudatory statements or articles used as propaganda. Foreigners are only allowed to inspect a restricted number of Potemkin Village–type model prisons. All labor reform camps are given ordinary farm or factory enterprise names. They are a closely guarded secret from the average Chinese citizen—let alone people outside mainland China.

These circumstances undoubtedly make accuracy in the research of labor reform difficult. I hope specialists in various fields will kindly offer corrections for the occasional unavoidable mistakes and deficiencies of this book. I also hope that someday the Chinese Communist authorities will fully reveal to the world the true extent and nature of the *laogaidui*.

The materials cited in this book are all from newspapers, magazines, official documents, and internal documents of the Chinese Communist Party of the People's Republic of China. My personal experience in twelve labor reform camps over nineteen years and what I have seen and heard over the past forty years in mainland China are naturally other important sources of information.

I would like to thank all those who helped—directly or indirectly—make this book a reality, especially the following institutions and individuals: The Hoover Institution on War, Revolution, and Peace; The Pacific Cultural Foundation; The Institute of International Relations; Prof. Wu Yuan-Li; Dr. Ramon Myers; Prof. Li Ta-Ling; John Creger; Ted Slingerland; Huang Lin; Lin Dan; Prof. Chiu Hungdah; Martin Husmann; Prof. Andrew J. Nathan; and Chen Ching-Lee. Thanks also to Abraham and Hershel Edelheit for their review. I would also like to thank Susan

McEachern, Libby Barstow, and all the people at Westview Press for their patience and understanding.

Hongda Harry Wu

Notes

1. Eugen Kogon, *The Theory and Practice of Hell* (New York: Farrar, Straus, and Giroux, 1950), p. 254.

2. Ibid., p. 254. Kogon includes Jews and Gypsies, but not Soviet POWs, in this figure.

3. The best introductory overview of the Nazi concentration camps is Konnilyn Feig's *Hitler's Death Camps* (New York: Holmes & Meier, 1981).

4. James Bunyan, *The Origins of Forced Labor in the Soviet State, 1917–1921* (Baltimore, MD: Johns Hopkins University Press, 1967).

5. Robert Conquest, *The Great Terror* (New York: Macmillan, 1973).

6. Avraham Shifrin, *The First Guidebook to Prisons and Concentration Camps of the Soviet Union* (New York: Bantam Books, 1982).

7. Faxue (Legal Studies) (Shanghai: Huadong, June 1985), p. 12.

1

Introduction

The labor reform system in the People's Republic of China (PRC) consists of three distinct categories: convicted labor reform (CLR; *laogai*), reeducation through labor (RTL; *laojiao*), and forced job placement (FJP; *jiuye*). Generally referred to as labor reform camps (LRCs; *laogaidui*), the labor reform system functions as the prison system of the Chinese Communist Party (CCP). It serves an important organizational role in the autocratic system of the PRC; indeed, labor reform camps are a necessary product of the Chinese totalitarian state.

The labor reform system is governed by three policies that have remained essentially unchanged for over thirty years. Their influence and the extent of suffering they have caused is incalculable. These policies are

1. Labor Reform Policies, approved by the People's Republic of China State Council on August 26, 1954, and promulgated on September 7 of the same year.[1]
2. Temporary Disciplinary Methods for the Release of Criminals Completing Their Terms and for the Implementation of Forced Job Placement, approved by the twenty-second plenary session of the Government Administration Council on August 29, 1954, and promulgated on September 7 of the same year.[2]
3. Reeducation Through Labor Policies, approved at the seventy-eighth plenary session of the National People's Congress (NPC) and promulgated by the State Council on August 3, 1957. It was amended on November 29, 1979, by the issuing of Supplementary Reeducation Through Labor Regulations.[3]

After Deng Xiaoping came to power in 1978, new policies in government, economy, culture, and law as well as the appeals for "reform" and "openness" have attracted the attention of the world. But the labor reform policy established in Mao's era, except for some slight modifications in measures and regulations, has remained essentially unchanged. In fact, certain aspects of the labor reform policies have been expanded and strengthened.

When the CCP came to power in 1949, the regime relied on the Marxist-Leninist theory of class struggle as its guiding principle. Although the power of the CCP has been firmly established for many years, the CCP still maintains that "class struggle is very intense in China" and that "the problem of who shall emerge victorious" has not yet been resolved. Therefore, the leadership claims, it is necessary to employ various methods, including suppression by police powers and the establishment of the *laogaidui* system, to eliminate all "class enemies" and "anti-socialist elements."

In 1957, Mao proclaimed "six criteria for political words and deeds" for the Chinese people: (1) words and deeds should help to unite, not to divide, the people of all ethnic groups in China; (2) they should be beneficial and not harmful to socialist transformation and socialist construction; (3) they should help to consolidate, and not undermine or weaken, the people's democratic dictatorship; (4) they should help to consolidate, not undermine or weaken, democratic centralism; (5) they should help to strengthen and not weaken the leadership of the Communist Party; and (6) they should be beneficial and not harmful to international socialist unity and the unity of all the peace-loving people of the world.

Mao went on to say that "of these six criteria, the most important are the two concerning the socialist path and leadership of the Party."[4] In mainland China, whoever does not act or speak in accordance with these six criteria is an "enemy of the people."[5] Mao further stated, "Towards enemies, the people's democratic dictatorship uses the method of dictatorship . . . [that] compels them to engage in labor, and, through such labor, be transformed into new men."[6]

In 1978, Deng Xiaoping, the leader of the PRC for the past ten years, announced the "four cardinal principles": "First of all we must uphold the socialist path; secondly, we must uphold the dictatorship of the proletariat; thirdly, we must uphold the leadership of the Communist Party; fourthly, we must uphold Marxism-Leninism and Mao Zedong Thought."[7] He continued, "In our socialist society [there is a] special form of struggle. . . . It is still necessary to exercise dictatorship over these anti-socialist elements. . . . This dictatorship is an internal struggle and in some cases an international struggle as well. . . . So long as class struggle exists and so long as imperialism and hegemonism exist, it is inconceivable that the dictatorial function of the state should wither away."[8]

There is little difference between Deng Xiaoping's four cardinal principles and Mao Zedong's six criteria for political words and deeds. Both of them uphold class struggle and Lenin's theory: "Dictatorship is based directly upon force and unrestricted by any law."[9] It is inconceivable that labor reform in the PRC will be abandoned or changed before the dictatorship itself is abandoned or changed.

Even before 1949, the CCP had already established a certain type of labor reform camp. However, the Party did not immediately formulate related laws or establish labor reform teams across the country upon its assumption of power. In the Agrarian Land Reform[10] and Suppression of Counter-revolutionaries[11] movements of the early 1950s, millions of people were publicly arrested or executed without the benefit of any legal process whatsoever because the CCP believes that "law does not have this kind of power." The Party must rely on mass movements . . . for thorough elimination of "class enemies."[12] This phenomenon occurred again during the Cultural Revolution (1966–1976) when millions of people were arbitrarily persecuted beyond the framework of any legal process.

Nazi Germany's concentration camps lasted more than ten years. To support a war economy, the Nazis often forced camp prisoners to labor for a limited period of time and then brutally eliminated them. The Nazis also ran slave labor camps (such as the factories in Auschwitz III/Monowitz—also known as the Buna-Werke). However, they did not apply systematic methods derived from political theories to impose "mind reform," as they were uninterested in long-term productive tools.

The Soviet labor camps were founded in the period from 1917 through 1921. The system was formally codified under the Legal Code for Labor Reform of 1933. In 1961, the Soviet Union promulgated Decrees for Strengthening the Struggle with Social Parasites Who Avoid Beneficial Labor and Lead Anti-Social Lives, similar in content to the CCP's Reeducation Through Labor Policies of 1957. Today the Soviet Union has labor camps of various forms: labor camps for general labor reform, labor reform camps for special punishment, labor reform camps for juveniles, territories for exile, territories for labor reform of migrants, and prisons. Yet the absolute and proportionate number of Soviet labor camps and the number of prisoners they contain is less than in the People's Republic of China. The purpose of the Soviet labor camps is suppression and punishment—not the systematic, complete "thought reform" emphasized by the PRC camps. Furthermore, the economic value of the products from the Soviet camps is only a small percentage of total national production, and currently available sources, including *The Gulag Archipelago,* suggest that the treatment prisoners receive in

CHART 1.1 The Public Security–Judiciary–Labor Reform Camp System of the People's Republic of China

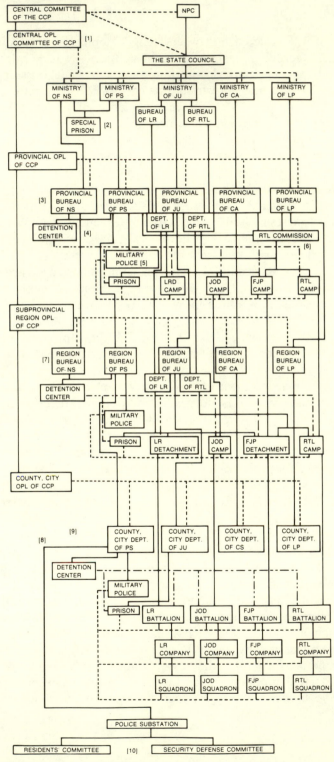

[1] At all levels in the CCP there is a commission of politics and law (OPL) for supervising the same level's administrative department. [2] Special prisons are directly under the control of the National Security Ministry (NS) and Public Security Ministry (PS) and unrelated to the Judiciary (JU). The number of the special prisons is secret. [3] Provincial level refers to the cities directly under the central government, provinces, and autonomous regions. This is the departmental (bureau) level. [4] Detention center: All levels of prisoners in the detention centers are under the control of Public Security and National Security. The prisoners are, through various means, sent to prisons, labor reform disciplinary production camps, juvenile offenders disciplinary camps, and RTL camps, which are under the control of the Judiciary. [5] People's military police headquarters, brigades, companies, and platoons are responsible for suppression, arrest, and execution. They are directly under the control of the Public Security Department. The military police force is part of a system that is distinct and separate from that of the labor reform camp police force. [6] RTL commission: In every province, municipality, autonomous region, and large and mid-sized city, a commission for the administration of reeducation through labor is organized by the departments of Public Security, Judiciary, Civil Administration, and Labor and Personnel. This commission is responsible for inspection and approval. The RTL camps are administered by the RTL Bureau of the Judiciary. [7] Region level refers to regions, cities, and autonomous prefectures. This is the bureau level. [8] County level refers to counties and autonomous counties. This is the level of bureau divisions. [9] There is no National Security Department at the county level. [10] In all districts, on all streets of all cities, there are many residents' committees, and each working unit there has a security defense committee; both committees are under the control of CCP branches and police substations.

CCP: Chinese Communist Party; NPC: National People's Congress; OPL: Office of Politics and Law; NS: National Security; PS: Public Security; JU: Judiciary; CA: Civil Administration; LP: Labor and Personnel; LR: Labor Reform; LRD: Labor Reform Disciplinary Production Camp; JOD: Juvenile Offenders Disciplinary Camp; FJP: Forced Job Placement Camp; RTL: Reeducation Through Labor Camp; ——: Command channel; ---: Supervisory channel; —--: Transfer channel.

---

the Soviet labor camps is better than that in the CCP labor reform camps.

The *laogaidui* system consists of six parts: detention centers, prisons, labor reform disciplinary production camps, juvenile offenders' camps, RTL camps, and FJP camps (see Chart 1.1).

Politically, the labor reform system of the CCP is the same as its Soviet and Nazi German counterparts. All use violence to suppress political dissidents. However, the labor reform system of the CCP differs from the other two in its conception and means of suppression—"mind reform through forced labor." In economic terms, the labor reform system of the CCP also differs from the other two in that it forces work not only from prisoners but also from those who already have completed their term. In the PRC, labor reform camps are an economic enterprise. The products of the prisoners' labor are sold in domestic as well as foreign markets and have become an indispensable component of the national economy.

For all these reasons, I believe that it is time for the international community to become as aware of the labor reform system of the CCP as it is of its two more infamous counterparts.

The Organization and Distribution
of Labor Reform Camps

Laogaidui, or labor reform camps (LRC), is a political term invented by the CCP after it came to power in 1949. Though the term literally means "labor reform team" in Chinese, it actually refers to a labor reform camp or prison under the control of the CCP Public Security Ministry. The meaning of the term was broader during the Cultural Revolution, when it also meant "cowsheds," "May 7 cadre schools," and "bases for the sent-down" founded by all levels of party organizations, Red Guards, and rebels. Except during this particular period, the term *laogaidui* refers to labor reform camps controlled by six organs under the auspices of Public Security and the Judiciary (see Chart 1.2).

Laogaidui hold three types of personnel (*sanleirenyuan*). This term, for internal use by the Public Security Bureau, refers to (1) prisoners who have been arrested, convicted, and subjected to labor reform (so-called convicted labor reform, or CLR); (2) prisoners subjected to reeducation through labor (RTL); and (3) people subjected to forced job placement (FJP) in their original labor reform or RTL camps upon completion of their sentence. However, in recent years the CCP has begun using the term "double labor personnel" (*lianglao renyuan*), referring only to CLR and RTL personnel, in an attempt to pretend that those subject to FJP are treated as ordinary citizens.

In fact, all of these "three types of personnel" have been denied their citizens' rights. They are under the control of the Public Security Bureau and are treated as "subjects of the dictatorship of the proletariat." There are between 16–20 million "three types of personnel" in the PRC.

The six organs that constitute the LRC system are described in the sections that follow.

Detention Centers

The main purpose of detention centers is to house criminals who have not yet been sentenced. A vast majority of criminals sentenced to terms of under two years are also confined to detention centers.[13] All criminals, whether sentenced or not, are required by law to engage in forced labor.[14]

In accordance with official regulations,[15] detention centers are established at central, provincial, autonomous regional, and municipal levels as well as in each county-level work unit. At present there are a total of

CHART 1.2 Public Security and the Judiciary

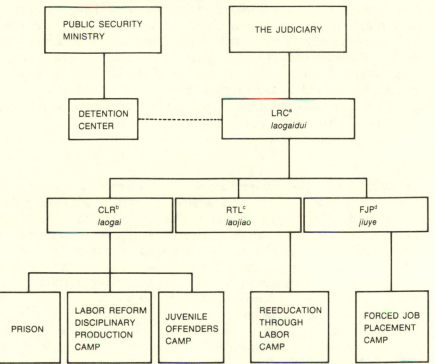

^aLabor Reform Camp. ^bConvicted Labor Reform. ^cReeducation Through Labor. ^dForced Job Placement.

2,046 county-level work units in mainland China. Shanghai Municipality, for example, has about 12–20 detention centers. There are a total of between 2,500 and 3,000 detention centers throughout China.

The number of criminals in detention centers awaiting sentencing fluctuates greatly, often in response to various "political movements" promoted by the Communist government. Most unsentenced prisoners in detention centers either have already been convicted and are waiting to be sent to a prison or labor reform production battalion or an RTL camp, or they are being detained for a certain period of time before being released. There are no statistics indicating how many sentenced prisoners are held in detention centers. If the average number of prisoners in a typical detention center is about 200, the total number of such prisoners in mainland China could be as high as 500,000–600,000.

According to article 92 of China's judicial code (1982), arrested criminals must be tried and sentenced within sixty days. In reality, however, this regulation is completely ignored by the Public Security Bureau. For instance, Yang Wei, a student who spent time abroad studying in America, was arrested on January 11, 1987, and not sentenced until December 1987, approximately eleven months later. There are large numbers of people in detention centers who languish for months, even years, before being sentenced. Some prisoners even spend the rest of their lives in detention centers and die there without ever having been sentenced. One can only imagine how much worse this situation must have been before 1982, when the sixty-day regulation did not even exist.

Prisons

Only criminals who have been arrested and sentenced are confined to prisons. Unfortunately, a lack of available information precludes a discussion of the Communists' secret prisons, although the extent and importance of the secret prison system is significant. For example, a former head of state, Liu Shaoqi, was charged as a counter-revolutionary and eventually died in a building that previously had served as a bank in Kaifeng Municipality, Henan Province. There is no way of telling when or how the old bank was converted into a secret prison.

Mainland China's various provinces, municipalities, and many counties have established only a few prisons. For example, Beijing Municipality has only five publicly acknowledged prisons (not including detention centers or LRCs)—No. 1, No. 2, No. 3, and two other prisons.

Except in name, there is no basic difference between prisons and labor reform disciplinary production camps. According to internal Communist documents, 13 percent of criminals are confined to prisons, 87 percent to labor reform disciplinary production camps. A CCP internal regulation states, "Prisons will house criminals sentenced to death with a two-year reprieve; counter-revolutionaries sentenced to life terms or terms of over five years; common criminals sentenced to terms of over ten years; and special cases such as spies, foreign criminals, criminals with knowledge of classified material, and female criminals."[16] The presence of more serious offenders in prisons is due to the greater degree of strictness and higher level of security in the prisons. For this reason, many special political prisoners—such as Mao's wife, Jiang Qing; Kuomintang high officials Shen Zuei and Du Liming; the former puppet emperor of Manchuria, Pu Yi; democracy activist Wei Jingsheng; Catholic priest Hong Pinmei; and *Life and Death in Shanghai* author Cheng Nian—were confined to prisons. A certain percentage of counter-revolutionaries and common criminals, after displaying "good reformed behavior" for a certain period of time, are sent to continue their terms in labor reform

The entrance of No. 2 Prison of Hunan Province (LRC-08-02). The left signboard reads "The CCP Committee of the No. 2 Prison of Hunan Province." The right signboard reads "Hunan Heavy Truck Plant." In 1987, the plant produced 3,000 heavy trucks, model HN150.

disciplinary production camps. Some labor reform disciplinary production camps, such as those established in the desert regions of Qinghai Province and Xinjiang Uygur Autonomous Region, specialize in handling serious offenders with life terms or with sentences of over ten years. One example is Xinjiang Uygur Autonomous Region's Koria Labor Reform Detachment (LRC-15-17), which is located in the northern regions of the Takelamagan Desert (in the Uygur language, "Takelamagan" means "those who go in don't come out"). One-third of this camp's prisoners have suspended death sentences or life terms.[17]

All prisons house factories or workshops in which all prisoners are forced to labor. Each prison also has an alternate production unit name. For example: Beijing No. 1 Prison (LRC-03-09) is also called Beijing Plastic Factory; Xinjiang No. 3 Prison (LRC-15-21) is also called Xinjiang No. 3 Mechanical Tool Factory; Shaanxi Province No. 2 Prison (LRC-17-14) is also known as Shaanxi Boiler Factory; Shanxi Province No. 3 Prison (LRC-01-07) is also called Fenhe Automotive Factory; Hunan Province No. 2 Prison (LRC-08-02) is also known as Hunan Heavy Truck Factory; Hubei Province No. 3 Prison (LRC-19-28) is also called Jingzhou Textile Dyeing Factory; etc.

The total number of prisons is estimated to be from 1,000–1,500; the number of prisoners confined in each prison can range from 200–5,000. If 400–500 is used as an average number, the total number of criminals confined in prisons would be between 500,000–700,000.

Labor Reform Disciplinary Production Camps

As was stated earlier, 87 percent of the prisoners are confined to this type of camp. For this reason, the term *labor reform camp,* which formally refers only to this type of Convicted Labor Reform Detachment, is often used when discussing the Chinese labor reform system as a whole.

Camps are organized along military lines; prisoners are divided into squadrons, companies, battalions, detachments, and general brigades. Each squadron consists of 10–15 prisoners, with two prisoners appointed by Public Security police to act as squadron leaders. One of these leaders is responsible for "labor production," the other for "thought reform and political education." Companies are the basic organizational unit of the LRC and are rather similar to a military company. Each company consists of 10–15 squadrons. From 3–5 public security cadres are assigned to each company, one acting as overall chief, one as political instructor, and the others as captains. Battalions generally consist of 8–12 companies, with a total of over 1,000 prisoners. Battalions have a commander, a political commissar, and a few "discipline cadres" and administrative personnel. One level above the battalion is the detachment. The detachment corresponds well to the county level of PRC administrative organization. The size of detachments varies greatly. Examples of large detachments include Beijing Municipality's Qinghe Farm (LRC-03-12), Xinjiang Uygur Autonomous Region's Koria Detachment (LRC-15-17), and Qinghai Province's No. 2 Labor Reform Detachment (LRC-16-07), which have a combined prisoner and FJP personnel population of 50,000–80,000. There are also detachments that, because of environmentally limited production capacity, have smaller prisoner populations, for example, Shanxi Province, Huoxian County's Wangzhuang Coal Mine (LRC-01-09), which has approximately 1,200 inmates and is called Shanxi Provincial Labor Reform Production No. 4 Independent Detachment. A detachment is a complete entity unto itself, an independent administration and work unit that under various names manages its own financing, production, sales, and cost accounting. In the past ten years, with Deng Xiaoping's economic reforms, each detachment has become individually responsible for profits and losses. Detachments have a detachment chief and a political commissar as well as disciplinary, production planning, financial, personnel management, technical, and economic departments. The detachment chief and political commissar not only have control of all prisoners in the detachment but moreover are responsible for every aspect of the detachment's public security personnel, including their children and family members as well as their political and economic treatment and benefits.

Some provinces and autonomous regions, like Hubei Province, have established general brigades. General brigades correspond closely to the provincial or regional level of PRC administrative organization and have been under the direct control of the Labor Reform Bureau of the Judiciary since 1983.

How many labor reform camps are there in each province or autonomous region? It is very hard to say with any certainty, in part because Public Security's regulation that provincial labor reform camps be given numerical designations (like Shanxi Province No. 13 Labor Reform Detachment—LRC-01-37) is not always observed. Public security personnel and prisoners usually refer to a given labor reform camp by the name of its location (for instance, Hunan Province No. 5 Labor Reform Detachment, LRC-08-10, is usually referred to as Hengyang Labor Reform Detachment). If we assume each province and autonomous region has on the average 20 labor reform camps, then nationwide there should be a total of approximately 600 labor reform camps and a total prisoner population of 3–4 million.

Juvenile Offender Camps

In accordance with Communist regulations,[18] juvenile offender camps are organized on provincal, municipal, and autonomous regional levels. Statistics show that there is a total number of approximately 50–80 camps, with a total prisoner population of approximately 200,000–300,000.

All juvenile offenders are forced to labor like other prisoners, and are organized along the same military lines as LRCs.

Reeducation Through Labor Camps

Like prisons and labor reform detachments, reeducation through labor (RTL) camps are not organized by the central government. Communist government policy is that RTL camps "should be established according to the needs of provincial, autonomous regional, and municipal people's governments . . . however, records must be filed with the Public Security Bureau."[19] According to article 1 of Supplementary Regulations Regarding Reeducation Through Labor, announced on November 29, 1979: "Reeducation Through Labor work and RTL commissions established by provincial, autonomous regional, special municipal and large and middle size municipal governments will be organized, led and managed by the local People's Government, Public Security and Labor Bureau."[20] According to the *China Statistical Yearbook,*[21] under mainland China's administration system there are 353 large and middle-sized municipalities, so there are presumably over 353 RTL commissions. Each commission is allocated several RTL camps according to the population in the area under its jurisdiction.

RTL regulations specify "a distinction between county and regional levels. County levels can establish battalions or companies; regional levels can establish companies or branches. A company is composed of approximately 150 people, and branches of approximately 50 people."[22] This sort of organizational structure is exactly the same as that of CLR camps. So the RTL camps at a county level are equivalent to large CLR prisons or labor reform detachments and at a regional level to small CLR prisons or battalions.

In accordance with government regulations,[23] RTL camps take their names from their location—for instance, Liuzhou RTL Camp (LRC-07-09). There are also certain provinces, Shandong Province for one, that give their RTL camps numerical designations such as Shandong Province No. XX RTL Camp (LRC-21-06). However, each RTL camp has at the same time an alternate name based upon its production unit; for example, Shandong Province No. 1 RTL Camp is also known as No. 83 Factory.

Based upon an analysis of this situation and other information sources, the total number of RTL camps can be placed at somewhere between 400–600.

Before 1983, only somewhere around 20–30 percent of RTL camps existed independently; most were integrated with a CLR general brigade or detachment in the LRC system. For example, Beijing Municipality's Tuanhe Farm (LRC-03-11) in the 1960s consisted of three battalions and a few auxiliary companies. Among these, No. 1 battalion was CLR prisoners (consisting of about 2,500 people), No. 2 battalion was FJP personnel (about 2,000 people), and in addition, there was one company of RTL prisoners numbering about 500 and the No. 3 battalion of juvenile offenders numbering about 1,500. After 1983, the Communists decided to segregate RTL and CLR prisoners into separate production brigades. However, the practices of thirty-some years are slow to change; for production, labor allocation, and managerial reasons about 30 percent of RTL groups are still integrated with CLR camps.

According to a public Communist legal document,[24] RTL commissions are the sole organs responsible for investigation, rectification, notification, and nullification of RTL sentences. Moreover, members of these commissions include the People's Government's Labor and Personnel Bureau and the Civil Administrative Bureau (refer to Chart 1.1). These commissions are portrayed as "educational organizations" capable of resolving "the internal contradictions of the people" by means of high-level government disciplinary boards with "an ability to allocate work."[25] The true nature of these boards will be discussed in Chapter 3. From an organizational standpoint it seems RTL serves an important educational and peacekeeping function, but the real picture is quite different. A Communist internal regulation[26] states that "Reeducation Through Labor have instituted specialist service organizations (offices), to take responsibility for daily work while the board is adjourned, as follows: it is permissible that this office be so established that the provincial, autonomous regional, special municipality and large and middle sized municipal Public Security Bureau and Reeducation Through Labor Bureau are one organization with two names . . . the organization that actually implements RTL . . . should be established in the Public Security Organ, and be organized as a department of Public Security, and should carry out Reeducation Through Labor under the practical direction of Public Security officials." From this it can be seen that RTL is entirely under the control of the Public Security Bureau. The unmistakable purpose of RTL camps is to serve the needs of preserving the political dictatorship of the Communist regime. Indeed, this is one of the primary purposes of the LRC system as a whole.

The situation has even reached the point where a few provinces have abolished outright RTL commissions in order to institute a "one name, one organization" system; Liaoning Province took such a step in November 1986. This move was not well received by some of the top figures in the Communist party.[27]

Forced Job Placement Camps

FJP camps were established on September 7, 1954, in accordance with the Party Congress's proclamation, Temporary Management Methods for Job Placement of Criminals Who Have Completed Their Terms (usually referred to as Policies on Job Placement). Policies on Job Placement and Labor Reform Policies were announced at the same time. It seems clear that the Communists planned to deprive "class enemies" of their rights and freedom and force them into slavery on an indefinite basis.

Before 1961, Policies on Job Placement was applied only to CLR prisoners who had completed their terms, because according to the RTL regulations formulated in 1957, RTL had no fixed term. Therefore, RTL was, in itself, job placement.

After RTL policies had been in effect for four years, the CCP decided to establish a fixed RTL term. Announced in an internal document of March 1961, Public Security Supplementary Regulations Regarding Ten Current Problems in Public Security Work, this decision subsequently created the problem of what to do with those who had completed their RTL terms. At this time Policies on Job Placement was expanded to include those who had completed RTL terms, and FJP personnel were organized into those who had completed CLR terms and those who had completed RTL terms.

This sort of forced job placement occurs when the prisoner's local "Labor Reform organ . . . requests permission from the governing Public

Security Agency." A simple procedure that does not require the consent of the prisoner, FJP is also very convenient because the large majority of such people are simply kept within the confines of their original LRC. If the prisoner's particular LRC is a large one and already has an FJP battalion or company, he is simply transferred into it. In the above-mentioned Tuanhe Farm, for example, in No.1 battalion, prisoners who had finished their sentences were simply transformed into a battalion of FJP personnel. If a particular LRC has very few FJP personnel, it is possible that they will be organized into a squadron with FJP personnel from other LRCs and attached to another CLR or RTL company.

Given this system, it is not surprising that very few prisoners have actually been released. The exceptions include those who during certain periods were considered "wrongly accused" or "reformed" and thus set free; or those prisoners from small villages who had lost their ability to labor, had relatives on whom they could depend, and posed no threat to the Communists and were thus allowed to return to the countryside. Their ranks are small, however, and thus the number of FJP personnel has snowballed over forty years. In certain LRCs, FJP personnel have even become a majority, and other prisoners have been simply transferred to new regions, resulting in an LRC composed entirely of FJP personnel. For example, Wangzhuang Coal Mine in Huoxian County, Shanxi Province (LRC-01-09) before 1970 accommodated CLR personnel; after 1970, it was composed entirely of FJP personnel. Shanghai's Huadong Electric Welding Machine Works is another example.

Communist public and internal documents do not contain stipulations regarding the manner in which FJP is supposed to be organized. FJP simply exists, and grows as the LRC system expands. It is virtually impossible to estimate how many FJP personnel there are in LRCs in the various provinces, autonomous regions, and special municipalities or how many LRCs are composed entirely of FJP personnel.

FJP camps are arranged along exactly the same military lines as CLR and RTL camps.

After more than ten years of research based on various sources, I have compiled a report, "List of the Labor Reform Camps of the People's Republic of China," which contains information about 990 labor reform camps (see Appendix 1).

The Population of the Labor Reform Camps

In the past forty years, there has never been any statement or report from the Communist Party, the legislative organs, or the Department of Statistics regarding the total number of people who have been sent to LRCs during these past forty years or even how many of the three types of personnel are currently detained in these camps. Because this is one of the Chinese Communists' most closely guarded secrets, it is impossible to obtain reliable statistics.

The Communist government's highest legislative organ, the National People's Congress, only in 1984 began to receive judicial reports from the head of the Supreme People's Court and chief of the People's Procuratorate. Information in these reports pertaining to the LRC is very limited (see Chart 1.3). In the National People's Congress, essentially a rubber-stamp body, when the delegates raised their hands to approve Labor Reform, Reeducation Through Labor, and similar measures—except in 1954, 1957, and 1980—they never raised any proposals, inquiries, or opinions regarding the issue they were voting upon.

The information contained in Chart 1.3 is extracted from ten years of reports given to the National People's Congress by the Supreme People's Court. Because upon taking power, Deng Xiaoping announced that he wished to overhaul the judicial system and institute judicial procedure, since 1984 the head of the Supreme People's Court and the chief of the People's Procuratorate have made reports to the Congress. However, the information contained in these reports is often fragmentary or misleading.

Despite certain oversights and omissions, the statistics contained in these reports are not entirely without value to a researcher. The author, on the basis of various reports and information gathered over ten years and from his own personal experience, can make a conservative estimate that during the past forty years, at least 50 million people have been sentenced to labor reform camps; moreover, at present 16–20 million are still confined in these camps.

Now a brief analysis of these numbers, broken down with respect to the three types of personnel:

Convicted Labor Reform (Laogai) Criminals

As can be seen by examining lines 8–11 in Chart 1.3, from August 1983 to December 1988, the highest annual average number of criminals arrested and sentenced is 598,000, the lowest 325,000. Comparatively speaking, however, the annual averages from lines 8 and 10 are a bit more useful; looking only at these two time periods, we can see that the average number of criminals arrested and sentenced is about 500,000. There should be a directly proportional relationship between the crime rate and the number of criminals arrested and sentenced. On the basis of its own information, the Communist Party established the crime rate to be about 5 in 1,000 (looking at the 1988 report, comparatively lower rates were reported in 1956 and 1965—3 in 1,000; comparatively higher rates in 1981—8.9 in 1,000—and 1982—7.4 in 1,000). It can be postulated that

CHART 1.3 Number of Persons Sent to Labor Reform Camps

ITEM NO.	PERIOD Mo/Yr	No Mo	SENTENCED/PERIOD	SENTENCED per yr	SENTENCED >5 YEARS %	>5 YEARS no	SENTENCED <5 YEARS %	<5 YEARS no	CRIMINAL RATE %	DATA SOURCE[a]
1	1956		**		**		**		.03%	ROSC-ZTS 6thNPC, 4thCO 04/08/1986
2	1965		**		**		**		.03%	same
3	1981		**		**		**		.089%	same
4	1982		**		**		**		.074%	same
5	1983		**		**		**		.06%	same
6	1984		**		**		**		.05%	same
7	04/84-02/85	10 Mo	470,000	564,000	**		**		.052%	ROSC-ZTS 6thNPC, 3rdCO 04/03/1985
8	08/83-12/85	28 Mo	1,395,000	598,000	42%	251,000	58%	347,000	.052%	ROSC-ZTS 6thNPC, 4thCO 04/08/1986
9	01/86-12/86	12 Mo	325,000	325,000	**		**		.052%	ROSC-ZTS 6thNPC, 5thCO 04/07/1987
10	03/83-12/87	52 Mo	2,047,800	472,600	38.18%	180,400	61.1%	292,100	.052%	ROSC-ZTS 7thNPC, 1stCO 04/01/1988
11	01/88-12/88	12 Mo	368,800	368,800	30.8%	113,500	68.7%	253,200	**	ROSC-RJX 7thNPC, 2ndCO 03/29/1989
12	01/89-12/89	12 Mo	482,700	482,700	**		**		**	ROSC-RJX 7thNPC, 3rdCO 03/30/1990

**: No Information

[a]ROSC: Report of Supreme Court; ZTS: the Chief of Supreme Court, Zheng Tian-Xiang; RJX: the Chief of Supreme Court, Ren Jian-Xing; NPC, _____; CO: the _____ Conference of the _____ National People's Congress.

when the crime rate is about 5.2 in 1,000, the average number of arrested and sentenced criminals is 500,000. If we extend this estimate to cover the remaining forty years of Communist rule, the total number of those arrested and sentenced to LRCs is approximately 20 million.

It must be emphasized that these figures are based completely upon analyses of official Communist government information and, as such, do not accurately reflect the true state of affairs. The figure of 20 million should be used as a lower limit of the actual numbers arrested over forty years of Communist rule. There are two major categories of arrests for which even the Communist authorities themselves have trouble obtaining accurate statistics. In the past forty years, during the many political movements—for example, during the 1966–1976 Cultural Revolution period; the 1950–1951 Movement to Suppress Counter-revolutionaries period; the 1955 Liquidate Counter-revolutionaries period; and the 1959–1961 Three Years of Natural Disaster period—frightening numbers of people were arrested and persecuted. Also, there have always been numerous secret arrests. The numbers involved in the two types of situations described above can only be estimated in the millions. The most conservative estimate: Over forty years, between 30–40 million people have been arrested and convicted.

As can be seen from Chart 1.3, among those arrested and convicted, the annual average of those sentenced to terms of over five years or to unlimited terms or put to death can be determined from an analysis of lines 8 and 9 and can be fixed at about 250,000 (similarly, this period's crime rate was about 5.2 in 1,000). If we assume that this type of criminal is incarcerated for an average of ten years, we can postulate that of those incarcerated in Communist LRCs in 1980, in 1990 somewhere around 2,200,000 still remain. Analyzing this information in a similar way, we can see that the annual average of those sentenced to under five-year terms is about 320,000; calculating on the assumption of three years as an average term, any given year there should be 1 million of these types confined in the LRCs. These two types together total about 3,200,000 (we should also consider the huge numbers in detention centers who have not yet been sentenced). This 3,200,000 figure should be viewed as the lowest estimate on the numbers of arrested and sentenced criminals confined in the LRCs. According to the author's research, the number of arrested and sentenced criminals currently in the LRCs is between 4 and 6 million.

Reeducation Through Labor (Laojiao) Subjects

RTL policies have been in effect since 1957—already thirty-three years—a slightly shorter period of time than labor reform policies.

Because the Communist Party announced that RTL policies are "high level government disciplinary actions," they are not considered judicial punishment, and so subjects do not go through judicial procedures such as arrest, examination, or sentencing, and therefore local public security bureaus do not have to submit reports to the courts or the Office of the Procuratorate. Thus, there is no way for us to know exactly how many people, over the course of thirty-three years, have been sentenced to reeducation through labor.

The author, on the basis of personal experience and judging by the manner in which RTL policies are carried out and by the fact that RTL camps exist in every province, estimates that in thirty-three years at least 20 million people have been sentenced to LRCs in the name of reeducation through labor. Moreover, in the LRCs today, there currently remain 3–5 million RTL prisoners.

In summary, the cumulative number of CLR and RTL subjects confined to LRCs during the past forty years is over 50 million.

Forced Job Placement (Jiuye) Personnel

According to a 1984 Communist announcement entitled, Forced Job Placement Policies, of all the convicts who had served their entire term before 1980, about 80–90 percent were subjected to forced job placement. Over the span of forty years, about 40 million of these convicts were subjected to FJP within their own *laogaidui*.

Before 1980, only a very small number of people—special convicts such as the former puppet-emperor of Manchuguo, Pu Yi, or high-level Kuomintang generals, Tu Li Ming and Shen Zuei, etc.—after completing their terms or receiving amnesty were not subjected to FJP.

In the *laogaidui* a popular saying was "There is an end to *laogai* (or *laojiao*); *jiuye* is forever." Regardless of the severity of their sentences, CLR or RTL subjects could endure their hardships because they always knew the day would come when their term would be over. Instead, when they were released, they were merely informed that they would be forcibly settled in a job within the confines of the *laogaidui*. The meaning of "job placement" is, "You are free, you have become a citizen once again, but you will work in a *laogaidui*, live in a *laogaidui*; your overseers will be public security police, you must continue to acknowledge your crimes, work hard, and reform your way of thinking." The 40 million people described previously endure years of suffering and misery, torture and hardship. A few older convicts, no longer able to labor, are sent back to their villages; some are announced to have been wrongly accused and are "rehabilitated" and sent back to their original work units. These are exceptions, however; in 1980 there still remained in the LRC somewhere from 6–8 million FJP personnel.

After 1980 changes were made in the FJP policies and there was a decrease in the number of CLR and RTL personnel who were subjected to FJP after their terms were completed. But FJP policy was not abandoned, so the total number of FJP personnel (who go in but don't come out) continued to rise dramatically; in the past ten years it can be estimated that another 2 million people have been added to their ranks.

On the basis of this analysis, the number of FJP personnel in Communist LRCs must be somewhere between 8–10 million.

The Political Function of Labor Reform Camps

The essential nature of the Chinese Communists' LRC system is not like that of other nation's prisons or detention centers. The purpose of the Chinese LRC is not simply to maintain order in society or to punish criminals in accordance with the law but also to protect and consolidate the dictatorship of the Communist Party. As the Communists themselves freely admit, "Our *laogaidui* system constitutes an important part of our public security system; it is one of the tools of the dictatorship of the proletariat; it serves to punish and reform all counter-revolutionaries and other criminals."[28] For forty years the main target of punishment meted out by the LRC was "counter-revolutionaries." With regard to criminal acts in general, the CCP class and class struggle theories hold that "crime . . . is a single individual's struggle against the government."[29] Because this sort of criminal phenomenon also tends to undermine communist rule, it must be suppressed.

Since the 1950s, the LRC system's main function has been to systematically detain and punish counter-revolutionaries. Because during the past forty years, the so-called landlords and capitalists left behind by the Kuomintang government have gradually disappeared, the proportion of counter-revolutionaries in the LRCs has declined from 90 percent in the 1950s to 10 percent in the 1980s. As a Public Security Bureau document[30] describes: "Of those currently detained, counter-revolutionaries comprise almost 10 percent; those with a historical counter-revolutionary background comprise only 1.6 percent of the total inmates."[31] This 400,000 figure does not include those imprisoned under the auspices of RTL; the number of RTL convicts is probably not much less than 400,000. RTL is very convenient for dealing with counter-revolutionaries and "anti-socialist elements."

Before the bloody suppression of the Democracy Movement on June 4, 1989, the media had reported that many LRCs (prisons) in the Beijing area were transferring prisoners out of the region in order to be able to

Five defenseless lamas surrounded by fifty to sixty military policemen equipped with helmets, electric cattle prods, and gas masks. The photograph was taken in 1988 in Lhasa, Tibet.

accommodate those students and protesters soon to be arrested in the crackdown. To this day there are still no reliable figures indicating how many were thrown into the LRCs after the "June 4th Incident." The following bit of news reveals the political function of the *laogaidui* during this bloody crackdown:

On October 17, 1989, the Ministry of Justice at a conference in Shanghai publicly praised "National Ministry of Justice collectives outstanding in preventing chaos and controlling violence"; the announced list contained 52 work units, 30 of which were LRCs (see Chart 1.4). Obviously, these 30 *laogaidui* imprisoned many students and protesters involved in the 1989 Democracy Movement. LRCs named in this list include those as far south as Hainan Island's Qionghai Prison; as far north as Heilongjiang Province, Mudanjiang Municipal Reeducation Through Labor Camp; as far west as Xinjiang Uygur Autonomous Region's No. 1 Prison; and as far east as Jiangsu Province Dalianshan Reeducation Through Labor Camp. These facts show that the crackdown was not limited to the North but extended all over the country.

A photo from Chinese Central Television Station, June 14, 1989, showing Communist authorities arresting two men for RTL during the suppression of the Tiananmen Democracy Movement. The person on the right, named Wu Zhijun, was accused of "obstructing traffic and stirring up trouble" and was sentenced to *laojiao*. The person on the left, named Chang Shaoyin, was accused of "stirring up trouble and attacking a police department" and was also sentenced to *laojiao*.

Political Prisoners in the *Laogaidui*

Although the Communist regime has consistently denied the existence of political prisoners, it does admit the existence of "counter-revolutionaries" (*fangeming fenzi*)—those who protest or disagree strongly with the government. The Soviet Union was the first regime to create the concept of counter-revolutionary crimes; Communist China soon followed suit. In recent years, the Soviet Union has replaced counter-revolutionary crimes with crimes against the state. At present, Communist China is the only country in the world that has specific counter-revolutionary crime provisions written into its legal system. Counter-revolutionary crime is obviously a political concept; it therefore follows that counter-revolutionary criminals are political prisoners. In the past forty years, over 30–40 million people have been sent to LRCs for various political reasons. This number does not include the three types of situations described below:

CHART 1.4   The List of National Ministry of Justice Collectives Outstanding in Preventing Chaos and Controlling Violence by the Judiciary Ministry of the PRC, October 17, 1990

No.	Unit's Name	Code No.
1.0	Bureau of Judiciary, Daxin County, Beijing	
2.0	Bureau of Judiciary, Xiuwu District, Beijing	
3.0	Leading group of Law propaganda, Beijing	
4.0	Propaganda and Education Section, Political Department of Labor Reform Bureau, Beijing	
5.0	Beijing No.1 LRD	*(LRC-03-12)
6.0	Beijing Tiandonghe RTL	*(LRC-03-13)
7.0	Bureau of Judiciary, Hexi District, Tianjin	
8.0	Tianjin No.3, LRD	*(LRC-04-01)
9.0	Notary office, Tianjin	
10.0	Hebei Provincial No.1 LRB	*(LRC-05-05)
11.0	Hebei Provincial No.1 Prison	*(LRC-05-01)
12.0	Xuajazhong RTL, Hebei Province	*(LRC-05-11)
13.0	Shanxi Provincial No.13 LRD	*(LRC-01-37)
14.0	Inner Mongolia Autonomous Region Prison	*(LRC-25-26)
15.0	Bureau of Judiciary, Fuxing City, Liaoning Province	
16.0	Labor Reform Department, Linyuan City, Lianoning Province	*(LRC-27-23)
17.0	Chuncun Prison, Jilin Prison	*(LRC-26-19)
18.0	Haoerpin Prison, Heilungjiang Province	*(LRC-24-26)
19.0	Motanjiang RTL, Jilin Province	*(LRC-24-05)
20.0	Bureau of Judiciary, Jinan District, Shanghai	
21.0	Discipline Section of Labor Reform Bureau, Shanghai	
22.0	Public Security Section of Labor Reform Bureau, Shanghai	
23.0	Shanghai No.1 Attorney office	
24.0	Judiciary School of Jiangsu Province	
25.0	Labor Reform Police School of Jiangsu Province	
26.0	Dalianshan RTL, Jiangsu Province	*(LRC-23-39)
27.0	Ninxiu Autonomous Region Law School	
28.0	Zhangjiang Province No.1 Prison	*(LRC-20-03)
29.0	Labor Reform Police School of Anhui Province	
30.0	Bureau of Judiciary, Sanyuan District, Sanming City, Fujian Province	
31.0	Fujian Provincial No.4 Prison	
32.0	Labor Reform Police School of Jiangxi Province	
33.0	Politics & Law Management School of Shandong Province	
34.0	Labor Reform Police School of Shandong Province	
35.0	Shandong No.1 RTL	*(LRC-21-06)
36.0	Loyang RTL, Hunan Province	*(LRC-28-43)
37.0	RTL Department of Judiciary Bureau, Wuhan City, Hubei Province	
38.0	No.5 LRD of Hubei Province No.1 LRB	*(LRC-19-30)
39.0	Bureau of Judiciary, Yuanjiang City, Hunan Province	
40.0	Hunan Provincial No.5 LRD	*(LRC-08-10)
41.0	Guangzhou Fuzibao Press, Guangdong Province	
42.0	Jihuangdon LRD, Guangdong Province	*(LRC-02-43)
43.0	Junhai Prison, Hainan Province	*(LRC-02-108)
44.0	Forging Battalion of Yinshan Prison, Guangxi Autonomous Region	*(LRC-07-12)
45.0	Sichun Provincial No.1 Prison	*(LRC-18-42)
46.0	Guizhou Provincial Jizishan LRD	*(LRC-06-20)
47.0	Yunnan Provincial No.41 LRD	*(LRC-11-30)
48.0	Yunnan Provincial No.3 RTL	*(LRC-10-64)
49.0	Discipline section of Shaanxi Provincial No.9 LRD	*(LRC-17-16)
50.0	Gansui Provincial No.1 Prison	*(LRC-12-09)
51.0	Qinhai Provincial No.2 LRD	*(LRC-16-07)
52.0	Xingjiang Autonomous Region No.1 Prison	*(LRC-15-27)

*(LRC-02-15): See the list of LRC of the PRC (Appendix 1); LRB: Labor Reform General Brigade *laogai zhongdui*; LRD: Labor Reform Detachment *laogai zhidui*; RTL: Reeducation Through Labor Camp *laojiao suo*.

1. Since 1949, the Communist government has launched several political movements during which many people, denied any sort of
   legal procedure, suffered direct persecution at the hands of the
   Communist Party leaders, the Public Security Bureau, the Red
   Guards, the "proletariat rebel masses," or the "revolutionary masses."
   A typical example: During the Land Reform Movement (around
   1950), between 2–3 million landlords and rich peasants suffered
   from persecution at the hands of the "peasant masses" under the
   direction of the Communist leaders. During the 1966–1976 Cultural
   Revolution, approximately 10 million people were persecuted by
   Mao Zedong's Red Guards and "proletariat rebel masses." Obtaining accurate numbers concerning these types of movements is virtually impossible.
2. Whenever possible, the Communist regime does its utmost to avoid
   using the label "political criminal." When the individual being
   persecuted can be charged for a crime other than a political one,
   this other crime usually becomes the rationale for imprisonment.
   After being sentenced and sent to a labor reform camp, however,
   this type of prisoner is treated as a "doubly charged bandit"—such
   as "hoodlum and counter-revolutionary" or "corrupt and counter-
   revolutionary background."
3. In accordance with the Communist regime's class struggle theory,
   the ultimate goal of the revolution is to abolish all classes, beginning
   with the exploiting classes. How is this to be accomplished? The
   labor reform camps is one way. Usually any criminal activity of
   "capitalists" or "landlords" (regardless of its political or criminal
   nature) is viewed as counter-revolutionary class opposition that
   must be severely repressed. Similar types of criminals, then, will
   be sentenced to terms of differing severity based upon their class
   status or political background. Suppose someone steals twenty pecks
   of corn from a commune. If this person is from a landlord family,
   it is possible his sentence could be as high as ten years, the rationale
   being "This act should be considered a counter-attack by the landlord class, a hostile and destructive counter-revolutionary act against
   socialist public property." If this person is from a poor or middle-
   class peasant background or from the family of a Party cadre, it is
   possible that no disciplinary action would be taken.

Before 1980, at all levels of the Communist judicial system, verdicts
were required to include information about the class status and political
background of all sentenced criminals. This was a very important factor
in determining the length of the sentence.

Those political prisoners sent to labor reform camps can be classed into four rough categories, briefly described below:

Landlord and Rich Peasant Counter-Revolutionaries

According to Party statistics, when the Communist regime seized power in 1949, mainland China had approximately 20–25 million landlords and rich peasants (including their children). By 1980, this class had already dissappeared. In the 1950s, 10–15 percent of the LRCs' prisoners, about 2–3 million people, were landlords or rich peasants. By the 1980s, this class of people had already disappeared from the LRC.

Historical Counter-Revolutionaries

"Historical counter-revolutionaries" refers to all those people who before 1949 had served in the Kuomintang (KMT) regime at any level above secretary in the KMT Party, section chief in the government, company commander in the military, or chief in the police or had been a member of the military police were treated as counter-revolutionaries. Regardless of whether or not they had ever, at that time or in the past, directly resisted the Communist Party, they were all either punished or arrested and thrown into labor reform camps. Later this category gradually expanded so that anyone who had served in the Kuomintang regime at any level, even as an ordinary staff or Party member, was treated as a counter-revolutionary. In the 1950s, 50–60 percent of the prisoners in the *laogaidui* belonged to this category, totaling about 10 million in all. This category of political prisoner has gradually disappeared with time. Following a major change in Communist policy in 1978, most of the remaining prisoners of this type were released. At present, 20,000–30,000 still remain in custody.

Active Counter-Revolutionaries

The term "active counter-revolutionaries" refers to those people whom the Communist government considers to be involved in activities "whose purpose is to overthrow the dictatorship of the proletariat and the socialist system, and to endanger the People's Republic of China."[32] In the Communist government's published Criminal Code, there are fourteen articles concerning counter-revolutionary crimes.

Of course, the words and actions of those who have counter-revolutionary backgrounds, that is, those who were born into landlord, rich peasant, or capitalist classes, are very easily interpreted as counter-revolutionary crimes, and hence these types of criminals often incur harsher sentences. Although those without this type of "class" or "political" background are in the majority, if their words and actions do not meet the political requirements of the Communist government they also can be labeled as active counter-revolutionaries.

What exactly constitutes active counter-revolutionary activity, changes with the tides of Communist Party doctrine. Some examples of anti-counter-revolutionary movements in the past include

- 1955 persecution of the Hu Feng Counter-revolutionary Clique[33]
- 1952–1955 purge of Catholics and Protestants. In 1955, in the case of the Catholic Gong Pin-mei Counter-Revolutionary Clique alone, over 3,000 people were arrested.
- 1957 Anti-Rightist Movement purge of at least 550,000 "counter-revolutionary rightists"
- On January 13, 1967, Communist officials announced Six Public Security Regulations.[34] Under the auspices of Regulation No. 2 alone, which labeled any person who attacked Mao Zedong or Lin Biao an active counter-revolutionary, approximately 10,000 were punished. In 1970, while the author was confined at Huoxian County Wang-zhung Coal Mine in Shanxi Province (LRC-1-09), FJP subject Yang Baoyin was summarily executed by a firing squad for writing the words, "Overthrow Chairman Mao," and his brain was eaten by a public security cadre.
- In the past such Communist Party leaders as Liu Shaoqi, Lin Biao, and Jiang Qing have also been labeled active counter-revolutionaries and punished accordingly.
- During the Democracy movements that emerged in the late 1970s, many prominent figures such as Wei Jingsheng, Xu Wenli, and Yang Wei were sentenced as counter-revolutionaries.
- In 1989, after the suppression of the Tiananmen Democracy Movement, students and activists wanted by police—such as Wang Dan, Chai Ling, Wuer Kaixi, and Yan Jiaqi—were labeled counter-revolutionaries.

Most of the three types of counter-revolutionaries are arrested and sent to labor reform camps.

Anti-Socialist Elements and Ideological Reactionaries

Before the Cultural Revolution, the Communist Party often used the term "ideological reactionary"; after the Cultural Revolution, however—especially in the past few years—the term "anti-socialist element" has become more common. Although this type of person is essentially no different from an active counter-revolutionary, from a political standpoint his activity is considered a less serious offense. This type of person generally has no obvious political goals or plans, and the influence of his or her actions does not extend beyond a purely personal sphere—for instance, those who in their personal diaries, correspondence with friends or relatives, or in the course of daily life express dissatisfaction with certain leaders, governmental policies or measures (the so-called discontented grumbling). The Communist government considers anti-socialist elements to be politically unstable and deals with them in a dictatorial fashion. A typical example: during the Three Red Banners Movement (Great Leap Forward, People's Communes, and General Line for Socialist Development) that began in 1958, anyone who expressed dissatisfaction with the hardships caused by Mao Zedong and the Communist Party leaders' impractical policies or anyone who showed resentment over the following three years of hunger and food shortages was seen as directly threatening the stability of the Communist Party's dictatorship. The Communist authorities responded with draconian measures of suppression, imprisoning approximately 10 million people in the *laogaidui* as "ideological reactionaries." About 70 percent of these were imprisoned under the auspices of RTL, not CLR.

For many years the Communist government has had regulations concerning the segregation of political counter-revolutionaries and common criminals. According to the author's nineteen years' experience, however, in most *laogaidui,* there is actually no such segregation. Common criminals, political counter-revolutionaries and even FJP personnel are mixed together without regard for the nature of their crimes.

In the LRC, political prisoners are usually treated much more harshly than common criminals. Although political prisoners tend to be more obedient and are less frequently involved in fights or jail breaks, their sentences are still relatively longer. In addition, a much higher proportion of political prisoners are reprimanded and beaten and more often than in the case of common criminals have their sentences extended or are forced to remain as FJP personnel after their terms have expired. The difference in treatment—including food rations, visits from relatives, sentence reductions—is also very large. The reasons for this include the following:

1. The Communist regime has repeatedly warned the Public Security Bureau that political prisoners are "the most dangerous enemy of the party and the nation." These types of persons have deeply rooted ideological consciousnesses, very carefully concealed, so it is difficult to "mold them into new socialist people."
2. Because most political prisoners have definite cultural values, a strong sense of morality, and good analytic ability, it is difficult for them to accept Communist propaganda.

3. Most political prisoners are not accustomed to physical labor and therefore often fail to meet their production responsibilities, reducing the profits of their LRC and thus incurring the wrath of the Public Security Bureau.
4. A large number of political prisoners have a traditional conception of morals and values and therefore have difficulty adapting to the treacherous, dog-eat-dog environment that prevails in the LRCs.
5. The economic and cultural level of most political prisoners is somewhat higher than that of most public security personnel, a fact that often arouses jealousy and resentment.

The public security cadres in the LRCs have a greater trust in the common criminals, considering them to be more ideologically pure and more easily reformed. In addition, common criminals are often used to maintain order and control other inmates in the prison. Under the encouragement of government policies, common criminals often engage in the torture and punishment of other convicts and serve as an indispensible tool of the Public Security Bureau.

Thought Reform in the Labor Reform Camps

Communist leader Mao Zedong's guiding principles were the maxims "Political power grows from the barrel of a gun" and "Only with guns can we reform the world."[35] The Communist regime certainly came to power through force and relies on force to maintain its rule. The use of tanks by Mao's successor, Deng Xiaoping, to suppress the Tiananmen Democracy Movement in 1989 once again revealed the true nature of the Communist regime. However, Communist leaders understand very clearly that the use of violence alone is not enough to maintain a dictatorial rule; it is essential that the thoughts of the populace be controlled as well. The barrel of a gun may obtain the submission of many people under many situations for a certain period of time; however, it is not sufficient to obtain the long-term submission of all people under all situations. In addition, submission obtained through use of force breeds secret resentment.

Over forty years, the Communist regime has established a thought reform system on a national scale, a system that reaches into every area of society, from the educational system to the agricultural and industrial systems, from kindergarten students to retired seniors, from Party cadres to criminals. Using secrecy, isolation from the outside world, spreading of superstition, repetition of lies, distortion of truth, and other similar methods, they plan not just to obtain the populace's blind obedience but to inspire in them a willingness to follow the Communist Party and to believe in socialism.

Thought reform in the *laogaidui* is designed not only to remove ideological objections to the present regime but also to preserve order and encourage production. As such, it is quite similar in content to that promoted on a national level. The main difference is that thought reform in the *laogaidui* is a much more violent affair. The purpose of the compulsory thought reform practiced in the LRC is to radically change a person's consciousness, political views, religious beliefs, and moral values.

Labor Reform Camp Thought Reform Measures and Methods

"Acknowledge Your Crimes, Acknowledge Your Faults, Submit to Superiors, Submit to the Law" (renzui fufa). A Public Security Bureau internal document[36] describes this process very clearly: ". . . if a criminal does not acknowledge his crimes and submit to the law, then accomplishing thought reform is out of the question. . . . Criminals cannot submit to the law until they acknowledge their crimes, and only when they have acknowledged their crimes and submitted to the law can they accept thought reform. Acknowledging one's crime is a prerequisite to submitting to the law, and submitting to the law is the beginning of reform. Acknowledging their crimes and submitting to the law are the first lessons criminals must learn upon entering prison, and this consciousness must be present throughout the process of reform."

Upon entering an LRC, most CLR or RTL subjects do not immediately begin physical labor. Instead, they are first placed into "study groups" (also called introductory teams). This "study" period may be anywhere from half a month to three months, the length of time depending upon the prisoner's confession (a process in which he reviews the history of his crime), his consciousness of and judgments about his crime, and his level of repentance. New prisoners are organized into small groups, and public security cadres select an older convict to manage the group and act as group leader. Under the direction of the team leader (a public security cadre) those in the group who are educated—who speak well and can write—arrange to hear the prisoners' confessions, acknowledgments of guilt, and self-appraisals and organize all documents and self-criticism letters into a report that is submitted to the public security cadre. The other portion of the group are hardened criminals, most of whom were formerly gangsters or hoodlums. Under the direction of the group leader, they try to extract more confessions by beating and torturing the new convicts.

There is absolutely no freedom in the study groups. Talking, standing, and walking about are all prohibited. While sitting, one must raise one's hand and obtain the group leader's permission before changing one's sitting posture. Once in the morning and once again in the afternoon there is a ten-minute rest period. There are two meals a day, enough food to keep one alive, but hunger is a constant fact of life. During the morning, afternoon, and evening periods one is forced either to sit together with one's group or to study governmental orders and LRC regulations or is forced perhaps to listen to some prisoner's confession or engage in struggle sessions. Generally speaking, there are three stages in a study group.

1. The first stage is acknowledging one's crime; acknowledging one's guilt (*jiaodai zuixing*). In the small study groups each new prisoner is required to relate the story of his crime (if the case is of a sensitive nature the convict relates his story privately in an interrogation room). The group leader mobilizes the other new prisoners to apply pressure on the subject. If the subject's story does not agree with the information possessed by the public security cadre or the subject claims to be innocent, he is accused of "denying guilt and resisting reform." The Communist Party is "glorious, noble, and correct," so how could it possibly be guilty of wrongly accusing a "class enemy?" Usually those who deny their guilt are punished, either by being forced to undergo struggle sessions and beatings or by being placed in solitary confinement; sometimes their sentences may even be extended. Most who deny their guilt are not allowed to leave the study groups and go labor. This is a critical point for prisoners. During this process of confession, two common situations occur: The first case is one in which a certain prisoner has been sentenced to labor reform or RTL based upon certain definite facts, but the Public Security Bureau is still unsure about certain aspects of the case and wishes to investigate further, particularly if it hopes to uncover information leading to the incrimination of others. In this situation Public Security uses persuasion and torture to extract confessions and obtain information. The second type of situation is where a criminal, out of fear of torture or punishment, relates information previously not possessed by Public Security. This information possibly is fictitious, invented in the hopes of being seen as willing and cooperative. It is also possible that this information is true, in which case it bears further investigating by Public Security. In this situation the criminal will face many problems, because until the case is cleared up he will not be allowed to leave the study group and begin work. So the best course of action is neither to say too much nor too little—to avoid the intimidation, threats, and beatings by telling Public Security only what it already knows. This way the study group period can be passed through quickly and easily. It is only learning to bear the physical and emotional torture that is difficult.

2. Second is the stage of recognizing and criticizing (*pipan renshi*). One must recognize and make criticisms of one's crimes. Not only counter-

revolutionaries but most petty thieves and hoodlums as well must recognize that their criminal behavior is capitalistic in nature, anti-socialist, and counter-revolutionary. They must also criticize themselves as class enemies because their behavior aids the capitalists in their battle against the proletariat and their attack on socialism. The group leader, under the direction of the public security cadre, encourages the other criminals to criticize the subject. Generally speaking, if it is announced that the subject is progressing well in his self-criticism and raising his consciousness, he will quickly pass through this stage. However, under no circumstances can the subject make such excuses as "I was momentarily confused" or "I was misled by others," "I was young and foolish" or "It was only this one time that I strayed from the proper party line." One must ruthlessly criticize and attack oneself, while at the same time expressing gratitude for the magnanimity of the Communist Party and the belief that one feels "reformed" and a "new person."

3. The third stage is that of submitting to authority; submitting to teaching (*fuguan fujiao*). In the study groups, in addition to engaging in acknowledging one's crimes and in self-criticism, one is forced to study the rules and regulations of the LRC. If prisoners have acknowledged their crimes and criticized themselves, they are expected to show repentance, obeying the rules and submitting to authority. Their self-criticisms, along with other plans to reform, must be submitted in writing by the prisoner. Of course, these essays must all be approved by the public security cadre, after which they are put in the prisoner's file.

"Expose Treachery and Show Allegiance to the Government" (kaolong zhengfu). This basic demand has two aspects. The first is that because the prisoner has acknowledged his guilt, engaged in self-criticism, and expressed repentance, all of this should be manifested in his behavior. A prisoner's behavior should thus uniformly reflect his political attitudes and ideological consciousness. For instance, he should immediately expose any and all behavior or comments that might disturb political order, harm Communist leaders, or undermine socialism. In order to express his change in class position and his firm allegiance to the government, he should struggle against "bad elements and harmful acts." A criminal who fails to pay attention to such things, taking a "see no evil, hear no evil" stance, will be judged as "protecting bad elements" and having a "faulty political stance"—in other words, as unreformed.

The second aspect is that those who wish to control the ideology and behavior of a large group of people know that depending purely upon force is not the most reliable or clever method. The best method is to use the individual members of the group to control each other. Obviously, a small number of public security police are unable to turn a large group of living, thinking people into tools in the service of socialist production;

This photograph taken at Yuci Chemical Plant (Provincial No. 4 Prison, LRC-01-14) of Shanxi Province shows prison authorities awarding several female prisoners the title of labor reform activist in a thought reform summary meeting. In order to receive this type of commendation, one must have an exceptional political and production record.

it is necessary to utilize the prisoners themselves to control each other. This type of policy is commonly and clearly implemented in every LRC. For example, criminals "providing cadres with intelligence or preventing illegal behavior on the part of other convicts"[37] or "exposing and controlling other criminals' illegal behavior or acting as a source of intelligence."[38] are given commendations or material rewards. LRC authorities refer to this type of behavior as "aiding in the reformation of others."[39]

The *laogaidui* have been very successful in utilizing prisoners to control other prisoners. An example of this type of mass control[40] is Shanghai's No. 2 RTL Camp, Division 9, which in March of 1988 instituted the categories of light, heavy, and general supervision. These divisions were not designed to separate those prisoners with good behavior from those with poor behavior. Rather, the behavior and performance of work units as a whole are evaluated and on this basis receive light, heavy, or general supervision treatment from Public Security. Differential treatment in these different levels of supervision extends to every aspect of a prisoner's life—monthly living allowance, food rations, granting of furloughs, family visits, etc. A group that has attained light supervision status can lose this privilege if one of its members breaks the rules, refuses to work, or displays poor behavior, thus affecting the privileges of the entire group. "This type of policy has mobilized the reform spirit of reeducation through labor prisoners and encouraged labor reform production. In 1988 this division had no escapes or unusual deaths or similar misfortunes. In 1988 the average level of wheat production per *mu*[41] was 330 kg, that of barley 402 kg, an increase over previous years of 28.9 percent. Production of soybeans increased 61.5 percent, that of rape 150 percent."[42]

In the *laogaidui* there is no concept of false incrimination. Government policies encourage informing and betrayal. Even if the evidence brought against a person proves to be totally false, the accusor is nonetheless praised by public security cadres. The reason for this lies in the fact that the authorities view the ultimate truth or falsehood of an accusation as secondary in importance; most important is the allegiance to the government shown by the act of accusation. The encouragement of blind accusations and "ratting" not only changes convicts' political ideology but alters their sense of conscience and moral character. This phenomenon is frequently seen in general society as well; in this sense, the LRC system is a microcosm of mainland Chinese society as a whole under Communist rule.

Redemption of Sins Through Bitter Toil (jiangong shuzui). Forced labor is justified by the Communist government on two principles.

1. Basically speaking, the basis of labor reform enterprise production is low-wage, slave-like labor. Moreover, labor reform production constitutes a large portion of China's socialist production planning. Therefore, the basic purpose of forcing criminals to engage in hard labor is to produce wealth for socialist society.

2. The theory behind labor reform holds that all crimes, no matter what their political or criminal nature, stem from the ideology of the exploiting class. Only through hard toil can this ideology be eradicated, while at the same time cultivating a feeling of solidarity with the Communist proletariat. If "resisting work" or "lazy work attitude" are tantamount to "resisting reform," Communist logic holds that such a criminal has neither fully recognized the seriousness of his crimes nor changed his reactionary viewpoint; nor has he made the resolution to pass through hard labor in order to become a "new socialist person." According to Communist labor reform regulations: ". . . during the period of labor reform, any prisoner who displays a poor work attitude, repeatedly violates jail regulations, or commits acts that indicate he has not yet been reformed or has the potential to become a threat to society after his release, may on the recognizance of the labor reform organization, and after investigation by the Public Security Bureau and legal review by the local People's Court, be forced to continue the process of labor reform beyond the limits of his original term."[43]

Education Under Deng Xiaoping's Four Cardinal Principles (sixiang jiben yuanze jiaoyu). In the opinion of the Communist regime, all criminals, whether counter-revolutionaries or common offenders, have incorrect political views and attitudes. "Some have extreme reactionary ideologies; others have decadent political thoughts, dominated by idealism and corrupt feudal and capitalistic ideologies. Given this, it is imperative that the four basic educational principles be instituted—to turn the criminal's political thoughts in a normal direction, towards Marxism-Leninism, a belief in Maoism, a belief in socialism, faith in the Communist party and the democratic dictatorship of the people."[44]

In the LRC, freedom of religious belief is nonexistent, for it is opposed to the education under the four cardinal principles and labor reform regulations. Communist propaganda, however, claims that prisoners have freedom of worship. For example, those LRCs that have Muslim prisoners provide them with their own separate food (pork fat is not used), employ Muslim prisoners as cooks and give these prisoners a day off on Muslim holidays, etc. However, rather than being an example of religious freedom, this is merely the exercise of common customs and traditions. In 1953, a Roman Catholic priest in the Shanghai LRC refused to cooperate with the Communists. He was arrested as a counter-revolutionary and thrown in prison for fifteen years. Two years after his release, in accordance with his religious beliefs, he performed the ceremony of baptism for two other prisoners and was again imprisoned. He was not released again until 1989, having spent a total of thirty-four years in prison. The Communists have decreed that in the LRC "studying the Bible, worshipping, or spreading of religion are prohibited."[45]

Forced Labor and Labor Production
in the Labor Reform Camps

The Communist government uses a sort of labor production "theory" to justify forcing convicts into slave labor: People commit crimes only because their thoughts are dominated by the ideology of the exploiting class; in order to remove the problem at its root, it is necessary to reform the criminal's ideology; and only by undergoing hard labor can a criminal be reformed into a "new socialist person." Over the course of forty years, how many criminals (what percentage of those in the LRCs) have been reformed into "new socialist people?" All we can see are people spending their last drop of sweat, their last drop of blood, only to die in disgrace; all we can see is countless LRCs spreading throughout mainland China; all we can see is LRC slave labor resulting in great profits for the Communist regime.

The CCP states: "The reform through labor of counter-revolutionaries and other criminals carried out by labor reform organizations should completely integrate punishment and thought reform, serving the purposes of both production and political education."[46]

The real purpose of forced criminal labor can be ascertained from two comments made by the Communist government's first Public Security Ministry chief, Luo Ruiqing: ". . . the process of reform through labor of criminals . . . *is essentially an effective method of purging and eliminating all criminals.* Labor reform production (*laogai shengchan*) . . . directly aids in the development of the nation's industries, and also saves the nation a great deal in expenses. *It is a dependable source of wealth*" (spoken in the Communist General Assembly, 1954, emphasis added). "Looking at it from an economic perspective, these counter-revolutionary criminals, if not executed right off, *are a source of labor,* and if we organize them and force them into the service of the nation . . . they will have a definite effect on national development"[47] (emphasis added).

These are the general conditions under which forced labor is implemented:

1. All able bodied convicts must participate in labor production.
2. Labor regulations must be observed.
3. All must meet or surpass production quotas.
4. All must obey orders and follow instructions.
5. Those who have a poor work attitude, consistently resist reform, attempt to escape, avoid work, or hamper production will be disciplined or punished.[48]

The LRCs' three types of personnel receive slightly different salaries (please see Chapters 2, 3, and 4 for details). But they are all turned into "objects of the dictatorship" by the Communist government, and all engage in labor production within the LRC.

All within the LRC system are forced into slave labor. Those awaiting sentences and short-term prisoners in detention centers are no exception. A few serious offenders are not allowed contact with the outside world and are forced to labor in solitary confinement. According to government regulations, convicts should "engage in nine-ten hours of labor a day" and seasonal work should not exceed twelve hours.[49] In practice, however, each LRC has its own regulations, and generally speaking most convicts labor at least twelve hours a day.

The LRCs hold FJP personnel as well as CLR and RTL subjects, and every year their labor pool is strengthened by a never-ending source of dependable labor drawn from mainland Chinese society. These laborers are largely young males from every class of society and with widely differing cultural levels and abilities. Barring any major political shifts or changes in policy, these people will engage in ceaseless slave labor unless they fall ill or die. Not surprisingly, labor reform enterprises have developed into an essential component of the economy of the People's Republic.

This "achievement" of the Communist regime—segregating people into classes and political categories, taking away their freedom and rights as well as destroying their bodies, turning them into tools of production and forcing them to engage in slave labor—is historically unprecedented.

The Communist regime's regulations are clear: Labor reform production is included in overall national production planning.[50] Labor reform production (*laogai shengchan*) is controlled by various levels of the People's Government Finance and Economic Committee and can also fall under the direction of the Ministries of Agriculture and Forestry, Industry, Finance, Transportation, Water Conservancy, Commerce, etc., depending upon the nature of production.[51] At the same time, labor reform production planning is carried out under the supervision of central, provincial, and municipal levels of the financial organs and public security and judicial bureaus, from which a labor reform production supervisory committee is organized.[52]

The LRCs also serve a few special functions for the Communist regime. For example, a few LRC farms in Yunnan and Guizhou Provinces grow opium poppy and refine opium; the LRCs in Xinjiang Uygur Autonomous Region and the Qinghai and Jiangxi Provinces excavate radioactive ore and gold. Certain sources have reported that the Communist government forces prisoners to enter nuclear test sites to perform dangerous work. A few LRCs are still involved in the printing of currency, government bonds, and high-level secret documents.

All of the prison and labor reform camp dormitories and a portion of the Public Security Bureau buildings were built after 1949, primarily by labor reform teams specially dispatched by the Public Security Bureau. Thus convicts built the very walls that confine them.

Methods Employed to Maximize Convict Production

Quality of Reform Linked to Production Output. The quality of a convict's labor output is often seen as an indicator of whether he has truly reformed. The government has designed various regulations to encourage or force compliance. Labor Reform Regulations, article 68 states,

> Criminals showing any type of behavior described below may be given praise, material rewards, citations, reduced sentences, parole, etc., depending upon the level of achievement attained. . . .

3. actively labors, meeting or surpassing production quotas,
4. conserves material resources; particularly careful about caring for public property, . . .

Article 69 of the above-mentioned regulations states,

Criminals showing any of the behavior described below may be issued warnings, given disciplinary notices, confined, or otherwise punished, depending upon the severity of the infraction. . . .

2. does not care for properly or damages production tools,
3. evidences a lazy attitude towards work, . . .

Similar regulations exist for RTL subjects, like Experimental Methods in Reeducation Through Labor, article 57:

Reeducation through labor subjects who, during the course of their term, show any of the behavior described below may be given praise, commendations, material rewards, reduced sentences, early release, etc.:

1. consistently obeys regulations, studies diligently, actively labors, expresses sincere repentance for all crimes, . . .
5. meets or exceeds production quotas on a regular basis,
6. practices conservation; is particularly conscientious about caring for public property,
7. discovers innovations or improvements in production techniques."

Article 58 of the regulations mentioned above states,

Reeducation Through Labor subjects showing any of the following types of behavior may be given warnings, disciplinary notices, extension of terms, and similar sanctions, depending upon the severity of the infraction: . . .

3. consistently poor work attitude, not following directions, unwillingness to engage in labor. . . ."

Setting of Quotas. In the *laogaidui,* for every type of work and every person there is a definite daily quota that must be met; otherwise, one is guilty of "not following directions," "lazy work attitude," "poor work attitude," or "unwillingness to engage in labor."

Usually divided into three types, production quotas in the *laogaidui* are specified very carefully. The first type is for labor for which there is no precise method of measuring, for example, managing irrigation dams in rice paddies, feeding pigs, inspecting vehicle parts, monitoring natural gas levels in coal mines, etc. Most of these types of jobs are given to those considered by public security police to evince reformed behavior.

The second type is for labor for which an individual quota cannot be set, for example, coal mining excavation, much agricultural work, foundation and other construction excavation, etc. In these cases small groups are organized, with a prisoners' group representative taking responsibility. The third type is for labor for which a definite quota is given to each individual, for instance, harvesting paddies, planting rice seedlings, sorting cotton, lathing machine parts, firing bricks in a kiln, etc.

Each group or squadron has a prisoner appointed by public security police who acts as group leader and organizes the group's efforts and also acts as a bookkeeper who carefully records daily attained quotas, which are submitted to the work team and put into each prisoner's file for later reference.

The quotas for each type of labor and step of production are specified very precisely and are also usually higher than those in regular enterprises. Brick production, as an example of how the production process is divided into steps, consists of digging soil (excavating yellow soil and delivering it to a specified place—measured in cubic meters per shift); brick molding (adding water and mud, shaping bricks—pieces per shift); stacking (piling up the rough bricks—pieces per shift); loading kiln (moving the rough bricks into the kiln—pieces per shift); firing kiln (specialized prisoners); removing from kiln (moving the finished bricks out from the kiln—pieces per shift).

Linking Food Rations to Production. Prisoners' food in the LRC is rationed. These rations are similar to those given to workers in regular farms and factories, except for the fact that the actual amount of a prisoner's ration is decided by the public security police. If one is unable to work due to sickness, the public security police take this as evidence of a poor work attitude; and such "work avoiders" may have their food immediately cut off or decreased by public security police, the rationale being "no work, no food" or "light work load, light rations."

Employing Other Sanctions ("the Stick"). The *laogaidui* have a few measures to force convicts to work, for example, revoking convicts' letter-writing privileges; revoking family members' visiting rights; decreasing the monthly living allowance; giving written demerits; solitary confinement; sending convicts to supervisory teams (mass education teams); confining to handcuffs or foot shackles while not working; calling meetings of the convict's work group to criticize his poor work attitude, etc. For example, in September 1965, at Tuanhe Farm (LRC-03-11), in No. 6 company of the second battalion, a life FJP inmate named Xiu was subjected to an on-the-spot criticism meeting in the grape vineyard due to his poor work attitude in applying fertilizer to the grapes. Captain Liu ordered Xiu to take off his clothes. His hands were then tied behind him to a cement post. Captain Liu directed the other people to speak out to

The vineyard at Tuanhe Farm. Xiu was tied to one of these cement posts.

"help" him through criticism. The autumn sun was setting and the mosquitoes were gathering, blackening his face and body. Xiu shouted and struggled against his bonds. After ten minutes, Captain Liu relented, announcing dismissal and releasing Xiu. Scratching deeply at his face and body, Xiu ran to a nearby irrigation ditch and jumped in. He mixed and smoothed mud, blood, and dirty water together, rubbing the mixture over his body to ease the pain. As a result, Xiu has permanent black scars on his face and body. Due to this scarring, Xiu became a reticent man. One year later, when he was thirty-two, Xiu disappeared. The grapes still grow year after year and are exported to foreign countries, being made into such wines as Dynasty, a product of a joint venture between China and the French cognac company Remy Martin that is sold all over the world. The sale of Dynasty wine grapes and other forced labor products to foreign countries enables the Communist regime to obtain hard currency with which they buy rubber bullets from West Germany to use against their own people.

From Paris wire services, June 8, 1990:

Peter Sonkovski, deputy managing director of Remy et Associes, admitted that prison labor had been used between 1982 and 1986 on the vineyard

Dynasty Dry Rosé Wine is produced by the Sino-French Joint Venture Winery, Ltd., Tianjin, People's Republic of China. This bottle was purchased in a supermarket in Santa Clara County, California, in May 1990. It is imported by Nan Yang Trading Company, Inc., Palo Alto, California.

that supplied the company's Tianjin plant but said the firm had been kept completely in the dark about this practice.

When asked why the use of convict labor had been stopped in 1986, Mr. Sonkovski said he imagined that "the Chinese municipality must have found a better source of [labor]." [The "better source of labor" referred to probably consists of FJP personnel.]

The author for many years served as prison labor in this camp, growing table grapes for export to foreign countries. In 1965, there were 8 million pounds of grapes from Tuanhe Farm exported to Hong Kong and Japan.

CHART 1.5   Coal Production Levels and Profits of Shandong Province Daizhuang Labor
Reform Branch, from 1984 through 1988

Year	Output (million ton)	Increase (percent)	Profit (10,000 yuan)	Increase (percent)
1984	7.0			
1985	15.3	118.5	106.2	
1986	20.87	36.4	200.42	88.7
1987	26.06	24.9	252.6	24.4
1988	31.11	19.4	480.7	90.3

Employing a System of Rewards ("the Carrot"). The *laogaidui* use a
few measures to encourage convicts to work, for example, increasing the
monthly living allowance; bestowing the title "active reformer"; giving
written commendations; reducing sentences; increasing food rations; giving family members special visiting privileges, etc.

Much of the forced labor in the LRC is carried out under the direction
of public security police, who employ various methods to encourage and
take advantage of a certain proportion of prisoners (or FJP personnel)
as well as other (often violent) methods to compel the large majority.
Usually the number of public security police is 10–15 percent of the total
population of prisoners and FJP personnel. A large number of the police
not only do not understand production techniques but also have no
understanding of labor management. Moreover, organizing and managing
a group of people with widely differing cultural backgrounds and from
every class of society into a team that can engage in agricultural and
industrial production is obviously no easy task. The Communist regime
has been very successful in utilizing criminals to control other criminals
and manage labor production.

Forced Labor Production

Because it utilizes low-wage or no-wage forced labor power, labor
reform production is highly efficient and, predictably, very profitable. For
example, Shandong Province's Laiyang Labor Reform Branch's (LRC-21-
23, established February 1984) production, profits, and exports over a
five-year period increased annually at rates of 28.5 percent, 48.3 percent
and 43 percent respectively. Similarly, Liaoning Province's Tile House
Labor Reform Branch's (LRC-27-12, established 1952) production in-
creases annually at a rate of 13 percent. Shandong Province's Daizhuang
Labor Reform Branch (LRC-21-44, established 1984) from 1984 to 1988
had production levels (of coal) and profits noted in Chart 1.5.

In the past ten years, LRC officials have been very concerned that
convicts learn production techniques and skills; this undoubtedly is necessary for the continued development of labor reform production. Those

convicts in the LRCs with specialized skills or knowledge are all greatly valued and their talents are fully utilized. Taiyuan City's (Shanxi Province) biggest hotel, Yinze Guest House, was not only built by the Shanxi LRC but was also designed by former architectural engineer Lin (last name), who was arrested in 1952. In 1965, two counter-revolutionary rightists who had been sentenced to RTL at Beijing's Tuanhe Farm (both with the last name Liu—one graduated from Shanghai's St. John's University, one from America's Columbia University) had originally been brought to Beijing City's public security school to teach English.

Labor Reform Enterprise's Place
in the Economic System
of the People's Republic of China

Labor Reform Regulations, article 30, states, "The production of labor reform should serve in the development of the national economy, and should be included in overall national production planning." Article 35 adds, ". . . in accordance with each district's criminal production situation and national development needs, unified plans will be drafted to govern the transfer of criminals and the distribution of labor power."

Labor reform camps' armies of low-paid, forced, highly efficient workers play a very important role in the Communist government's "socialist construction." The production of labor reform industries constitutes a large proportion of the PRC's national economy.

In accordance with official regulations, each LRC in the People's Republic of China has two names. Within the public security and legislative bureaus, each camp is known as XX Prison; XX Reeducation Through Labor Camp; Number X Labor Reform Team, Branch X, Detachment X; XX Education Camp for Juvenile Offenders; Number X Labor Reform Camp, Branch X, XX Job Placement Team; etc. Outside these bureaus, however, the camps are known to the general public by "production units names, determined by their type of production."[53] Each camp is thus publicly known as XX Farm; XX Coal Mine; XX Steel Mill; XX Electric Welding Device Factory; XX Air-Powered Tool Factory; XX Ceramic Factory; XX Chemical Plant; XX Tea Factory; XX Construction Company, etc. Of these two types of names, the first are used internally, the second publicly. With the exception of a few prisons or LRCs that display their prison or LRC names on their signs, the vast majority of display signs note only their industrial names and thus from the outside appear no different from regular factories, farms, or mining operations. The Communist government refers to labor reform enterprises as "special state-run enterprises." This uniqueness is mainly apparent in the fact that, although they are dictatorial organizations, they also have

Very seldom is the internal name of a labor reform camp used publicly. This is one such instance. The signboard on the left reads "Shanghai Baimaoling Farm"; the one on the right reads "Shanghai No. 2 Labor Reform Disciplinary General Brigade" (LRC-29-11). The camp is located in Anhui Province and includes at least seven battalions. One of its branches is a valve factory that produces low-pressure valves that are exported to foreign countries, including the United States.

attributes of state-owned enterprises; their purpose is to carry out reform first, production second. The labor power of these enterprises comes entirely from criminals; in other aspects, they are very similar to other state-run enterprises."[54] Labor reform enterprises have full-scale production planning, financing systems, wage and benefits packages, etc. All labor reform enterprises are under the control of the Public Security and Judicial bureaus, but at the same time come under the central direction of the Bureau of Production.

Communist labor reform enterprises constitute a vast system of production, encompassing agriculture, industry, transportation, and construction. This system's production planning, commodity exchange, allocation of natural resources, imports, exports, etc. are all organized in such a way as to play a part in the Communists' "socialist construction."

In the past forty years, labor reform camps played a large role in many important socialist construction projects, for example,

1. Hui River Valley Water Conservancy Project (1950s)
2. Heilongjiang River Valley Northern Wilderness Development Project (1950s and 1960s)
3. Subei General Irrigation Project (1950s)

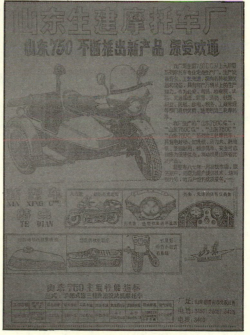

Above: The entrance of Shandong Province Shengjian Motorcycle Engine Factory (LRC-21-05). The left signboard reads "Shandong Province Taishan Yuxin School." *Right:* A motorcycle advertisement in *Chungguo fazi ribao* (China Legal Daily), February 12, 1987. The motorcycle pictured (model Sandong-750) is produced by Shengjian Motorcycle Engine Factory, which turns out 10,000 a year.

4. Xinjiang Public Road and Agricultural Development Project (1950s–1980s)
5. Qinghai Province Public Road and Agricultural Development Project (1950s–1980s)
6. Several mining operations in Shanxi province (Jinpushan, Yin-Ying, Xinzhi, Yangfanghou (1950s–1980s)
7. Inner Mongolia Jier Railway Project (Jining-Erenhot) (1950s)
8. Baolan Railway Project (Inner Mongolia Autonomous Region, Baotou City to Gansu Province, Lianzhou City, 1950s)
9. Chengyu Railway Project (Szechuan province, Chengdu City to Chongqing city, 1950s)
10. Lanqing Railway Project (Gansu Province, Lianzhou City to Qinghai Province, Xining City, 1960s)
11. Chengkun Railway Project (Szechuan Province, Chengdu City to Yunnan Province, Kunming City, 1950s)
12. Baocheng Railway Project (Shaanxi Province, Baoji City to Szechuan Province, Chengdu City, 1950s)

In recent years, it has been impossible to establish with any certainty what portion of the PRC's economy and production is made up of labor reform enterprises. However, certain aspects revealed in the following analyses may help in understanding the economic benefit provided by the labor reform enterprises.

Labor reform enterprises (*laogai qiye*)—whether factories, mines, or farms—are all enterprises under the control of the citizens of the People's Republic of China. As with other state-run enterprises, they are organized among the various departments of the Communist government. The only difference is that all of the laborers in labor reform enterprises are convicts and FJP personnel and the enterprise managers are public security and judicial personnel.

The average yearly salary of a worker in 1986 in one of the People's Republic of China's state-run enterprises was 1,329 *yuan*.[55] In labor reform enterprises, CLR convicts have no salary other than a prison cell, prison garb, and limited food provided by the authorities—the minimum necessities of life (please see Chapter 2 for details). Calculating this in terms of money, it is approximately equivalent to 20 percent of the earnings of a regular worker; RTL subjects receive a salary of approximately 30 percent of a regular worker (please see Chapter 3 for details). The salary received by personnel is approximately 60 percent that of a regular worker (please see Chapter 4 for details). A rough estimate places the average income of the three types of personnel at about 40 percent that of regular workers. If we calculate on the basis of an average salary of 1,329 *yuan,* workers in this type of "special state-run enterprise" (that is, the three types of personnel) are paid about 800 *yuan* less annually per person. Assuming that the total number of the three types of personnel is between 16 and 20 million, the Communist government is robbing between 12.8 and 16 billion *yuan* a year from these workers' salaries. To put this figure in perspective, the People's Republic of China's defense budget in 1987 was 20.02 billion *yuan*.

Although it is impossible to obtain statistics on the overall productive value of the labor reform enterprises, reference can be made to the following concrete statistics and information:

> . . . the two labor organizations [i.e., labor reform and reeducation through labor enterprises] in Jiangsu province . . . last year's [1985] industrial and agricultural production exceeded 247 million yuan and net profit was more than 30 million yuan, a more than 15 percent increase over the year before.[56]

> Shanxi province's Labor Reform work unit's . . . last year's [1983] end of year realized profits were 17.45 percent greater than in 1982; profits submitted to the government reached 10 million yuan. Industrial production was 120 million yuan [not including agricultural work units], an increase of 4.25 percent over 1982. Agriculture also exceeded projected production by 14.23 percent. These [labor reform] enterprises are included in [provincial] annual production planning for the fifteen essential commodities; the production of raw coal, bricks, air compressors, and low-pressure valves all greatly exceeded expectations.[57]

The chief of Beijing Municipal Labor Reform Bureau, Wei Xiang Ru, has noted

> Labor Reform work in Beijing Municipality was instituted earlier than in the rest of the country . . . in the past thirty years . . . it has resulted in great material accomplishments, creating industrial and agricultural production of more than 2.3 billion yuan . . . the Golden Horse nylon socks produced by the Beijing Municipal prisons are not only enthusiastically received by the domestic market, but have also entered the international market; Qinghe Machine Factory is first in the nation in the production of battery-driven vehicles, and its products are sold all over the nation, along with Tuanhe Farm's roses and green grapes, and Chinghe Farm's prawns.[58]

The Chief Justice of Fujian Province, Chen Zhen Liang, noted that

> In Fujian Province . . . since Labor Reform and Reeducation Through Labor began to concentrate on agriculture, all aspects of agricultural production in Fujian have developed greatly. Overall production has jumped from 13,610,000 yuan in 1982 to 42,500,000 yuan in 1987; from a deficit of 1,640,000 yuan to a surplus of 4,050,000 yuan.[59]

These photographs were provided by the Hubei Province Reform Bureau as part of a pictorial entitled "The Development of Xiangyang Machine Tool Factory of Hubei Province." *Above:* The entrance of the camp; the signboard reads "Hubei Province Xiangyang Machine Tool Factory." *Top Right:* Several certificates of commendation for machine tool quality bestowed by the Ministry of Machinery and Electronics, People's Republic of China; the Labor Reform Bureau of Hubei Province; and others. *Bottom Right:* A shaping machine, model B6050B; it has been exported to more than forty countries through intermediaries, including Dadong Company of Hong Kong, General Motors Company of Hong Kong, and Singapore Machinery Company.

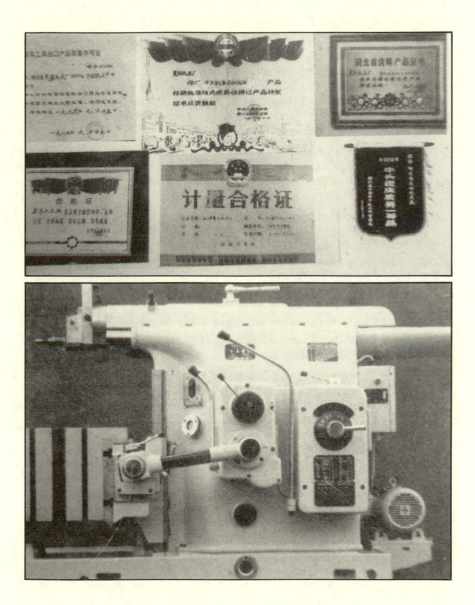

Guangdong Province's Labor Reform industrial and agricultural organizations' production in 1961 first broke the 100 million *yuan* mark . . . in 1988 the total production of all labor reform industries and agricultural concerns province-wide was 155.73 million *yuan,* an increase of 33.7 percent over the previous year.[60]

. . . . [Hubei Province's] Gengzhou Prison [this prison is also known as Xinsheng Dye Factory and specializes in confining serious offenders; in this book it is referred to as LRC-19-28], in the three years from 1986–1988, had an overall industrial production of 62,230,000 *yuan.* . . . Its products are already sold in a few foreign countries and autonomous regions, and have earned us $U.S. 8.49 million in foreign currency.[61]

[Shanghai Municipal] Huadong Electric Welding Machine Factory, a camp of FJP personnel [referred to in this book as LRC-29-07], in November [1985] reached a production level of 32,240,000 *yuan;* 14.56 million *yuan* in profits was submitted to the government.[62]

[Liaoning Province's] House Tile Enterprise, Labor Reform branch [referred to in this book as LRC-27-12] . . . houses over 2,000 criminals. . . . In 1988 its industrial production reached 26.23 million *yuan,* realized 7.06 million *yuan* in profits, and had total sales of 47.77 million *yuan.* Since 1952 it has grown by 13 percent every year, exporting machinery to the countries of Southeast Asia, and is considered one of our nation's Grade 2 Enterprises.[63]

The Judicial Bureau's deputy justice, Jin Jian, on December 7, 1988, at the National Convicted Labor Reform and Reeducation Through Labor Work Conference, noted that

. . . in the past 5 years, Convicted Labor Reform and Reeducation Through Labor work units everywhere have been undergoing re-structuring; expanded or newly-constructed mid- and small-scale production units number over 700, and over half of these have already begun active production. Last year the net value of fixed capital was 1.5 times that of 1983, and last year's industrial and agricultural production was 56 percent greater than in 1983. Among the CLR and RTL enterprises, there are already over 30 types of products that have received national awards for outstanding quality; 350 types of products are considered provincial or departmental outstanding products; 8 enterprises are considered Grade 2 National Enterprises; and over 60 enterprises are considered Advanced Provincial Enterprises.[64]

1983 statistics:

Labor Reform Enterprises' (LRE) industrial products total over 200 types, including light industrial products. Metal products include lead, zinc, tin, gold, copper and mercury; mining products include coal, iron, sulphur, and phosphorous; mechanical and electrical products include automobiles, machine tools, electrical components and electrical instruments; chemical products include chemical fertilizer, sulfur, recycled rubber and industrial chemicals; light industrial products include cotton cloth, fans, leather shoes and clothing. LRE also supply over 20 types of agricultural products, the most important being soybeans, oil products, tea leaves, fruit and fowl. In 1983, LRC nationwide produced over 12 million tons of raw coal, over 6,000 machine tools of various sorts, over 6,000 agricultural irrigation pumps, 16,000 tons of zinc, over 200 tons of mercury (one-fifth of the total national production), 25,000 tons of asbestos (one-fourth of the total national production), over 16,000 tons of cast steel pipes, over a billion *jin* [about 500 million kg] of grain, and 24 million *jin* [about 12 million kg] of tea leaves (one-third of the total national production).[65]

As a Communist legal scholar noted, "In the past forty years, the People's Republic of China's 'Labor Reform' production has already become a major force in such projects as water conservancy, road building, wasteland development, mining, construction, and other heavy labor intensive fields, in developing the handicraft industries and in increasingly mechanizing and automating all types of heavy and light industry. A few of its products have received national silver medals for quality and have entered the international market."[66] A glance at Appendix 2 will help us to understand this situation. Appendix 2 employs classifications used by the U.S. Department of Commerce for foreign trade, separating commodities into 99 categories. A lack of information precludes drawing conclusions about 35 of the categories; however, based on an analysis of current information, it can be proven that the other 64 categories all contain products provided by labor reform enterprises.

Never before has there been a nation with a prison system so extensive that it pervades all aspects of national production, has such careful planning and organization, and composes such an integral part of a people's economic and productive system.

The labor reform camps and labor reform production, then, are not only essential to the Communist government's political control but also constitute an integral part of the economy of the socialist society. It is apparent that if from a human rights point of view it was demanded that the LRCs be abolished, not only would this demand be rejected by the Communist dictatorship for political reasons but from an economic angle it would also be extremely difficult to accept.

Notes

1. Gongan fagui huiban 1950–1979 (Collection of the Public Security Regulations of the People's Republic of China, 1950–1979), Beijing: Legal Press, 1980, pp. 195–206.

2. Ibid., p. 207.

3. Ibid., pp. 209, 211.

4. "On the Correct Handling of Contradictions Among the People," in *Mao Zedong xuanji* (Selected Works of Mao Zedong), vol. 4, Beijing: People's Press, February 27, 1957, p. 393.

5. Ibid., p. 364.

6. Ibid., p. 371.

7. "Upholding the Four Basic Principles," in *Deng Xiaoping xuanji* (Selected Works of Deng Xiaoping), Beijing: People's Press, March 30, 1979, p. 87.

8. Ibid., p. 92.

9. *Liening quanji* (Lenin's Complete Works), Beijing: People's Press, 1965, Pp. 28, 218.

10. The Agrarian Land Reform was a revolutionary mass movement launched on a national scale in 1950 to redistribute land among the rural peasants.

11. The Movement to Suppress Counter-revolutionaries took place from 1950 to 1952 and was carried out by the CCP to suppress counter-revolutionaries, i.e., former military personnel and government officials of the nationalist regime in mainland China and others who maintained power from prerevolutionary times.

12. There are many accounts of persecutions during the Communists' "mass movements" from the victims themselves, relatives, or witnesses, but most of these reports and affidavits have been labeled by the Communists as works of class enemies, written "with ulterior motives." Here is an excerpt from one of these accounts: [During the Agrarian Land Reform Revolution. A scene from the "revolution" in a small village in Pinggu County, Hebei Province, now part of Beijing municipality]: "At dusk one September day, a village leader who had once served as a CCP functionary but was not terribly popular was tightly bound with his hands behind his back and hung by his neck from a tree. He kicked wildly, bloody foam coming from his mouth, as he shouted 'I've been wronged! I've been wronged!' His fellow villagers looked on impassively. In accordance with tradition, they voted on this man's fate by tossing soybeans into a bowl. Once the vote tallier shouted that a majority had been reached, the executioner raised a loaded rifle and fired. The old village chief's intestines flowed out onto the ground. Another big fellow had been bound and hung in a tree, but he died rather quickly. A group of elementary school students who were being encouraged to engage in revolutionary activity had been watching. At the encouragement of the adults, they used awls, scissors, small knives and nails to poke the man's eyes out, dig holes in his flesh, slash his body and smear mud on the wounds. One excited small boy leapt up and cut off the prisoner's ears as if he was cutting leaves from a tree. It was said that this prisoner's only crime was that it was discovered that during his grandfather's time his family had employed a farm worker; according to the spirit of government policy, this penniless peasant was thus considered to be a landlord, turning into an enemy of the people overnight . . . Agrarian Revolution activities in Pinggong county manifested themselves in random violence and killing, fields left until they were overrun with weeds, and forced arranged marriages . . . during the [Agrarian Revolution] movement a soldier's widowed mother was forced into re-marriage with a hired laborer."

This account is quoted from a paper entitled "The General Situation." The author of this document is a very reliable source—in 1947 he served in the Communist government as consignment officer in the Hebei Provincial Military Administration. In January of 1988 he was transferred by the Airforce Rear Logistics Bureau to Nanjing Military zone as a major general to serve as an air force administrator.

13. Gongan fagui huiban 1950–1979 (Public Security Regulations of the People's Republic of China, 1950–1979), Beijing: Legal Press, 1980, article 8.

14. Ibid., article 9.

15. Ibid., article 11.

16. Laodong gaizao gongzuo (Labor Reform Work), Beijing: CCP internally circulated document, 1985, p. 47.

17. *Fulu yi shenghuo* (Law and Life), Changsha: Legal Press, January 1989, p. 29.

18. Public Security Regulations, article 23.

19. Laodong jiaoyang shixing banfa (Experimental Methods in Reeducation Through Labor), Beijing: CCP internal document, January 21, 1982, article 7.

20. Public Security Regulations, article 1.

21. *China Statistical Yearbook, 1987,* Beijing: China Statistical Press, 1988.

22. Experimental Methods in RTL, article 8.

23. Ibid., article 7.

24. Ibid., article 4.

25. Public Security Regulations, article 2.

26. Laojiao gongzuo (Reeducation Through Labor Work), Beijing: CCP internal document, 1983, p. 66.

27. Dong Cunjiang, "Reasons Not to Abolish the RTL Commission," *Legal Daily,* Beijing: August 10, 1987.

28. Laodong gaizao gongzuo (Labor Reform Work), Beijing: CCP internal document, 1985, p. 1.

29. "An Examination of the Scientific Necessity of and Research Objectives in Establishing Labor Reform," Legal Research, 1985, first issue, p. 58. Beijing: Studies in Law, China Social Science Press.

30. Labor Reform Work, p. 6.

31. According to information contained in the document referred to in Note 30, assuming there are currently 4 million convicts in the *laogaidui,* 400,000 of them are political counter-revolutionaries; among these about 65,000 have a "counter-revolutionary background"—i.e., served with the Kuomintang government forty years ago.

32. Criminal Code of the People's Republic of China, in Collected Public Security Regulations, 1950–1979, Beijing: People's Publishing Society, p. 18, article 19.

33. In 1954 Hu Feng criticized the Communist Party for using Mao Zedong's thought to restrict the freedom of writers. This triggered a nationwide movement to eradicate Hu's and all other heterodox tendencies and ideas. In the course of the campaign, the Party propagandists encouraged the whole population to uncover any latent "Hu Fengism" within themselves and continued to use his case

in a general campaign to liquidate all unorthodox thinking and hunt out counter-revolutionaries.

34. CCP Central Politburo–State Council's Several Regulations Concerning a Strengthening of Public Security Work During the Great Proletariat Cultural Revolution, Document No. 19. Issued by CCP Central Politburo, State Council on Jan 13, 1967. The document has six regulations in total (it is often referred to in abbreviated form as Six Public Security Regulations); the second regulation reads as follows: "Any and all who send anonymous counter-revolutionary letters, secretly or publicly mount posters or distribute counter-revolutionary leaflets, write reactionary mottos or shout reactionary slogans, in order to attack or defame our great leader Mao Zedong or his close comrade-in-arms Lin Biao, will be considered Active Counter-revolutionaries and appropriately punished by law."

35. "Warfare and Strategy," in *Mao Zedong xuanji* (Selected Works of Mao Zedong), vol. 2, Beijing: People's Press, November 16, 1938, p. 535.

36. Labor Reform Work, p. 87.

37. Ibid., p. 63.

38. Experimental Methods in Reeducation Through Labor, No. 17, article 57.

39. Ibid.

40. *Fazhi ribao* (Legal Daily), Beijing: April 18, 1988, p. 3.

41. A *mu* is a measure of land equal to 733.5 square yards.

42. *Legal Daily,* p. 3.

43. Laogai gaizao tiaoli (Labor Reform Regulations), Beijing: September 7, 1954, article 72. According to the author's personal experience, the procedure for extending the term of labor reform is much simpler than it sounds. In the various *laogaidui,* about two or three times a year a meeting of prisoners is held (rewards and punishments meeting, annual ideology mass meeting, etc.). At these meetings a public security cadre reads off a list of prisoners who for "resisting labor" or similar reasons have had their sentences extended, the case having been investigated by XX Public Security Bureau and approved by XX People's Court. There is no legal procedure such as appeal, legal defense, etc. These prisoners are already in jail, so they need not pass through such procedures.

44. Labor Reform Work, p. 89.

45. Ibid., p. 48.

46. Laodong gaizao tiaoli (Labor Reform Regulations), Beijing: September 7, 1954, article 4.

47. *Renmin ribao* (People's Daily), Beijing: May 24, 1951.

48. Zuifan Gaizao shouce (Crime Reformation Register), Beijing: Central Judicial Ministry, Labor Reform Bureau, 1986, p. 133.

49. Labor Reform Regulations, article 52.

50. Ibid., article 30.

51. Experimental Methods in RTL, article 5; Labor Reform Regulations, article 31.

52. Ibid.

53. Methods for Conscientiously Implementing Reeducation Through Labor, article 7, Beijing: Communist government internal document, No. 17, January 21, 1982.

54. "Selections from Newspapers and Periodicals," Beijing: China People's University Periodicals Center, June 1987, p. 122.

55. *Renmin ribao* (People's Daily), Beijing: March 26, 1986.

56. Ibid.

57. *Fazhi ribao* (Legal Daily), Beijing: April 16, 1984.

58. Fazhi jianshe (Law and Order), Beijing: February 1988.

59. Fazhi jianshe (Law and Order), March 1988.

60. *Legal Daily,* May 29, 1989.

61. Fazhi jianshe (Law and Order), January 1989.

62. *Legal Daily,* February 8, 1986.

63. *Legal Daily,* October 5, 1989.

64. *China Annual Statistical Review,* Beijing: China Statistical Publishing Society, 1989.

65. *People's Daily,* April 20, 1986.

66. Laodong gaizao zuifan de lilun yu shijian (Labor Reform Criminals—Theory and Practice), Beijing: Legal Press, 1987, p. 268.

2

Convicted Labor Reform *(Laogai)*

Convicted labor reform *(laogai)* refers to situations in which a criminal is arrested by the Communist authorities and sentenced to reform through hard labor in a prison, a labor reform disciplinary production camp, or a juvenile offender camp. When the word "labor" is used in terms seen in Communist official documents or propaganda—such as "double labor personnel" *(lianglao renyuan)*, "double labor enterprises" *(lianglao qiye)*, or "double labor work" *(lianglao gongzuo)*—one "labor" refers to convicted labor reform, the other to reeducation through labor.

Laogai is the mainstay of the LRC system. Reeducation through labor *(laojiao)* is often seen as a supplement or auxiliary part of *laogai*. Forced job placement *(jiuye)* is a derivative of the two.

The General Development of Convicted Labor Reform

The LRCs were not only founded by the Communist regime after it took power in 1949. Back in the 1930s, when the Communists began their armed revolution, they would first capture a territory and establish a power base, then organize what amounted to LRCs under various names. Although these camps were on a much smaller scale than those of today, the basic organization, management techniques, slave-like hard labor, and harsh conditions were not much different. The LRC per se developed as the range of the Communist regime's power extended, following like a shadow in the wake of Communist liberation. The development of the LRC system before 1949 can be divided into three stages.

First Stage (1927–1937, the So-called Second Revolutionary Civil War Period)

During this period the Communists were subjected to a campaign of encirclement and annihilation by the Kuomintang and were practicing a strategy of guerrilla warfare. Near the border of Jiangxi and Fujian provinces they established a "Chinese-Soviet republic"; the arrangement of the public security, legislative, and labor reform organs is pictured in Chart 2.1. Most of the people confined in this period were guilty of "plotting to overthrow or destroy the Soviet regime and power of the peasant and worker democratic revolution—counter-revolutionaries hoping to preserve or restore the rule of the landlord and capitalist classes."[1] The Communists' "forced prison interrogations . . . often ended in . . . cases of serious torture and maltreatment."[2] According to statistics, at that time 95 percent of prisoners were executed without trial. Before being killed, "less serious offenders"—including those who had violated no laws but were treated as criminals merely because they belonged to the landlord or rich peasant classes[3]—were organized into "hard labor teams" that were sent to the front to perform military logistic duties as a special form of punishment. The Communists referred to this practice as "adapting to the needs of a revolutionary war."[4] In October of 1932, for example, there were over 900 hard labor team convicts (*kugongdui*) at Central Base in Jiangxi Province. This was the ancestor of the Communist LRC.

In June of 1932 the Communists began to consider slave labor in central production plans. According to a document released at Central Base in June 1932—Chinese Soviet Republic's Temporary Judicial Organizations and Regulations—a labor reformatory was to be established. A "labor reformatory" was "an organization to educate and reform criminals . . . and also function as a work unit . . . in order to further strengthen the People's Economic Organizations' control over labor reform production."[5] "Labor reform production was rapidly proving to be an important supplementary force in supplying materials to Central Base; in order to increase their control over production of the labor reformatory, the Central Worker and Peasant Government incorporated it into overall economic planning. . . . Under the poor production conditions and with dearth of raw materials possessed by the Central Base regime at that time, the labor reformatory still managed to produce a great deal of consumer goods and military products. . . . [The labor reformatory] not only relieved the financial burden of the [Central Base] regime, but also increased government's income."[6] This was the Communists' first attempt at labor reform production.

Half a century later, the purposes, achievements, nature, and organization of Communist LRC and labor reform production are essentially the same as those of the labor reformatory of 1932, only immensely larger in scale. At that time, although the Communist regime claimed to be established as a nation, there was still no legal system. The arrest and sentencing of so-called criminals was directly decided by various levels of Communist officials. Because the base areas were not very stable, often

CHART 2.1 The Arrangement of the Public Security, Legislative, and Labor Reform Organs

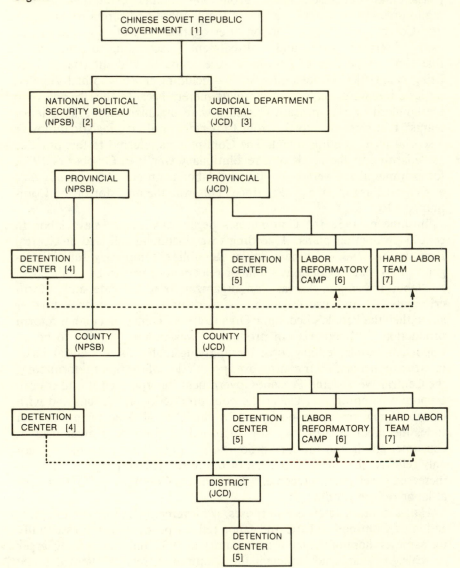

[1] Central base established by the CCP in Jiangxi and Fujian provinces, called the Chinese Soviet Republic. [2] The National Political Security Bureau (NPSB) *zhengzhi baoweiju* was the communists' organ for purging dissent. It was established at central, provincial, and county levels. Its responsibilities consisted of "arresting, detaining, and interrogating counter-revolutionaries." [3] The Judicial Department (JCD) was the CCP's judicial organ and was established at central, provincial, and county levels. Its responsibilities consisted of "punishing troublemakers among the revolutionary ranks and common criminal offenders among the masses." Some local CCP organs combined the National Political Security Bureau and the Judicial Department into one "Counter-Revolutionary Purging Committee" *sufan weiyuanhui*. [4] National Political Security Bureau's detention centers. At this time prisons had not been established. Detention centers housed sentenced counter-revolutionaries and those still awaiting sentencing. [5] The Judicial Department's detention centers generally housed common criminals who were awaiting sentencing. [6] Labor Reformatory Camps *laodong ganhua yuan* (referred to in some regions—such as E-Yu-Wan region and Chuanshaan region—as "prisons") specialized in detaining serious offenders. [7] Hard Labor Team *kugondui* housed short-term convicts. Its guidelines for inmates were as follows: (1) no serious counter-revolutionaries; (2) poor convicts with less than two-year sentences; (3) landlords with less than one-and-a-half-year sentences; (4) those sentenced to forced labor (most landlords and rich peasants). Hard Labor Team prisoners were sent to the front to serve the war effort.

---

when a threatening situation developed criminals were simply rounded up and executed.

Second Stage (1937–1945, the So-called War of Resistance Against Japan Period)

During this period the Communist regime strengthened itself politically and militarily, becoming comparatively stable. The number of jails and detention centers in the liberated areas increased dramatically, and the rate of execution of prisoners dropped somewhat. During this time the Communists also began to organize legislative and public security institutions. Although the jail system was still not complete, many LRC policies and organization systems already had begun to develop.

On November 6, 1942, the "Communist Party Central Committee's Explanation of Lenient Political Measures" mentioned "a blending of harsh and lenient political measures." This was the origin of the Communists' present emphasis on "leniency with those who cooperate, harshness with those who resist."

Another point of interest during this period was that besides strengthening slave labor production and organizing different terms of forced labor for criminals, the Communists also instituted previously unknown measures such as an organized "thought reform" process, an intensifying of Communist ideological propaganda, and an emphasis on thought reform as a basic goal to attain a "change in political standpoint, so that through true repentance one can become a new man."[7]

During this time "prison production work" (i.e, labor reform production) not only developed and expanded very quickly but became organized under a managerial system, a system that remains largely unchanged to this day. In the opinion of the Communist regime: "[labor reform production] . . . provided a great service in alleviating the material and economic hardships suffered during trying wartime conditions."[8] From the following examples we can see that slave labor production has played a consistently central role in labor reform policies:

- In 1940, the Communist's Shaanganning Mobilization Region organized all prisoners with sentences of over three years into a "hard labor team," which extended the roads in Shaanxi Province, Yan'an Prefecture, by 30 kilometers, brought under cultivation 1,000 *mu* of wilderness, established coal mines and shoe factories, etc.
- In 1942, the Pusui Mobilization Region Prison brought 30 *mu* of wilderness under cultivation, grew 10 *mu* of vegetables, built 40 spinning wheels and established an iron foundry, a weaving factory, a construction team, and centers to process wheat and bean curd. It expanded in 1946 to include a wool processing factory, a textile factory, a livestock farm, a sawmill, a charcoal factory, and other enterprises.
- Linbei County Prison had a coal-transporting team of prisoners that employed 70 small handcarts and 2 large carts.
- Taihang Regional Jail, starting from scratch, by 1946 had under cultivation over 2,000 *mu* of land and working capital of 1,400,000 *yuan*.
- Ciwu County Jail established a wool-processing factory, which produced woolen clothes, pants, hats, gloves, etc., for Communist Party cadres.
- Shaanganning Mobilization Region's earnings (calculated in rice) for 1940 were 329 *dan*[9]; for 1941, 450 *dan;* for 1942, 540 *dan.*
- Pingshan County Prison's 1945 profits (in grain) were 15,300 *dan,* cash profits 285,000 yuan—enough money to cover the jail's expenses for two years.
- Shexian County Jail's production of rice, over and above that which was consumed by the jail's prisoners and personnel, was over 6,000 pecks.[10]

Third Stage (1945–1949, the So-called War of Liberation Period)

The Communists during this period gained control of a large number of municipal jails and needed to deal with a large number of political counter-revolutionary criminals. At that time they announced "The Three 'In Order Tos'" (*sange weiliao*): "In order to reform prisoners, in order to overcome difficulties, and in order to prevent counter-revolutionary activists from sitting inactive and getting a free meal from the state."[11] Therefore, the Communists instituted a large-scale system of forced labor and organized labor reform production.

In 1947, in Heilongjiang Province's Harbin Municipality the Communists established a labor reform convicts' weaving factory, printing factory, military uniform factory, and even a factory to produce "6.0" artillery shells to support the war efforts. Some 27 percent of the income from this LRC in 1949 went toward maintaining the prison. The remaining 73 percent was submitted to the government or used to finance additional production.[12]

After 1948, the number of political counter-revolutionary prisoners increased dramatically in response to the political and military needs of wartime, and "due to the inability of existing prisons to accommodate the new influx of prisoners, the judicial organs of many areas began moving prisoners out of the jails and cities to the villages and mines, in order to establish new reformatory bases. . . . For example, Harbin Municipal Jail moved 55.75 percent of its prisoners to mines or farms to engage in hard labor."[13] For various reasons, in January of 1949 and beginning in the Northeast, the Communists established Shuangyaze Criminal Mining Labor Reform Camp, Lingdong Mine Criminal Labor Reform Camp, Songha Criminal Labor Reform Camp (farm), and similar institutions. These few LRCs were models for the next forty years of the Communist LRC system. The Communist Public Security Bureau announced the following four important points regarding LRCs: (1) they would not have confining jail architecture but rather broad industrial or agricultural production areas; (2) prisoners would be organized along military principles, with selected prisoners to manage and control those below them, thus cutting down on the number of public security cadres and police needed; (3) there would be specified general regulatory, organizational, labor, and reform measures; and (4) the government would seek to obtain the greatest profits with the least amount of capital investment.[14] Even more important was the suppression and purging of counter-revolutionary activists, and the resulting preservation and consolidation of the Communist regime.

With this experience and these principles as a model, after the Communist regime gained control of the entire nation in 1949, it instituted a system of LRCs at central, provincial, and county levels on a scale previously unprecedented. The Communists announced that "not only will this result in great savings in jail construction costs and personnel, but these prisoners will quickly become a major source of labor for society."[15]

The Development of Labor Reform Camps After 1949

In June of 1952, at which time the Communists called the First Plenary Labor Reform Work Congress (although official labor reform legal provisions were not publicly announced by the Politburo until September 7, 1954), there had already been established at a national level 640 labor reform farms and 217 mines as well as large labor reform units involved in the Zhihuai Water Conservancy Project and the Chengyu Railroad Construction Project.[16] This was the "first flourishing" of CLR.

Those sentenced to *laogai* for political reasons—such as nationalist soldiers and officials, landlords, rich peasants, capitalists, active counterrevolutionaries, rightists, etc.—constituted 90 percent of the total prisoner population (not including RTL personnel). The total number of *laogai* prisoners was between 10–20 million.

After 1958, production and daily life in the LRC were greatly affected by the Great Leap Forward movement promoted by the Communists and by the Three Years of Natural Disasters that followed. This was a very difficult period; many prisoners lost their lives during the intense forced labor of the Great Leap Forward period and during the famines that followed.[17]

After 1963, the national economy took a turn for the better and the LRC system began to develop again. By 1965, the Communists had established over 800 fairly large labor reform factories, mines, and farms.[18]

Nineteen sixty-six marked the beginning of The Great Cultural Revolution. One aspect of this period was the various levels of revolutionary committees, Red Guards, and rebels that arose throughout mainland Chinese society at the time who had no use for the courts or the dictatorial organization of labor reform camps—they were accustomed to taking people into custody, administering beatings, and performing interrogations and executions at will. At the time this type of direct action was referred to as The Entire People's Proletariat Dictatorship. Another feature of this period was the legal and public security organs, which were under the control of Liu Shaoqi, Peng Jen, and Luo Ruiqing. These three were not trusted by Mao Zedong, Lin Biao, and Jiang Qing, and the LRC system was paralyzed together with the public security system, the number of LRCs dropped to half their former level, land under cultivation dropped 60 percent, and over 2 billion *yuan* in fixed capital was lost. For example, a traditionally more developed "labor reform work" area, Heilongjiang Province, before 1966 had 4.8 million *mu* of land under cultivation and

every year submitted to the government an amount of grain that constituted one-third of the province's total grain production; however, during
the Cultural Revolution period land under cultivation dropped to 335,000
mu, and no excess grain was available to submit to the government.

In 1978 Deng Xiaoping took power and began a program of rectification, restoration, openness, and reform. The LRCs also began their own
"second flourishing." According to reports, from 1978–1980 the total
industrial and agricultural production value of the LRCs was 14 billion
yuan, with profits of 2 billion *yuan* (compared with 1958's total industrial
and agricultural production of 1.7 billion *yuan*).

For more information on LRC development in the past ten years, please
see Chapter 5.

Objects of *Laogai*

The CCP has made it very clear that the LRC system "is one of the
tools of the democratic dictatorship of the people. Its purpose is to punish
and reform all counter-revolutionaries and other criminals."[19] Therefore,
the first objects of labor reform were political counter-revolutionaries.
Changes in the nature of convicted labor reform prisoners over forty years
can be divided into four different time periods:

- The 1950s: 80–90 percent of CLR prisoners were military or government leaders left behind by the nationalist government, landlords,
  rich peasants, capitalists, and a few active counter-revolutionaries.
  Most of these prisoners came from "exploiting class" (*boxie jieji*)
  backgrounds.
- The 1960s: Besides remaining prisoners from the 1950s who had
  either not yet completed their sentences or had remained as FJP
  personnel (*jiuye*), during this period there was a great increase in
  the number of "active counter-revolutionaries" (*xianfan*) and "reactionary thinkers" (*sifan*). This group of prisoners, when lumped
  together with those "ox ghosts and snake spirits"[20] "dug out" during
  the early years of the Great Cultural Revolution, made up approximately 60–70 percent of prisoners in the LRC. At the same time, the
  number of imprisoned common criminals also increased.
- The 1970s: By the late 1970s, the original landlords, rich peasants,
  capitalists, and nationalist officials had largely died out.[21] Active
  counter-revolutionaries from the Cultural Revolution were in the
  majority, and there was a similar large increase in the number of
  arrested common criminals. There was also a large increase in the
  number of arrested criminals with Communist Party cadre family
  backgrounds.

- The 1980s: During this period arrested CLR criminals became the major component of the LRCs, constituting 90 percent of the prisoner population. A Communist internal document shows that active counter-revolutionaries make up only 10 percent of the general population (1.6 percent of which are "historical counter-revolutionaries," *lifan*). Recently, the Communists' viewpoint has been: "There are no longer really any of the landlord, rich peasant, or capitalist classes left. Class relations and conflict have undergone fundamental changes, and the objects and scope of the dictatorship have narrowed. However, there still remains counter-revolutionaries and enemies of the people, criminals who seriously disrupt the order of socialist society, degenerates, corrupt thieves and robbers, opportunists and exploiters, remnants of Lin Biao and Jiang Qing counter-revolutionary cliques, and a small number of unreformed landlords and rich peasants and other remnants of the old exploiting classes. Our battle with the 'Five Black Elements' and 'Two Remnants' is an important new stage in the history of class struggle; moreover, domestic class struggle is closely related to international class struggle. For this reason, various types of counter-revolutionary movements and other criminal phenomenon will be present for a long time."

It is particularly important to note that because concepts such as "counter-revolutionary rightists" (*fangeming youpai*), "bad elements" (*huai fenze*), "reactionary thinkers" (*sefan*), etc., created during the 1950s and 1960s had outlived their political usefulness, the Communists created two new political objects of the dictatorship to satisfy new political needs: "anti-socialist activists" (*fanshe fenzhi*) and "new exploiters" (*xinboxie fenzhi*).

Categories of Arrests in Mainland China

Category 1: Mass Movement Arrests. These were large-scale arrests conducted during one of the various political movements. On the basis of various guidelines sent down from the central government defining which sorts of behavior make one a "class enemy," "object of the dictatorship," or "object of investigation" (see Chapter 1 for details), the public security organs of the local village militia, residents' committee, and work unit defense bureau organize these arrests. On an average, there was a political movement every two years. Some of the major political movements over the past forty years include

- 1989: The suppression of the Tiananmen Democracy Movement and the Attack on Economic Criminals Movement

- 1986–1987: Movement to oppose "capitalist revisions"
- 1983: Swiftly and Severely Attack Criminals Movement
- 1982: Movement to oppose spiritual pollution
- 1979: Movement to suppress the Beijing Democracy Wall
- 1978: Movement to oppose the Gang of Four
- 1975: Counter-Attack on Rightists Attempting to Restore the Old Order and the suppression of the Qing Ming Festival Tiananmen Incident
- 1971 One Blow and Three Oppositions Movement
- 1966–1976: The Cultural Revolution
- 1964: Four Clean-Ups Movement
- 1960–1962: Three Years of Natural Disasters
- 1959: Oppose Rightist Opportunism Movement
- 1958: Great Leap Forward, People's Communes, General Party Line Movement
- 1957: Anti-Rightists Movement
- 1955: Eliminate Counter-Revolutionaries Movement and Anti-Hu Feng Counter-Revolutionary Clique Movement
- 1953: Collectivization of Agriculture Movement
- 1952: Three Oppositions, Five Oppositions Movement
- 1951: Suppress Counter-Revolutionaries Movement
- 1950: Agrarian Revolution Movement

So far there has been no official report or any authoritative investigation that has been made known to the public detailing exactly how many have been arrested, sentenced, and executed in the course of these various movements. But the total for each movement probably exceeds one million.

Generally those arrested in the course of political movements do not go through any sort of legal procedures.[22] The public security organs, under the direction of the CCP and the central government, gather together and register subjects, divide them into different groups, and confine them to detention centers. Some are even thrown directly into an LRC. Then, after a month, or a year, or longer, Public Security will finally announce a prisoner's charges and sentence. Over the course of forty years, this political movement style of arrest has proved to be the most common form of arrest.

Category 2: Formal Legal Proceedings. This is the smallest category (although it has grown slightly in recent years). Those in this category have been arrested and interrogated for whatever reason and then sent to court for sentencing. Such things as appeals or defense lawyers have appeared only in the past several years and are a bit more common in civil cases. The cases and sentencing procedures observed by foreign visitors and reporters are only those that have been thoroughly researched by the superior courts and approved by Communist legal committee members.

Category 3: "Preholiday" Arrests. It is the custom of the Communist regime before every major holiday (such as the October 1 National Holiday, May 1 Labor Day, New Year's, etc.), in order to show the stability of the social order and the government, to step up efforts to arrest suspects. Whether there is proof or not, with or without a warrant, the policy is to arrest first and ask questions later.[23] This type of political "better to err to the left" tradition is manifested throughout mainland Chinese society—the public security and judicial systems are no exception. The mistaken release of a criminal is the result of "an error in principles" or "a problem in class stance," whereas the mistaken arrest of a subject is merely the result of "a problem in work methods." After being arrested these subjects are held in detention centers. After the holidays they are cleared out, some. being sent to prisons, some sent to serve in labor reform disciplinary production camps or RTL camps. Only a minority are released. For this reason, every year at the holidays overcrowding becomes a serious problem in the LRCs and Public Security is forced to add extra squads and study periods.

Living Conditions Under Convicted Labor Reform

One of the most distinctive characteristics of prisons and labor reform disciplinary production camps is their organization along military lines and the use of prisoners to control other prisoners. Everyone is strictly supervised; the rate of protests or escapes is therefore very low. This type of close supervision is also a prerequisite of slave labor.

The number of prisoners kept in long-term solitary confinement is very small. Almost all live in groups where they can watch each other, working and living under constant surveillance. For twenty-four hours a day a prisoner has virtually no time alone.

The system of imprisonment is not the same for all prisoners; the conditions in various regions differ greatly. Generally, every year prisoners are issued one coarse black, dark gray, or dark red uniform and a pair of rubber or plastic shoes, but no underwear or undershirts. In the North during the winter, every other year a cotton coat and cotton hat are issued. For such daily necessities as underwear prisoners must rely on packages sent by relatives or must purchase these articles with the monthly 2.5–3 *yuan* living allowance.

An internal Communist regulation mandates that "Criminals who were orginally county or higher level Communist Party cadres, high level intellectuals or military commanders . . . should be stationed in camps with better living conditions, allowed to live individually, and cared for as they adapt to their new working and living conditions."[24] It seems that every province, autonomous region, and special municipality has one or two of these special prisons or LRCs. Beijing's Qingcheng Prison (LRC-03-22) is one of them.

All prisoner correspondence must bear a post office box number. It is not permissible to use the name of the labor reform organization or its enterprise name. For example, the post office box used for correspondence with Beijing Municipality's Qinghe Farm (LRC-03-12) is Jingshan Route Chadian Station P.O. Box X, with sub-boxes Y and Z. Box X designates Qinghe Farm's various work units; Box Y designates each work unit section; and Box Z each general brigade. Similarly, the P.O. Box for Yunan Province's Wulong Coal Mine (LRC-11-27) is Dongchuan City, P.O. Box 403. The conditions under which prisoners can engage in correspondence varies from place to place. Counter-revolutionaries can communicate only with family members.[25]

Visits from relatives are generally allowed once a month for about twenty to thirty minutes. Except for common daily necessities, the giving of food or books is very strictly controlled. Most *laogaidui* are located far from any cities or even located in isolated border regions where travel is exceedingly difficult. Also, relatives fear political sanctions by the Communists and wish to make clear political distinctions between themselves and the prisoner. For these reasons, the longer the prisoner's term the less frequent are visits from relatives. The author himself in nineteen years of confinement in the LRC received only one family visit.

The food rations provided by each LRC differ widely depending upon the region. To use Beijing as an example: The food ration for most prisoners involved in agricultural work is 13.5–22.5 kg per month. The exact amount of the ration depends upon the state of the prisoner's thought reform and labor performance and is decided by the company cadre. The rations are usually poor-quality corn and sorghum. Every month each prisoner also receives three ounces of cooking oil. No meat or eggs are provided. Every two weeks a "special" meal of white-flour steamed buns and pork-broth soup is provided. Every other month or so there are fried wheat cakes. At New Year's, National Day, or Spring Festival, prisoners are given a batch of meat dumplings. Aside from a few LRC factories and mines, there is no mess hall. Every day it is the responsibility of each company duty prisoner (*zhiban*) to load the corn bread or corn gruel and vegetable soup for his whole company into large wooden tubs and then transport them on pull carts to wherever the company happens to be working (if they are performing agricultural work it is brought out to the fields). Then each squadron leader takes the portion for the prisoners to his squadron and finds a place at the base of a wall or some other convenient spot for them to eat.

The expanded area of the Shanghai Laodong Steel Pipe Works (internal name Shanghai No. 7 LRD: located at Beidi Road, Shanghai City). The new wall is three feet higher than the old.

Prisoners have only this small portion of food on which to survive, and because of the constant hunger in the *laogaidui,* robbings, beatings, and fights over food are common occurrences. On August 18, 1984, 400 prisoners from Hubei Province were forcibly transferred to Kuytun County, Hongshan Coal Mine (LRC-15-29) in Xinjiang Autonomous Region. Because they were accustomed to eating rice, they demanded that the prison authorities respect their custom and provide them with rice. When this demand was refused, the prisoners protested by going on a hunger strike. The LRC dispatched armed police to suppress the strike and had the leaders of the strike removed from the prison and executed.

The living conditions of prisoners varies from north to south and between factories or mines and farms. The few LRC farms in the Beijing area are an example: Most prisoners sleep on earthen *kangs*[26] with about 2.5 feet of room each. Ten people make up one squadron, and each squadron is assigned one room. Ten rooms constitute one platoon barracks. In a large LRC there are approximately 10–12 such platoon barracks. Each has a room set aside as a kitchen, and toilets are situated on all sides. Surrounding the LRC is a wall approximately 20 feet high topped by electric fencing with a sentry tower at each corner. Outside this wall is about 40 feet of open space and then another even taller wall, similarly equipped with electric fencing and sentry towers. In order to enter the compound one must pass through two sets of iron doors guarded by armed police.

Whether in the north or south, all LRC are infested with snakes and flies and the ever-present lice and bed bugs. Most LRC have no shower rooms, only a row of faucets or a well in front of the platoon barracks. There are a few mining LRC work units that have shower rooms, like Shandong Province's Jinpushan Coal Mine (LRC-01-34), but the water is incredibly polluted and odiferous.

Because of differences in the labor procedures of mining and agricultural LRCs, there are also differences in the procedures of daily life. Using Tuanhe Farm (LRC-03-11) in the Beijing area as an example:

Prisoners are roused from bed at 5:30 A.M., and at 6:00 the *zhiban* (duty prisoner) from the kitchen wheels in a cart with tubs of corn gruel and cornbread. Each squad then under the direction of its squad leader waits in turn for a bowl of corn gruel, a hunk of corn bread, and a piece of salted carrot. At 7:00 the company public security cadre (captain) comes in, gathers all the prisoners together, and authorizes any sick prisoners to remain in the barracks. A sick prisoner who does not obtain the cadre's permission is forced to go to work. The prisoners put on their broken straw hats, grab their cracked earthen bowls, count off, and then form four ranks. After passing through the iron doors and being counted by the sentries they are led under armed escort by the captain to the fields to work. Once at the worksite, the captain delegates production responsibilities and places four red warning flags in the ground to mark off the territory in which the prisoners are to work. Anyone wandering outside of this restricted area is considered an attempted escapee and is immediately shot.[27]

At lunchtime, the *zhiban* (or an FJP worker) arrives pulling a handcart with a large tub of vegetable soup, two hunks of cornbread for each prisoner, and a large tub of drinking water. When the food cart arrives the captain announces a lunchbreak and all the prisoners come in from the fields to take their portion. After about thirty minutes work is resumed until the company chief announces quitting time in the evening. No one may cease work until they hear the captain's order. Generally the prisoners return to the barracks at about 6:30 P.M.

Upon return it is once again a dinner of cornbread, corn gruel, and vegetable soup.

At 7:30, two-hour study period begins. Study period includes *People's Daily* study, the study of Mao Zedong's works, struggle sessions, ideological discussions, etc.

The prisoners in this picture have been escorted to the field to labor and are listening to a labor reform policeman issue production orders for the day. On the far left is a military policeman with his horse and warning flag. The person standing next to the flag is an FJP worker who is responsible for taking care of technical problems. The photograph was taken at Weibei LRD (LRC-21-01) in Shandong Province.

At 9:30, no matter what the weather, all prisoners gather together outside the barracks for roll call and a speech from the captain. At around 10:00 everyone goes to bed.

During the night no lights are allowed and no one is allowed to move about. One must remain in one's assigned sleeping place and wait until 5:30 the next morning before getting up, when the whole cycle begins again.

Mining LRCs are different in a few respects. Because the mine shaft is very narrow and blocked off with electric fencing, no armed escort is needed.

Punishment in Convicted Labor Reform

The CCP has historically denied that torture or maltreatment of prisoners occurs in the *laogaidui*. All public and internal documents uniformly claim that "All corporal punishment has been abolished,"[28] that "it is forbidden to insult, beat, or extort evidence or forced confessions from arrested subjects,"[29] and that "it is strictly forbidden for any labor reform organ to subject counter-revolutionary or any other prisoners to torture or corporal punishment."[30] In reality, various sorts of cruel punishments are widespread in the labor reform camps; indeed, a *laogaidui* without cruel punishments would not be a *laogaidui.*

In the past several years there have been several published Communist documents that have revealed occurrences of violence in the LRCs. For example, in Henan Province's Puyang Labor Reform Detachment (LRC-28-29), a quarrel broke out among some of the prisoners. The public security cadre, Yang Qiuxing, was partial to one group and so sent from the other group three prisoners with the names Lian, Shi, and Li to the company leader's office, where after being forced to kneel they were beaten and kicked. The prisoner named Shi was beaten to death. In Henan Province's No. 52 Farm (RTL, LRC-28-39) a prisoner with the surname Yan was late for evening roll call and was therefore beaten by the company leader, Liu Tao. Liu Tao broke Yan's back and then forbade the other prisoners to come to his aid. Yan was left lying there on the ground until the next morning, when he was found dead. Another example is a woman counter-revolutionary in Liaoning Province, Zhang Zixin, who before being put to death by a firing squad in 1976 had her larynx cut for fear she would complain or shout counter-revolutionary slogans.

Handcuffs and Shackles

The LRC have many conditions under which handcuffs and foot-shackles are employed, for instance, "planning to escape," "planning violence," "disobedience to orders," "speaking back to cadres," "resisting reform," "disrupting production," etc. Foot shackles come in various weights, such as 5 kg, 8 kg, 10 kg, etc. Styles of handcuffs include back handcuffs (where both hands are secured behind the back) and twisted handcuffs (where both hands are secured behind the back, one below the armpit, one at the waist). There is no time limit on the wearing of cuffs and shackles—it all depends upon the prisoner's "attitude." Many areas in mainland China have no handcuffs (this was especially true in the 1950s) and so customarily bind prisoners with rope. In Shanxi Province, for example, most LRCs commonly punish prisoners by binding them with rope. The method used for binding them is such that any strong prisoners within five minutes of being bound must have his bonds loosened or choke to death or become crippled. Recently, as the Communists have begun to "modernize," most public security and labor reform police have begun using electric cattle prods while interrogating or dealing with "reform resisters" (*fan gaizao fenzi*). Public security police often use these electric prods on prisoners' mouths and reproductive organs and on females' breasts. For example, on December 17, 1987, a Henan Province

Xinxiang Municipality middle-school teacher named Li Rongcheng was arrested by that municipality's public security officer, Cui Yuanwu, and others. His four extremities were bound so that his body was forced into the shape of a curved bow, his head stretched toward his back by a leather thong, and then he was subjected to shocks from five electric cattle prods. Cui Yuanwu ordered, "Shock his old buddy [his reproductive organ] so he won't be able to use it for twenty years." Li Rongcheng was dead by the next morning. These legally santioned warning devices are in actuality all used as tools of punishment.

Solitary Confinement

Regulations concerning solitary confinement in the LRC as described in Communist internal documents are as follows: "Solitary confinement chambers should not be smaller than three square meters, and the ceilings not lower than three meters . . . in northern regions there should be adequate protection against cold . . . during the confinement period prisoners will be given standard non-laboring prisoner rations . . . the term of confinement should generally be seven–fifteen days, not to exceed fifteen days."[31] The author's experience has been that solitary confinement involves not only emotional torture but physical torture caused by the starvation that results from trying to survive on "non-laboring prisoner rations." In the 1960s, for example, Beijing's Tuanhe Farm's (LRC-03-11) solitary confinement chamber was one meter wide, two meters long, and one meter high, made of cement with no "protection against cold"—no mattress, blankets, or even straw. There were two meals a day consisting of a bowl of corn gruel and a piece of salted carrot. Usually after seven days in confinement the rations are increased by a half a bowl of corn gruel. After being released from confinement prisoners are usually so weak from hunger that almost none can walk unassisted.

Capital Punishment

One of the Communist regime's important policies after seizing power in 1949 was Regulations Concerning the Punishment of Counter-Revolutionaries (February 20, 1951, approved by the Eleventh People's Central Congress). There are eighteen regulations in all, and twenty-five crimes defined as punishable by death. Somewhere between 10–15 million people have been put to death under the auspices of these regulations. By the 1980s, with the publishing of Criminal Law (1980), Resolutions Concerning the Severe Punishment of Criminals Who Pose a Threat to Society (1983), Resolutions Concerning the Severe Punishment of Criminals Who Disrupt the Economy (1982), Temporary Articles Regarding the Punish-

This photograph shows one male and one female prisoner being escorted by military policemen in an execution parade held in Baise Municipality of Guangxi Autonomous Region on August 29, 1990. This is a common practice in Communist China, referred to as "killing the chicken to scare the monkey."

ment of Soldiers Negligent in Their Duties, and similar laws, a total of forty-eight charges and thirty-nine articles called for the death penalty. The People's Republic of China has more charges and articles calling for capital punishment than any other country in the world. Although there are no official statistics, of this we can be sure: The total number of people over the past forty years put to death and the annual average number of those put to death in the People's Republic of China are the highest in the world.

Capital punishment is performed in only one way: death by firing squad. One executioner shoots the prisoner through the back of the head—no need to waste bullets. Generally, except for exceptional cases where a single person is secretly executed, several scores (or in the 1950s even several hundred) of prisoners are bound, dragged to the field of execution, and shot en masse. Moreover, prior to execution they are often paraded through the streets—kill the chicken to frighten the monkey. Mass participation is encouraged. The author on September 23, 1983, in Zhengzhou City, Henan Province, along with 100,000 citizens witnessed the mass execution of forty-five criminals.[32]

Military policemen executing seven people in Yunji County, Jilin Province, in December 1983. Three policemen work as a group: Two of them force each victim to kneel, and then the third steps forward and shoots the victim through the back of the head. The author witnessed an execution in Zhengzhou Municipality, Henan Province, on September 23, 1983. Forty-five people were shot. The style of execution was the same as pictured above, so it is possible that execution style follows directives from the Public Security Ministry.

Convicted Labor Reform Production

In the 1950s the entrepreneurial management of the *laogaidui* was not very developed. One reason for this was the special emphasis placed at that time upon maintaining the stability of the regime and suppressing counter-revolutionaries. Another reason was that by and large all labor reform work was directed toward railroad construction, mining, reclamation of wasteland, water conservancy projects, and similar large-scale, simple manual labor projects that required no special management. Examples include

- The reclamation of 250,000 *mu* of land in Jiangsu Province's Sheyang, Dafeng, and Binhai counties, which established the more than ten state-run farms that today constitute Subei New Village. Jiangsu Province transferred 150,000 prisoners from Shanghai Municipality for this project.
- The reclamation of 250,000 *mu* of farmland in the Bao'anzao reclamation area in Jalaid Banner, Inner Mongolia Autonomous Region, which involved the transfer of 150,000 prisoners from an LRC in Shanghai Municipality, Jiangsu Province, Fujian Province, and Zhejiang Province.

- The reclamation of 1 million *mu* of farmland in Heilongjiang Province, for which 300,000 prisoners were transferred from LRCs in Beijing and Tianjin municipalities.

Because of the emphasis on eliminating counter-revolutionaries, *laogaidui* at the time did not overly concern themselves with thought reform, concentrating instead upon ruthlessly pushing prisoners to meet their production goals. It is impossible to estimate how many prisoners were executed by firing squads for attempting to escape or refusing to work. From 1955–1965 there were two violent incidents involving prisoners starting an uprising due to excessive work loads, lack of food, and insufficient medical care. One of these incidents occurred at the Zhihuai engineering project in Anhui Province, where during the space of only two months over two thousand weakened prisoners died from infectious disease. The surviving prisoners with their remaining strength plotted an escape, for which they were all executed. In response to this incident the CCP Central Committee called a meeting of the Political Bureau, at which Public Security Ministry Chief Luo Ruiqing reported on his investigations into the matter, and labor reform policies were reviewed and discussed. Liu Shaoqi noted at the meeting that "The primary object of labor reform work is reform; production is of secondary importance." On July 13, 1956, Luo Ruiqing conveyed CCP Central's remarks to the public security and judicial organs—this was the beginning of the "reform first, production second" (*gaizao diyi, shengchan dier*) labor reform policy that continued until Deng Xiaoping's time. This became one of the basic national policies of the PRC. The essence of this policy concerns long-term political and economic benefits—fully employing the political usefulness of the *laogaidui* while at the same time making great contributions to the economic sector.

The various types of capital, production, planning, quality, technology, and raw materials management systems used by state-run enterprises in society at large were adopted in full by the *laogaidui*. Most public security cadres were organized into classes to study management techniques and business accounting. All adjustments and changes implemented in state-run enterprises were adopted in turn by the *laogaidui*. When in 1958 the National Congress, on the basis of profits, technology management, financing systems, and various other indexes, judged the performance of the nation's agricultural work units and named "forty nationwide outstanding red banner work units," Beijing Municipality's Tuanhe Farm (LRC-03-11) was one of them and sent a representative to the awards ceremony held by the Congress. Of course, the representative for this "outstanding model unit" was not one of the prisoners who daily paid for the unit's exemplary performance in sweat and blood.

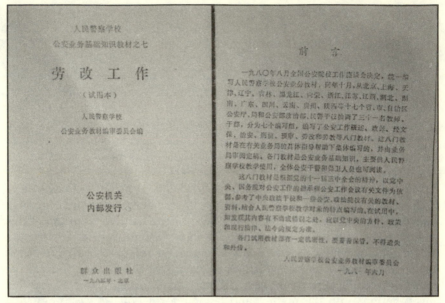

Title page of People's Police School No. 7 Textbook of Public Security Professional Knowledge, reading as follows: LABOR REFORM WORK (laogai gongzuo); (PROBATION) Edited by Public Security Professional Textbook Committee; RESTRICTED PUBLISHED IN PUBLIC SECURITY ORGAN; QUNZHONG PRESS, 1983 BEIJING

The prisons of the LRC system, because they are situated in cities, are necessarily limited in size. Additionally, those confined to prisons are usually more serious offenders to whom it would not be wise to give too much freedom of movement. Thus prison enterprises have gradually drifted toward handicraft industries such as shoe and clothing production, weaving, iron foundries, etc., for which industrial modernization is essential. Moreover, most prison inmates are serving comparatively long terms and therefore represent a stable labor force. For these reasons, in the late 1950s there began appearing many industrial labor reform enterprises that possessed a very high level of technical ability and a dependable production capacity. Examples include Beijing Municipality's Qinghe Textile Factory (Beijing Municipality No. 1 Prison, LRC-03-09); Shanxi Province's Fenhe Automotive Factory (Shanxi Province No. 3 Prison, LRC-01-07); Liaoning Province's Lingyuan Automotive Factory (Liaoning Province No. 1 LRD, LRC-27-23); Hubei Province's Wuhan Silk Factory (Hubei Province No. 1 Prison, LRC-19-25); Szechuan Province's Xinkang Asbestos Factory (LRC-18-35); etc. A few provinces have consolidated their capital and used it to develop mining enterprises. For instance, Shanxi Province has a large number of very technologically advanced labor reform mining operations, such as Xiyu Coal Mine

(Shanxi Province No. 3 LRD, LRC-01-15) and Yinying Coal Mine (LRC-01-21).

The LRCs have turned from heavy involvement in railroad and highway construction to the reclamation of farmland from waste areas. In already existing farms, besides engaging in agricultural production, they have begun to establish processing plants for agricultural goods. For example, Beijing Municipality's Qinghe Farm (LRC-03-12) has established a distillery, a dairy product plant, a paper processing plant, and similar enterprises. At the same time, large numbers of LRC prisoners are being forcibly resettled in such areas as Xinjiang Autonomous Region, Qinghai Province, and Inner Mongolia Autonomous Region.

Before 1980, important LRC enterprise products produced for export were agricultural goods such as cotton, fruit, meat, tea leaves, bristles, etc. All were handled by the provincial-level international trading companies. For example, the well-known Yingteh Black Tea sold since the 1950s in various Far Eastern countries is produced by Guangdong Province's Yingteh Tea Farm (also known as New Life United Enterprise Company, No. 7 Provincial Labor Reform Detachment, LRC-02-120). It is marketed by Guangdong Provincial Tea Import and Export Company under the name Guangdong Province Yingteh Tea Enterprise Company and in the past few years has been sold in the United States.

In 1952, the total value of nationwide labor reform production (LRP) was 200 million *yuan,* or *renminbi* (this number indicates only industrial production and does not include agricultural or construction enterprises). The 1958 LRP value (again, only industrial production) was 1.7 billion *yuan.* As far as agricultual production is concerned, in 1958 LRCs farmed 10 million *mu* of land, produced 1.4 billion *jin*[33] of grain, 16.59 million *jin* of cotton, 60.63 million *jin* of oil and 540,000 pigs. The government was very pleased by this state of affairs, noting that "Labor Reform Production (*laogai shengchan*) . . . has already become a production force in socialist construction whose importance cannot be denied" (a resolution at the Ninth Plenary Public Security Congress, August 1958).

The continued importance of LRP to the economy of the Communist regime can be further validated by the following facts:[34]

- 1953–1956: During the Communists' financial crisis, LRP provided 2.2 billion *yuan* to the economy, thus supporting the regime.
- 1960–1963: During an economic recession, LRP provided the Communist regime with 2.6 billion *yuan* in tax revenues.
- 1966–1976: When the Cultural Revolution had driven the economy to the verge of collapse, LRP value exceeded 20 billion *yuan.*
- 1953–1983: During these thirty years, the total tax revenues earned from LRCs reached 13 billion *yuan.* The Communist government

This box of Yingteh black tea costs $2.69 and is produced by Xinsheng United Enterprise, Provincial No. 7 LRD (LRC-02-120), Guangdong Province, China. It was purchased from a supermarket located in Santa Clara County, California, in May 1990.

acknowledges that these revenues greatly defray the cost of running the LRC system; indeed, not a cent of government money, even for prisoners or public security personnel salaries, is spent on maintaining the LRCs.

• Using Shanghai as an example: Up to 1983, Shanghai has had six mid-size labor reform factories and four labor reform farms, whose fixed capital and liquid assets totaled 150 million *yuan*. Production value over thirty years totaled 4.5 billion *yuan*. After providing for all their own expenses, these LREs still managed to provide the Communist regime with 1.8 billion *yuan* in revenues.

A very important factor in the technical development of labor reform production has been the effective utilization of prisoners with technical knowledge. Prisoners' areas of special ability are carefully noted in their files, and as long as they acknowledge their errors and crimes and accept reform they can be given a post in an appropriate labor reform enterprise or industry. For example, in 1952 a criminal in Shanghai with the surname Ling, originally an architect, was arrested for giving bribes and evading taxes. He was appointed to plan and oversee the construction of the biggest hotel built in the 1950s and 1960s—the Yingze Guest House, in

Shanxi Province's capital of Taiyuan. Another example is a prisoner named Yao, a counter-revolutionary rightist, who was originally a lecturer in the chemistry department of Beijing University and was responsible after his arrest for designing Beijing Municipality's Beiyuan Chemical Factory.

Notes

1. *Zhongguo jianyu shi* (A History of Chinese Prisons), Labor Reform Specialist's Teaching Material, Beijing: The Masses' Press, 1986, p. 325.

2. Ibid., p. 327.

3. Ibid., p. 326.

4. Ibid., p. 325.

5. Ibid., p. 331.

6. Ibid., pp. 331–332.

7. Ibid., p. 353.

8. Ibid., p. 367.

9. *Dan* is a dry measure for grain, equal to about 120–160 lbs.

10. *A History of Chinese Prisons*, p. 364.

11. Faxue (Legal Studies), Beijing: Selections of Published Material, Chinese People's University Periodical and Information Center, February 1987, p. 119.

12. *A History of Chinese Prisons*, p. 377.

13. Ibid., p. 382. Author's note: This refers to placing criminals to labor in regular societal mines and farms. These enterprises do not fall under the jurisdiction of public security or judicial organs. Many Western scholars have been under the impression that to this day criminals are forced to labor in regular societal mines and farms. However, this policy changed in November of 1949, when these types of operations were allocated to the Industrial Ministry, and the public security and judicial organs began managing their own large-scale, independent "special enterprises" and "two forced-labor enterprises."

14. Northwest Regional Gongchangling Labor Reform Camp, one of the models of the Communists' LRCs in the 1940s: When it was established in September of 1949, it had a population of 550 prisoners; by December this population had reached at least 1,700. When it began it had only 5 public security cadres and 19 armed guards. The organization was as follows: The first 550 prisoners were organized into 8 companies, each of which of had 65 people; each company was divided into 4 groups, each of which had 16 people; most of these groups were further divided into 3 smaller groups. Each company chief, group leader, and squad leader was responsible for allocating work to the prisoners under his direction. Policies such as "labor cooperation," "living cooperation," and "cooperation to prevent escapes" were instituted; moreover, from production profits a small amount was saved to give to the prisoners as rewards. Reduced sentences were given for such things as consistently exceeding production quotas, displaying reformed behavior, or apprehending or reporting other prisoners who attempted to escape or displayed destructive behavior. Still, punishments were meted out to those who did not meet their production quotas or did not follow instructions.

15. *A History of Chinese Prisons,* p. 384.

16. Laodong gaizao zuifan de lilun yu shijian (Labor Reform Criminals: Theory and Practice), Beijing: Legal Press, 1989, p. 229.

17. For example, at Beijing Municipality's Qinghe Farm, western end next to section 585, there was a huge area of wasteland that was used as a graveyard of sorts. Everyone called it field "586." It is estimated that during the space of two years 2,000–3,000 of the "three types of personnel" (mainly starvation victims) were buried there. Because the water table is near the surface of the ground there is no way to dig a deep grave, and at that time no preparations had been made to perform cremation and there was also no wood with which to make coffins; the bodies were simply all thrown together in a shallow grave. Before long, after wind and rain had worked on the graves, the bodies were dug up by wild dogs and soon bones were found scattered everywhere. Of those who had been to Qinghe Farm in the 1950s and 1960s, there were none who did not know of "586." The term "586" soon became synonymous with death. From 1961–1962, the author was confined to the western region of Qinghe Farm, in sections 583, 584, and 585, and buried his friend at "586."

18. "Labor Reform Criminals: Theory and Practice," p. 230.

19. Laogai gongzuo (Labor Reform Work), Beijing: CCP internal document, p. 1.

20. "Ox ghosts and snake spirits" is a derogatory term coined in the 1960s referring to anti-Maoists and bourgeoisie elements.

21. In July of 1983 Public Security announced that nationwide there was a total of 79,504 "landlords, rich peasants, counter- revolutionaries, and bad elements." Of these, 78,327 had already "removed their hat" (i.e., had their former charges dismissed). In 1950, there were around 20–25 million people classified by the Communists as landlords or rich peasants, around 10–15 million former nationalist officials, and about 3–5 million capitalists.

22. Labor Reform Work, p. 2.

23. For example, during the 1957 Anti-Rightists Movement the CCP Central Committee issued two documents (Deng Xiaoping was the head of the Anti-Rightists Office of the CCP): "CCP Central's Notification Concerning 'Standards for Defining Rightists'" was issued on October 15, 1957, and totaled 3,000 words. This document explained how to distinguish rightists in work units; analyzed recent problems in the distinguishing of rightists; explained acceptable methods of defining rightists and how to master and fully understand standards of analysis. "Standards for Defining Rightists" reads in part as follows: "Generally speaking, behavior falling under the following categories will be considered signs of a rightist: 1. Opposes the socialist system; opposes the socialist revolution in the cities and villages and the basic economic policies of the People's Republic's government (such as industrialization, centralization, etc.); denies the achievements of the socialist revolution and socialist construction; supports capitalism and promotes the capitalist system and exploitation by the capitalist class, 2. Opposes the dictatorship of the proletariat and the democracy of the masses; attacks the anti-imperialist struggle and the foreign policy of the people's government; attacks the struggle to purge counter-revolutionaries; denies the achievements of the 'Five

Great Movements' [initiated from 1949–1952, consisted of the Land Reform Movement, Movement to Resist U.S. Aggression and Aid Korea, Movement to Suppress Counter-Revolutionaries, Three-Anti and Five-Anti Movement, and the Ideological Remodeling Movement; opposes the reform of capitalists and capitalist intellectuals; attacks the personal control and cadre policies of the communist party and people's government; and demands the replacement of the socialist political, legal and cultural education systems with capitalist ones, 3. Opposes the leading role of the communist party in the political life of the nation; opposes the leadership of the communist party in economic and cultural areas; takes the opposition of socialism and the communist party as a goal and maliciously attacks the leading organs and individual leaders of the communist party and the people's government; slanders workers' cadres and revolutionary organizers; belittles communist party revolutionary activities and organizational principles, 4. Takes as a goal the opposition of socialism and the communist party and attempts to destroy the unity of the people; incites the masses to oppose the communist party and the people's government; causes divisions among the workers and peasants; incites ethnic conflicts; belittles the socialist camp and incites divisiveness among the socialist camps of various nations, 5. Organizes or actively participates in anti-socialist or anti-communist party cliques; harbors plans to topple or overthrow the communist party leaders of any bureau or at any level; incites anti-communist party or anti-people's government unrest, 6. Makes suggestions to, curries favor with, expresses sympathy with, or reveals revolutionary organizational secrets to a rightist who has evinced the above described behavior." The document goes on to say "Anyone falling into the following categories should be classified as an extreme rightist: 1. a leader, planner, hardcore member, or one with ambitions in any rightist activities, 2. one who proposes and actively promotes any general anti-socialist principles, 3. one who encourages or promotes particularly serious anti-socialist activities and particularly determined activists, 4. those with histories of consistently opposing the communist party and the people, and in this particular rightist action actively promoted reactionary activities."

The second document was CCP Central's Regulations Concerning the Distinction of Rightists; please see the rest of this chapter for details.

24. Labor Reform Work, p. 48.

25. Ibid., p. 53

26. A *kang* is a raised earthen sleeping platform that can be heated from below, commonly used in North China.

27. Li Zhirong, originally a platoon commander in the Nationalist Sixteenth Army, Ninety-fourth Division, involved his troops in a peaceful uprising in January of 1949 and joined the Chinese People's Liberation Army. In 1958, a Beijing Municipality middle court found him guilty of having a "counter-revolutionary background" and sentenced him to a fifteen-year term. On April 15, 1969, while Li was stationed at Heilongjiang Province's Nenjiang Farm (LRC-24-03) Subfarm 7, No. 3 brigade, he and over 100 other prisoners were led by company chief Li Chuenqi and three armed escorts to harvest fields two kilometers to the southeast of their barracks. The "restricted area" within which it was permissible to work was a square 400–500 meters on a side. Every prisoner had

a quota of 300 kg/day. About 2:00 p.m. Li, cutting grass with his head down, wandered three meters out of the restricted area, where he was stopped by an armed guard. The guard asked, "What is your crime?" Li replied, "Counter-revolutionary." "Have you ever killed a man?" he was asked. Li replied, "While in the military, yes." The guard, after ordering Li to march forward, immediately shot him in the lower back, killing him.

28. Official Order No. 16, Chinese Soviet Central Acting Congress, December 12, 1931.

29. Regulations for Safeguarding Human Rights and Property in the Shaan-ganning Border Regions—Selection of New Democratic Revolution Period Basic Laws and Documents, vol. 1, p. 35.

30. Labor Reform Regulations of the People's Republic of China, article 5.

31. Labor Reform Work, pp. 59–60.

32. "Execution Day in Zhengzhou," in *Orthodoxy, the American Spectator Anniversary Anthology*, New York: Harper & Row, p. 277.

33. A *jin* is a unit of weight equal to 0.5 kg.

34. Labor Reform Criminals: Theory and Practice, p. 230.

3

Reeducation Through Labor *(Laojiao)*

RTL *(laojiao)* is an "innovation" created by the Communist regime after it seized power in 1949, so it does not have a long history like that of CLR. The rationale behind RTL is to "create a level between peace-keeping management and legal sentencing . . . to bridge the gap between light and serious offenses by creating a closely knit, reasonable three-tiered system . . . [RTL] will allow us to avoid complicated judicial procedures . . . and serve a useful function in allowing a swift response to societal threats."[1] RTL is one of the Communists' *lianglao*—"two types of labor reform work." This special sanction as defined in CCP announcements can be summarized as follows:

- RTL is a government policy designed to force remedial education upon criminals whose offenses are not serious but who have repeatedly resisted reform and are in need of additional discipline.
- No judicial procedure need be involved in RTL; all that is necessary is for the case to be organized by public security, judicial, people's government, or labor reform bureaus and examined and approved by the appropriate provincial, autonomous regional, special municipal, or large or middle-sized municipal RTL committee.
- The term of service of one sent to RTL is determined by the appropriate provincial, autonomous regional, special municipal, or large or middle-sized municipal RTL facility.
- RTL does not "deprive one of freedom," it merely "limits one's freedom"; moreover, it does not deprive one of one's political rights.
- RTL subjects are referred to as personnel, not criminals. They are merely "under strict supervision in order to remove contradictions among the people."[2] RTL "personnel" receive "appropriate salaries," and "those with good behavior may, at the discretion of the RTL

81

facility, be allowed to take holidays in order to return home to visit relatives."
- Those with poor behavior have their sentences extended. Also, those who have served their sentences may be subject to FJP.

RTL policies went into effect in 1957. Communist propaganda tools managed to conceal RTL policies somewhere among the categories of "contradictions among the people" and "high-level administrative disciplining." The outside world had very little understanding of RTL or misunderstood it completely, thinking it was an educational administrative regulation. Actually, RTL policies play a very important role in the functioning of the Communist dictatorship, providing an inestimable service to the regime.

The Historical Background and Theoretical Basis of Reeducation Through Labor

Historical Background

In 1957 the Communists put RTL policies into effect. This year was a watershed in the historical development of the Communist regime.

The Communist regime was established in 1949, so by 1957 had already been in existence eight years. During these eight years the Communist regime went through the Agrarian Revolution, Suppress Bandits and Oppose Hegemonists Movement,[3] Suppress Counter-revolutionaries Movement,[4] Three Anti's, Five Anti's Movement,[5] Collectivization of Agriculture Movement,[6] Public and Private Joint Ownership Movement,[7] and similar political movements, which basically wiped out the nationalist government's power base in mainland China and destroyed its political strength and influence. The political and economic strength of the landlords and capitalists was dealt a fatal blow. These political movements were based upon the class struggle theories of Marx, Lenin, and Mao Zedong, employing such methods as "mass struggle" and the revolutionary "red terror" to remove approximately 20 million people from Chinese society. Shortly afterward, in 1955, the Communists began their Purge Counter-revolutionaries Movement,[8] the purpose of which Mao Zedong explained as follows: "Because during the great storm of revolution we emerged victorious, there are many types of people who would like to gather around us. It cannot be denied that we have gathered much dirt and confused foe for friend; it is not too late, however, for us to perform this last, thorough cleaning" (May-June 1955). After passing through the Purge Counter-revolutionaries Movement, the Communists' political order was completely and firmly established.

At the conclusion of the Korean War in 1953, mainland China's economic situation (especially in 1956) was showing signs of strong development, and society in general was very stable; the cultural and intellectual worlds were also flourishing. However, the land finally obtained by the peasants was suddenly snatched away by the Collectivization of Agriculture Movement, which relegated the peasants to the role of low-class, slave-like laborers. The workers not only had received no tangible economic or political benefits but found themselves under the control of Communist cadres, who were even harsher than the old capitalists. Intellectuals were discriminated against and considered in need of "reform." In all, the peaceful, democratic, free, unified, and prosperous socialist society hoped for by the Chinese people did not appear. At the same time, what did appear was an immense bureaucratic ruling class— the Communist Party. This ruling class wanted not only to maintain the privileges and powers already obtained but also to greedily use the tools of the state they controlled to seize even more economic and political power. As the people gradually came to recognize the violent and corrupt nature of this regime, discontent and protest began to increase and spread.

The political strength of the landlord and capitalist classes had already been destroyed. Most of them had been purged, and their sons and daughters were on "special lists."[9] They spent their lives in constant fear; during the frequent political movements they had to ceaselessly express the difference between exploiting families and themselves, criticize their own family origin and reactionary ideology, sincerely beg to undergo difficult reform, express their endless devotion to "the Party and Chairman Mao," and beg for their lives. However, these movements did nothing to decrease the amount of societal discontent and protest; indeed, more and more of this disenchantment was being expressed by the worker, peasant, and even Party cadre families, not from those attacked "exploiter classes" who "longed for their past glory" and dreamed of a return to capitalism. In order to adapt to this new situation it was necessary to come up with a new class struggle theory to explain it and a new set of policies and methods of suppression to preserve the dictatorship.

After 1949 the Communist regime adopted a "lean to one side"[10] policy, domestic and foreign policies all falling in line with the Soviet Union. It was announced that China had entered the international socialist army, the enemy being "American imperialism," which included the "imperialist armies" of Japan, West Germany, England, and France. Citing the "imperialist armies'" support of the nationalist regime in Taiwan, it was claimed that these forces planned to overthrow and destroy the People's Republic of China. In mainland China the words and actions of anyone protesting the dictatorship of the Communist party were considered part of "The movement plotting to restore American imperialism and nation-alist reactionaries" and were savagely suppressed.

In 1955 the Poznan Incident occurred in Poland, where workers went on strike to protest the Communist government, provoking a bloody confrontation. In 1956 in Hungary there was an armed uprising of intellectuals, workers, and peasants, and Soviet Red Army tanks were needed to pacify Budapest. The impact these incidents in Poland and Hungary had on mainland Chinese intellectuals and Communist Party organizations was very great. Despite the Communist regime's news blackout and propaganda claiming that the incidents in Poland and Hungary were instigated by imperialists, the people saw an example of a bloody, confrontational clash in a socialist country between the worker and peasant masses and the Communist regime that claimed to represent them. This presented a new problem for Marxism-Leninism class struggle theory.

After the death of Stalin in 1953, Khrushchev at the Twentieth Soviet Congress in 1956 gave a secret report detailing the violence of the Stalin period. Although the Chinese Communist regime strictly banned this report (even to this day it cannot be found in mainland China), the people managed to piece together the essence of the report from various channels, especially Chinese Communist Propaganda Bureau reports critical of Khrushchev. This engendered doubts and dissatisfaction among the people toward such Communist propaganda as "today's Soviet Union is tomor-row's China," "the everlasting Soviet-Chinese friendly alliance," and the true nature of Stalin, who was praised along with Mao Zedong as a great revolutionary leader.

Mao, who was in no way inferior to Stalin as a dictator and despot, naturally felt that any criticism of Stalin might reflect unfavorably upon him and have political and societal consequences. Under these conditions, it was imperative for the Communists to come up with a way to control the intellectuals and strengthen their dictatorial system and means of suppression.

Generally speaking, Marxism-Leninism class struggle theory holds that resistance to the socialist revolution comes only from those former ex-ploiter classes who "dream of returning to their past days of glory." However, in mainland China the Communist regime in the space of only six or seven years destroyed the power of the exploiting classes and saw the triumph of the socialist revolution, only to have new discontent and protest spring up everywhere among the people. This situation forced the Communists and Mao Zedong to seek for a new theory and new political measures to maintain the dictatorship.

This is the reason for the historical watershed in the development of the Communist government that occurred in 1957 and the reason for the main object of suppression changing from the already defeated nationalist regime, landlord, and capitalist classes to the great mass of the people themselves. In 1957 the Anti-Rightists Movement[11] and the announcement of "reeducation through labor policies" were two important signs of this historical change.

The Theoretical Basis of Reeducation Through Labor

Mao Zedong's 1957 publicly issued document "On the Correct Handling of the Problem of Internal Contradictions Among the People," which dealt with class struggle, internal contradictions among the people, and contradictions between ourselves and the enemy,[12] is the theoretical basis of RTL.

In this document Mao stated, "The revolutionary period of large scale, violent, mass class struggle has basically ended. However, there still remain remnants of the overthrown landlord and capitalist classes, and small capitalists are still in the process of reforming. Class struggle has actually not ended. The class struggle between the proletariate and capitalist classes, the class struggle between the various political groups, and the ideological class struggle between the proletariate and capitalist classes are long term, full of ups and downs, and even at times very fierce . . . the question of who will emerge victorious—socialism or capitalism— has still not been really decided."[13] Mao also stated that "the two types of contradictions presently facing our society are the contradictions between ourselves and our enemies and the internal contradictions among the people."[14] "The nature of these two contradictions is not the same, and the methods for resolving them are also not the same."[15] Mao later noted that "at this stage, while socialism is in the process of being established . . . all those who protest or are hostile to the socialist revolution and all powers or societal groups that disrupt the establishment of socialism must be considered as enemies of the people."[16] Mao Zedong's conclusion was that after the exploiting classes have been stripped of their property and after they have been politically, economically, and even physically destroyed, in a socialist society there still may continue to exist a classless class struggle. It is possible for any societal force or any individual to be classified by the Communist Party organs (or at times Mao himself) as an anti-socialist, an enemy of the people, and so suppressed in accordance with the principles of "contradiction between ourselves and our enemies."

When discussing "contradictions between ourselves and our enemies and the dictatorship," Mao stated that "dictatorial methods should be used to deal with enemies."[17] Mao also emphasized that "Under most conditions, contradictions among the people are not of an antagonistic nature; however, if they are dealt with improperly or insensitively, with no regard for their larger significance, it is possible that they may become antagonistic in nature."[18] This explains how contradictions among the people can turn into contradictions between the people and their enemies—it all depends upon the changes in the needs and desires of the Communist governing organs. Mao's comments indicate that the contradictions between the Communist governing organs and the people had already become a daily fact of life. For this reason, it was necessary for the Communists to come up with more effective, more convenient, and more subtle means of maintaining their dictatorship—such as the RTL policies instituted in 1957.

The Political Background of the Institution
of Reeducation Through Labor

In August of 1956, a CCP Central document Directives Concerning the Thorough Purging of Hidden Counter-revolutionaries noted, "two methods may be employed to deal with those purged during the Liquidate Counter-Revolutionaries Movement. One method is arrest and conviction followed by labor reform. The other method is Reeducation Through Labor."[19] The Liquidate Counter-revolutionaries Movement affected approximately 500,000 people. These people, after being investigated by their various work units' Party organizations, were arrested by Public Security. In the detention centers approximately 60 percent were convicted, executed, or sent to the *laogaidui*. The other 40 percent were not formally charged but were also not released and so were subjected to RTL without being formally committed to RTL. Shortly afterward, in January of 1956, CCP Central announced Directives Concerning the Immediate Preparation of Provincial and Municipal RTL Organizations.[20] (This directive was issued before the National People's Congress passed Reeducation Through Labor Regulations on August 1, 1957, and before its public announcement on August 3. This reflects the Communist regime's lack of regard for human rights or legal process.) All over the country the various local public security bureaus moved quickly to establish RTL battalions and detention centers in many LRC facilities. At that time, RTL prisoners were entirely under the control of the various LRCs.

The first group of prisoners subjected to RTL in the PRC were basically political prisoners who had been labeled counter-revolutionaries and numbered approximately 200,000. They were those "not worth sentencing but too dangerous to leave around,"[21] purged during the Liquidate Counter-revolutionaries Movement of 1955. Obviously, though, they were not merely vagrants and petty criminals overlooked by civil law.

In May of 1957 the struggle against rightists began, and by February of 1958, 550,000 capitalist-class rightists and over 400,000 rightist sympathizers, protectors of rightists, and reactionaries who had departed from the correct stand had been punished, as well as over one million intellectuals. Mao Zedong announced: "Capitalist-class rightists are . . . anti-communist, anti-masses, anti-socialist capitalist reactionaries."[22] Deng Xiaoping (who was at that time Central Party general secretary) in a report given to the Eighth Central Committee Congress's Third Plenary Session on September 23, 1957, "Regarding the Rectification Movement," noted, "The contradiction between capitalist-class rightists and the people is a contradiction between the enemy and ourselves, and its antagonistic nature cannot be mitigated, for it is a life-and-death confrontation." CCP Anti-Rightist Office chief, Deng Xiaoping, and CCP politburo member and political politic and law commissar, Peng Zeng, together drafted a plan to dispose of one million capitalist rightists and anti-socialist elements.

This persecution of one million intellectuals was the first time since the Communist regime seized power in 1949 that it dealt with dissidents "among the people" rather than those who had been associated with the nationalists. These intellectuals, concerned for their nation, had expressed unorthodox political opinions under the auspices of Mao Zedong and Party Central's Let a Hundred Flowers Bloom and a Hundred Schools of Thought Contend Movement, where intellectuals were encouraged to criticize the Party, to "speak what they think, without reserve or fear of reprisal, so that the hearers may be suitably chastened." Among these intellectuals were those who were not happy about Mao Zedong's anti-rightist struggle and who merely expressed sympathy for a few convicted rightists as well as core members of the CCP, for example, the author Liu Binying, who to this day is still a fervent proponent of Communism; Wang Meng, head of the Cultural Bureau from 1986–1989; and various itinerant propagandists for the Communist Party.

Even in March of 1980, Deng Xiaoping insisted, "We must acknowledge the importance of the anti-rightist struggle of 1957. Even after the completion of three great reforms, there definitely still existed anti-socialist forces and trends of thought that were fundamentally capitalist in nature. It was imperative to attack these trends. As I have said repeatedly, at that time there were those who were very militant, who sought to repudiate the communist party leaders and subvert the path of socialism. If they had not been counter-attacked we would not have been able to progress."[23]

The Communists' plan for punishing these rightists declared that although rightism was of the nature of "contradictions between the enemy and ourselves," they were to be dealt with using the administrative disciplinary measures usually reserved for dealing with "contradictions among the people." Furthermore, the punishments were classified into five levels of severity.[24] Most of the more hardcore rightists—"extreme rightists"— were arrested and sent to RTL camps. After 1958, a constant flow of rightists were arrested for RTL or sentenced to CLR for "resisting reform," "stubbornly refusing to change," and similar charges and thrown into LRCs.

From this it can be seen that RTL's early success was in dealing with those with unorthodox political views and dissidents. RTL has proved very successful in dealing with counter-revolutionaries and rightists. By avoiding the complication of trials and sentencing for hundreds of thousands of people, and with its violent suppression of political and human rights, RTL has been very effective in purging those with different ideas or whose existence was a problem for the dictatorial regime.

Similarly, as with CLR, besides the obvious political benefits provided by RTL, the Communist regime has also enjoyed considerable economic benefits.

General Development of Reeducation
Through Labor *(Laojiao)*

RTL's development can be divided into five stages.

First Stage: 1957–1958

This was the period of RTL's conception. Actually, back in 1955 there were approximately 200,000 "minor counter-revolutionaries" purged during the Liquidate Counter-Revolutionaries Movement who were being held by Public Security in "labor teams" (*laodong dadui*), "detention centers" (*kanshousuo*), and "production teams" (*shengchan dadui*) and being forced to engage in hard labor. So RTL was already being implemented at a very early time.

In August of 1957, immediately after the National People's Congress announced the implementation of RTL, all production teams hurriedly changed their names, and detention centers quickly began sending their charges off to RTL facilities. Many of these were rightists purged during the Anti-Rightist Struggle. At this stage, the population of RTL facilities was approximately 300,000–400,000. The rules and regulations at this point were not clearly established. Seventy to eighty percent of RTL subjects were counter-revolutionary political prisoners.

At this point in time, RTL facilities were established only at the provincial, autonomous regional, or special municipal levels, or at sites approved by these high-level people's governments. Comparatively speaking, the scope of RTL at this time was rather limited.

Second Stage: 1958–1962

This was the "golden age" of RTL.

As a result of 1958's Three Red Banners (the General Line for Socialist Construction, the Great Leap Forward, and the People's Communes) policy, RTL also experienced a "great leap forward." RTL facilities were established everywhere, from the provincial, autonomous regional, special municipal, and county levels all the way down to local village communes. These village commune-level RTL facilities were referred to as "commune-run reeducation through labor." "In August of 1958, CCP approved legislation to the effect that 'village people's communes and agricultural collectives can also establish Reeducation Through Labor facilities.' In 1959, CCP decreed that 'commune-run RTL facilities should be abolished; RTL subjects in communes should be sent to the county level for disciplining. . . .' In 1961 CCP ruled that 'The main purpose of RTL is to detain those purged from large and mid-size cities, mines, enterprises, organizations and schools,' as well as ruling that RTL facilities should no longer be handled at a county level"[25] (another example of CCP arbitrariness: before RTL was formally approved by the highest legislative organ— the National People's Congress—public security organs, under the direction of the CCP, had already established RTL facilities; even after RTL policies were formally announced, CCPCC still had authority over the expansion or cutting down of the RTL system). According to statistics, during this period ten million people were sent to RTL facilties.

If we look at it from a historical perspective, the period of time from the late 1950s to the early 1960s was a critical time for the Communist regime before the Cultural Revolution. With the gradual expansion of the Purge Counter-Revolutionaries and Anti-Rightists political movements, the factory closings, famine and economic collapse that accompanied the Three Red Banners campaign, the international isolation caused by the rift between the PRC and the Soviet Union, and the internal party conflict caused by the Peng Dehuai Rightist Anti-Party Clique,[26] the Communist government found itself faced with an immense political and economic crisis. During this period there was great social turmoil and a lack of public confidence, and the Communist Party seemed on the verge of collapse.

The Communist regime employed arrest and sentencing procedures to suppress this unrest but also used RTL policies to charge people with vagrancy, pilfering, spreading reactionary ideology, attacking the Three Red Banners, slandering socialism, obstructing production, and similar crimes that required no legal procedures, thus suppressing the waves of protest and discontent. RTL was undoubtedly one of the important methods the Communist regime employed to weather this threatening storm.

However, among these 10 million RTL subjects, besides a small number of potentially "dangerous elements" that needed to be kept under strict guard, most were peasants driven to drastic action or rebellion by hunger or dissatisfaction with living conditions. These peasants were from the countryside, and thus in the past did not consume commodity grain (that is, the regime did not provide them with food). However, once they became RTL subjects they had to eat public commodity grain, gradually increasing the amount of grain that needed to be supplied by the government and thus becoming a financial burden to the regime. Another problem was that the great increase in RTL facilities during this short period of two or three years created a demand for production tools and know-how that was extremely difficult to meet. The 10 million RTL subjects "detained" during the Great Leap Forward thus became a burden on the Communist regime—this is the reason for the 1961 order to cut-back on the scale of the RTL system and eliminate the commune-run RTL facilities.

Third Stage: 1962–1966—Eve of the Cultural Revolution

This was a stable period for RTL. During this period, the population of RTL subjects was steady at approximately four million. The management and production of the various RTL facilities were standardized in accordance with CCP's Public Security Bureau Resolutions Concerning Ten Recent Policy Problems in Public Security Work.[27] During this period several regulations were passed that unified and clarified such aspects as length of RTL terms, salaries of RTL workers, etc. Most RTL subjects were still mixed in with CLR criminals in the LRCs. In Beijing Municipality's Tuanhe Farm, for instance, No. 1 Battalion was CLR, No. 2 Battalion was FJP and RTL subjects, and No. 3 Battalion was juvenile offenders.

The CCP had ruled that RTL facilties could be established as far down as the mid-size municipality level. In reality, many provinces had RTL facilities established only at relatively larger county levels, such as Shandong Province's Pingyao County.

Fourth Stage: 1966 (Beginning of the Cultural Revolution)–1978

This was the low point for the RTL system. During this stage, because the public security organization was not trusted by Mao Zedong, the entire organization was attacked and expropriated by the Red Guards and Rebels, nearly dealing a fatal blow to the RTL system. At the same time, the Red Guards and Rebels in various work units began establishing "cow sheds,"[28] "labor reform camps," "study groups," and "May 7 cadre schools"[29] to serve in the place of RTL facilities.

During the second half of this period, near the end of 1970, after Mao Zedong had used the Red Guards and Rebels to defeat his political opponents, there was an immediate return to order and the public security system was strengthened. In early 1971, the "Summary of the Fifteenth Plenary National Public Security Meeting," approved by CCPCC, clearly called for the return of RTL.

Fifth Stage: 1978–Present

After Deng Xiaoping took power, RTL was again looked upon as an important means of preserving "public security and unity," and began its second golden age.

Contemporary with the development of large-scale economic and political reforms, in November of 1979 the CCP announced the implementation of Supplementary Reeducation Through Labor Regulations, and in 1980 reissued 1957's RTL policies. Shortly afterward, in June of 1981, the CCP announced the implementation of Resolutions Regarding the Disciplining of Escapees or Repeat Offenders Among CLR or RTL Subjects. The announcement and promulgation of these documents by the National People's Congress, and their establishment as formal law, reflects the Communists reaffirmation of the over twenty-year-old RTL policies.

The practical form and principles behind RTL policies during the period of Deng Xiaoping are reflected in the internal document Public Security Bureau Report Regarding Proper Methods in Reeducation Through Labor Work,[30] approved by the CCP. The subsequent Experimental Methods in Reeducation Through Labor was based upon this document (which was issued in January of 1982). This is the most exhaustive and complete document concerning RTL since 1957 and is the basis for the present implementation of RTL policy.[31]

The scope of RTL in Deng Xiaoping's period is much broader than it was in 1957. RTL was originally limited to large and mid-sized municipalities (except for 1958's "commune-run RTL facilities"); however, article 9 of 1982's Experimental Methods in Reeducation Through Labor states that ". . . offenders from the countryside who commit their offenses in cities, along rail-lines or in large factories or mines, and who after examination prove to meet the specifications for RTL, may be subjected to Reeducation Through Labor." The RTL system is presently much more developed than it was in the time of Mao Zedong, on a much larger scale and with a much greater population.

Reeducation Through Labor Subjects and Arrests

Over thirty-three years, the types of criminals subject to RTL have changed along with changes in the political and societal climate.

Before RTL policies were formally announced on August 1, 1957, the scope of RTL was limited to two types of criminals: those "petty counter-revolutionaries" purged during the Liquidate Counter-Revolutionaries Movement and "bad elements" removed from CCP posts.

The 1957 RTL document included four types of criminals;[32] 1982's Experimental Methods in Reeducation Through Labor expanded to include six types.[33] RTL subjects may be discussed using the distinctions employed in these two documents.

Type 1

Type 1 persons "cannot hold responsible jobs, [are] hoodlums and thieves not worth prosecuting, swindlers, violators of public security, and proven incorrigibles" (The second, third, fourth, and sixth types of criminals enumerated in Experimental Methods in Reeducation Through Labor all fall under this category). Communist authorities emphasize that this type of public security problem is a reflection of class struggle. According to Deng Xiaoping: "In a socialist society . . . various types of criminals who disrupt the socialist order . . . are a special manifestation of class struggle."[34] Therefore, the Communist regime must use one of the methods of the "dictatorship of the proletariate"—RTL—to confine these criminals to the *laogaidui*.

It cannot be denied that in mainland China there are those petty criminals who—because of deficiencies in upbringing, or personal error, or societal factors—come to constitute a threat to society and so should receive punishment. This is one matter. However, the Communists turn these people into "objects of the dictatorship of the proletariate" and throw them into LRCs under the name of RTL, not only depriving them of freedom but also forcing them to labor and undergo thought reform, giving up all their rights as human beings, and even in many cases forcing them to remain their entire lives in the *laogaidui* as slaves.

Type 2

Type 2 offenders are those who "commit petty offenses, [are] counter-revolutionaries not worth prosecuting, and anti-socialist reactionaries." Actually, this type can be further divided into three categories.

***Category A: Historical Counter-Revolutionaries* (lishi fangeming fenze).** Historical counter-revolutionaries were generally those who had served the Nationalist regime in some official capacity, many of whom had already been suppressed or arrested and sentenced. A large number of these people, however, had served some sort of minor post, with no obvious political aspirations or motivations, and moreover had never committed any actions that could be in any way be considered counter-revolutionary.

Most of these people escaped being purged during the suppression movements of the early 1950s. They were not so lucky as to be forgotten by the Communists, however, who labeled them as historical counter-revolutionaries, accused them of petty offenses and threw them into the *laogaidui* under the auspices of RTL. This especially applies to the 200,000 purged during the 1955–1956 Liquidate Counter-Revolutionaries Movement.

Category B: Active Counter-revolutionaries (xianxing fangeming fenze). Many in this category had nothing to do with the Nationalist regime. Many were openly opposed to the Communist Party but had never actually engaged in any important counter-revolutionary activities or were merely dissatisfied with or opposed to certain Party leaders—generally speaking, not really worth arresting and convicting. However, in order to not take any chances, the Communists confined these individuals to LRCs under the auspices of RTL.

Category C: Ideological Reactionaries or Anti-Socialist Elements (fandong fenze). This category of people merely complained or made some disparaging comments, expressed dissatisfaction with a certain party leader, revealed some dissident ideas in personal letters or diaries, or even merely held some rather immature political concepts (i.e., ones that differed from Communism). The label ideological reactionary is considered less serious than that of active counter-revolutionary. The disciplining of thought offenders is a unique feature of RTL. Back when the National People's Congress passed RTL policies, few could have imagined that they would one day be used as a tool against the rightist elements of the intelligentsia.

Type 3

Type 3 people are those who "have been dismissed from their jobs and have no means of making of a living." This type of person not only is unlikely to have any sort of political or historical problems but probably also has no problems with ideological consciousness—yet can still be arrested by Public Security and sent to RTL. All work units in mainland China are controlled by Public Security. Any worker who is considered by his work unit to be "obstructing public order," "violating the rules" or "obstinately shirking labor" can at any time be dismissed by his work unit. Being dismissed means one has no means of making a living and thus can be sent to RTL. This regulation illustrates very clearly how the freedom and rights of every person in mainland China are controlled entirely by the Communist Party organizations. Any who do not go along with this arrangement can be tossed into labor reform camps by Public Security.

Type 4

Type 4 offenders are those who "do not obey work allocation orders or job transfers" (this was the article removed from the 1982 Experimental Methods in Reeducation Through Labor). When this resolution was established in 1957, there were special circumstances that warranted its adoption. In 1955 the Communists were in the process of purging work units of all those who had served the nationalist government, including nationalist soldiers who had rebelled and defected to the Communists, former public officials, and intellectuals who were not trusted by the CCP. These people were subjected to "new job allocation," "alternate job placement" or "job transfer," removed from any relatively important jobs or official posts and transferred out of the central and large cities to more remote regions. Anyone who did not comply with or protested this sort of "transfer" was subjected to RTL. Thirty years later, the situation that called for this resolution no longer existed.

In summary, it can be seen that the objects of RTL are rather diverse and that the Communists can employ RTL to deprive any person they perceive as uncooperative of his freedom and subject him to slave labor without the complication of any sort of judicial procedure. This is one of the special features of the CCP's dictatorship.

Regarding Reeducation Through Labor Arrests

According to the CCP, RTL is based upon article 100 of the Constitution: "The citizens of the People's Republic of China must respect the constitution and laws, abide by the regulations, preserve public order and uphold public virtue."[35] This article is from the sections concerning citizens duties and rights.

If citizens do not perform their "duties" to the fullest, they then may be subject to compulsory reform through RTL, thus losing their freedom and rights. Because RTL is not comparable to such academic, industrial, or organizational administrative measures as demerits, demotions, or dismissals, the Communists refer to it as the "highest level administrative disciplinary action" (*zuigao xingzheng chufen*). However, it is not a criminal disciplinary action, so there is no need for formal arrest or such legal procedures as prosecution by the procurate, trial by the courts or sentencing—the whole process is entirely under the control of the Public Security Bureau. With regard to RTL, the authorities speak of "detaining" (*shourong*) rather than "arresting" (*daibu*), and "personnel" (*renyuan*) rather than "criminals" (*fanren*), in order to distinguish RTL (*laojiao*) from CLR (*laogai*). These are merely word games. RTL involves the same type of police, the same type of shackles, and the same type of LRC as CLR—there is no fundamental difference.

It is interesting to note the following fact: On June 10, 1981, the standing committee of the National People's Congress announced Resolutions Regarding the Disciplining of Escapees or Repeat Offenders Among CLR and RTL Subjects.[36] Looking at this from another angle, it can be seen that the "administrative measure" of RTL is in actuality considered together with CLR—there is no basic distinction made. Both *laojiao* personnel and *laogai* criminals are "objects of the dictatorship." It is obvious that RTL is a far cry from a simple administrative measure.

After the suppression of the 1989 Tiananmen Democracy Movement, the arrest of certain well-known leaders was made known in the media; it is unknown, however, how many youthful idealists were arrested under the auspices of RTL. Most likely the whole lot was imprisoned in one fell swoop.

The images presented by the Beijing television station are a concrete example: young people being arrested (or, to use CCP terminology, "detained") by public security police without the need for any legal procedures.

The Realities of Reeducation Through Labor

Because RTL involves no judicial process, it is difficult for the outside world to clearly understand the actual situation.

Reeducation Through Labor Consideration and Approval

The third article of 1957's Reeducation Through Labor states, "Those in need of Reeducation Through Labor may be recommended by the People's Government, Public Security Bureau, the appropriate organization, collective, enterprise or school work unit, or a parent or guardian, and must be approved by the provincial, autonomous regional or special municipal People's Committee or an organ appointed by this committee."

The "four types of people" (*sezhong ren,* see Chapter 3) set forth in RTL regulations are used to determine who is "in need of Reeducation Through Labor." However, nowhere is there any specific or concrete definition of exactly what sort of behavior characterizes one of the "four types of people." Therefore, who is "in need of Reeducation Through Labor" is simply decided by one of the various CCP branches or directly by Public Security. Then one of the following three types of procedures is employed to subject the individual in question to RTL:

In the first type the individual for whatever reason is placed by Public Security in a detention center and passes through an examination procedure. If it is decided that RTL is appropriate, it is announced in the detention center and the individual is sent directly to a *laogaidui.*

The second type involves recommendation by the appropriate organization, collective, enterprise, or school work unit. In mainland China every administrative work unit functions under the direction of a Party committee, all of which have a public security committee that functions as a branch of the Public Security Bureau.

Once the work unit's Party committee has decided that a certain individual's actions reveal him to be one of the "four types of people" and that he is in need of RTL, the Public Security Committee makes secret arrangements with the Public Security Bureau. As soon as the work unit's Party committee announces the dismissal of that individual, public security police suddenly appear, announcing that the people's government has already issued a "reeducation through labor notification," and thus take the individual into custody. The person in question not only does not know when he is suggested for RTL or when it is approved but is not even necessarily notified until the day of his arrest.

The third type involves recommendation for RTL by a parent or guardian. This type occurs very rarely, probably constituting less than 1 percent of RTL arrests. In the early 1960s, because of the famine and confusion of the time, in some cities parents lost the ability to adequately educate or control their teenage children, who often turned to crime. In these cases, many parents were pressured by Public Security to "recommend" their own children for RTL. For example, in Shanghai in 1961 there were about two thousand teenagers whose parents were pressured into recommending them for RTL and were thus sent off to a *laogaidui* in Shanxi Province.

In the 1980s this type of parental recommendation increased. Most cases involved the children of high-level cadres who committed some kind of crime that normally would warrant judicial proceedings. In these cases, the parents themselves took the initiative and recommended their children for RTL. This way they could avoid the anger and censure of public opinion as well as avoid the complications of arrest and sentencing. More importantly, after the expiration of their child's RTL sentence they could use their influence and position to arrange their child's return and job placement.

From the time RTL was established in 1957 there has been no such thing as an appeals process. Like the virtual absence of appeals in the history of the PRC's legal and judicial procedures, this phenomenon can be explained by the nature of the Communists' dictatorial system. Any decision or action by the Party or government is to be considered absolutely correct and cannot be doubted.

Nineteen eighty-two's Experimental Methods in Reeducation Through Labor contains provisions regarding examination and review procedures; however, these examination and review procedures are handled by the work unit that originally instituted the proceedings in the first place and therefore are a mere formality. Indeed, in the LRC an appeal by a prisoner is often considered "not acknowledging one's crime" (*bu ren zui*)—anti-reform behavior that is likely to cause even more trouble for oneself.

Experimental Methods in Reeducation Through Labor also outright abolished the "recommendation" procedure, stating instead that "all those in need of Reeducation Through Labor must be examined and approved by the provincial, autonomous regional or special municipal Reeducation Through Labor Committee."[37] Because the Reeducation Through Labor Committee is merely a front for Public Security, this means that arrests, examination, sentencing, and imprisonment are all completely controlled by the Public Security Bureau.

Reeducation Through Labor Terms

The 1957 RTL policies specify no limits to terms. RTL as it was defined in those days was a "job placement method" (Reeducation Through Labor, article 2; this article was removed from the 1979 document). Therefore, those purged during the Liquidate Counter-revolutionaries Movement in 1955 and those counter-revolutionary rightists sentenced to *laojiao* in 1957 upon being sent to the LRC were told, "This is your job, this is your home, work hard, try to reform, and redeem your crimes . . . looking at it from a broad perspective, reform is a life-long endeavor . . . you will receive appropriate pay, you will have the right to work, the right to rest, what else could you want?"

Before 1961, those subjected to RTL served unlimited terms. *Laojiao* was lifetime job placement.

"In order to aid in the reformation of Reeducation Through Labor personnel, CCPCC has authorized that, beginning April, 1961, Reeducation Through Labor will have terms of two-three years."[38] This set a definite term limit for every person subjected to RTL before and after April of 1961.

In 1979's Supplementary Reeducation Through Labor Regulations (*laodong jiaoyang buchong guiding*) this limit on term length became public knowledge. Up to that point it had been a CCP internal regulation.

The Communists' "criminal law" is very thorough and precise in defining the various types of criminal behavior that result in terms of five years and under. Similarly, Public Order Punishment Regulations (*zhian goanli chufa tiaolie*) also specifies in great detail minor criminal behavior. In contrast, however, with regard to RTL—which can deprive a citizen of his freedom for up to three years—the only guidelines are the "four types of people"—there are no specific regulations defining what these "four types of people" might be. This cannot be attributed to an oversight or lack of consideration by the CCP; rather, it reflects very well the political goals and necessities of implementing this type of policy.

The 1982 Experimental Methods in Reeducation Through Labor and 1979s Supplementary Regulations state that RTL terms may be extended, but not past one year.[39] Before 1979, CCP internal regulations stated that RTL terms could be extended up to three years. Moreover, there was no limit on the number of times it could be extended. On the basis of the author's personal experience, using the Beijing area as an example, in the 1960s and 1970s over 10 percent of *laojiao* subjects had their sentences extended twice or even three times.

It is essential to note that there is often a rather large discrepancy between what the Communists preach on paper and how they actually act. With regard to the length of RTL terms, we can look at one such example, Tuanhe Farm (LRC-03-11), under the jurisdiction of the Beijing Municipal Public Security Bureau: Among the No. 2 battalions here there is one branch referred to as *San yu zhuang* (Three Left Village), which consists of 143 *laojiao* rightists, all of whom were sentenced to three years, starting May 24, 1961, (before May 24, 1961 RTL had no term; at that time these people had already been there two or three years). On May 24, 1964, at the expiration of their terms, the 143 received notification from the Beijing Public Security Bureau: "We must wait for approval from higher authorities in order to commence procedures to release you. Until notification is received, you will continue to be treated as RTL subjects. This is a political necessity."

Not only was no reason provided for the extension of their RTL sentences but the length of this extension was also not specified. Just for the sake of CCP political expediency their terms were extended five more years. In August of 1969 they were finally split into three groups and it was announced that their RTL terms were complete. They were then immediately sent to different LRCs for *jiuye*—FJP.

During an RTL term it is very easy for one to have one's term extended because of "poor behavior." The reasons for extensions of terms are noted in article 58 of Experimental Methods in Reeducation Through Labor. There are ten types of behavior specified, including refusing to acknowledge guilt, resisting reform, violating rules, not submitting to discipline, passive work attitude, etc. Any of these types of behavior can be used as justification for extending an RTL term.

Before 1979, the procedure for extending an RTL term was very simple: The general brigade submitted information to the battalion, which gave the approval and then required the appropriate branch to submit a report. The was no such thing as an appeal. After 1979, regulations for extending RTL terms required the approval of the Reeducation Through Labor Commission, which is basically a part of the Public Security Bureau.

The procedures for ending an RTL term involved the general brigade submitting a report to the battalion regarding the subject's political behavior, thought reform, and labor performance. After being approved by the battalion the appropriate branch filed a report. Recent regulations have made the RTL Commission responsible for approval. This also has very little relation to reality because many provincial and municipal RTL commissions exist only in name.

The problems of returning to society or being subjected to FJP (*jiuye*) will be discussed in Chapter 4.

Monetary Remuneration of Reeducation Through Labor Subjects

RTL policies as announced by the CCP encompass only "internal contradictions within the people" (*renmin neibu maodun*) and "highest administrative disciplinary actions" (*zuigao xingzheng chufen*). Therefore, though on the one hand Public Security employs "dictatorial methods" to deprive these people of their freedom and force them to engage in labor reform, on the other hand it is also legislated that they must provide "appropriate" salary. This is the greatest point of difference between RTL and CLR.

Before 1962, RTL subjects were merely given monthly living expenses at three pay levels: 18 *yuan,* 22 *yuan* or 24 *yuan.* They were given no salary. After 1962 a few regions—like Beijing Municipality—began providing salaries. Chart 3.1 details the salary situation in the Beijing area from 1964–1965.

As can be seen from Chart 3.1, after deducting for food, clothes, shoes, and other basic necessities from an RTL subject's "appropriate" salary, the situation is actually not much different than that of CLR convicts, and the salary is only about 40 percent that of a regular worker.

Political Treatment of Reeducation Through Labor Subjects

When the Communists instituted RTL policy in 1957, they avoided the question of RTL subjects' political rights. According to official explanations, RTL is not a criminal proceeding—it is "highest level administrative disciplinary action." RTL subjects are not criminals, they are "personnel" or "students," and RTL camps are referred to as "special schools" (*teshu shuexiao*). Moreover, it is claimed that those subjected to RTL are still citizens and have not lost the rights granted to them by the Constitution—for example, they still have the right to vote, etc. However, an analysis of the actual situation in the over twenty years of RTL before 1980 reveals that

CHART 3.1 Details of Income of Beijing Municipality Area in 1962–1965

Item	Laogai *CLR* Convicts	Laojiao *RTL* Subjects	Society at Large
1. Income (farms)	No pay.	13–41.60 yuan/mo.	41.60–78 yuan/mo.
2. Income (factories)	No pay.	17–47.60 yuan/mo.	47–109 yuan/mo.
3. Bonuses	2–5 yuan/mo. Not given to all.	3–5 yuan/quarter in 3 levels of bonuses. Not given to all.	Average 15–20 yuan/mo.
4. Basic necessities	Prison provides shoes, blankets, clothes, etc.	All items self-provided.	All items self-provided.
5. Food	Provided by prison.	Provided by prison, deducted from convict's income. Average 16.5 yuan/mo.	Self-provided.
6. Sick leave	No pay, approved by police.	For short-term leaves, deducted from income. Long-term leaves, provide 13 yuan/mo.	Given sick leave pay.
7. Benefits/ Insurance	None.	Legally should provide family; in actuality none given. No workman's compensation or overtime; income increases or decreases depending on reform behavior, approved by police.	Family visits, overtime, workman's compensation, family support, opportunity for pay increase; generally no pay cuts.
8. Working	Work by law, 9–10 hrs/day, often 12 hrs. Every 2 wks, one day off.	Same as *Laogai*.	8 hrs. by law, 6 days a wk.

Pages of a security document. Right-hand page reads Selected Works of Security Management Work Documents (Volume 2); RESTRICTED DOCUMENT; HANDLE CARE-FULLY; Edited by Public Security Bureau of Fujian Province, Department Three, August 1984. Left-hand page reads Notice from the State Council to the Public Security Bureau [Experimental Methods in Reeducation Through Labor] National Document (1982) # 17; People's Police School Basic Public Security Professional Knowledge Textbook #8; REEDUCATION THROUGH LABOR WORK (laojiao gongzuo) (TRIAL DRAFT) Edited by Public Security Professional Textbook Committee; PUBLIC SECURITY ORGAN INTERNAL DOCUMENT; QUNZHONG PRESS; 1983 BEIJING.

- RTL is part of the *laogaidui* system and thus entirely under the control of the Public Security Bureau.
- Those subjected to RTL enjoy no rights as citizens (and no voting privileges).
- Those subjected to RTL are "objects of the dictatorship of the proletariate."
- In practice, there is no basic difference between RTL and CLR.

In 1982 the public security internal document Experimental Methods in Reeducation Through Labor contained new regulations concerning the political treatment of RTL subjects. Article 2 of that document states, ". . . [RTL] is a method of dealing with internal contradiction among the people." Article 19: "RTL subjects during the course of their terms shall enjoy the voting privileges accorded to them by law." The actual state of affairs, however, is somewhat different. On page 19 of 1983's "Reeducation

Through Labor Work," a teaching material published internally by the Public Security Bureau for the training of public security police, we find

> . . . RTL subjects during the course of their terms . . . should enjoy the privileges accorded to all citizens . . . with regard to certain political rights and freedoms, however, necessary limits should be imposed, for instance, revoking of voting privileges or the right to run for office, the right to assemble, the right to demonstrate, the right to strike, etc., as well as the right to come and go as one pleases . . . the limits on rights described above are only temporary administrative measures, not legal deprivation of rights.[40]

This reflects

- First, the rights granted to citizens by the constitution can be revoked at any time by administrative regulations or policies—an interesting note on the amount of authority possessed by the CCP's constitution.
- Second, the dictatorial Communist regime uses RTL as a means to recklessly deprive citizens of their freedom and rights.
- Third, there is a great discrepancy between what the CCP legislates on paper and the manner in which these laws are actually carried out.

The Realities of Reeducation Through Labor

RTL subjects are organized in exactly the same military fashion as CLR convicts. The styles and methods of labor production and thought reform are also exactly the same. The only minor difference is the lesser degree to which RTL subjects are under armed surveillance.

The escape rate in the *laogaidui* (including CLR convicts) is very low for the following reasons: (1) prisoners are encouraged to inform on each other; (2) through the use of a strict household registration system and rationing of basic daily necessities as well a successful system of thought control and propaganda, the Communist regime has complete control of all aspects of society. Counter-revolutionaries very rarely manage to escape. Escapes among those sent out to labor are also much more common than escapes from prisons.

Money is deducted from the salaries of RTL subjects whenever they are in study sessions, absent from work, or in solitary confinement.[41] Salaries are determined by the company public security cadre and issued by the battalion along with a detailed inventory. From this salary is deducted the monthly food expenses and the remaining amount is given to the duty prisoner (an RTL worker), who then deposits it in each individual's bank account. None of the money is actually given to the individual.

RTL subjects must pay for all their own clothes, blankets, and shoes; the amount of money left over after this is very small. Although CLR convicts receive no salary, every month they are given a subsistence allowance, and all food and clothing is provided by the LRC. In comparison, then, the living conditions of RTL subjects and CLR convicts are basically the same.

Hunger is a constant problem in the *laogaidui*. According to regulations, RTL subjects doing the same type of work as a regular worker in society at large should receive the same amount of food. The problem is (1) the grain supplied to RTL subjects is coarse, rotten, and unhulled; (2) various levels of food embezzling are involved, for all company and battalion public security cadres eat and drink for free from the provisions meant for the prisoners, and the cooks (who are criminals) not only snatch extra food for themselves but also steal food for the Public Security cadres to curry favor; (3) very little oil and meat are provided in the first place, and after food embezzling almost none reaches the prisoners' bowls. Generally every two weeks there is a "supplement" in diet, where each prisoner receives vegetable soup with a few strips of fatty pork. In Beijing's Qinghe Farm there was a popular saying: "eat cabbage broken, spinach tall, and chives once a year" (the outside leaves of cabbage are broken off and given to the prisoners to eat while the cadres eat the hearts; spinach is not given to prisoners to eat until it has grown into "trees" because it is sold to the LRCs by weight; chives are considered a higher-quality vegetable and are only given to prisoners once a year as dumplings at the Spring Festival).

RTL subjects are limited by regulation to sending two letters a month, which must be handed in to the company for inspection and mailing. Letters from the outside are opened and read first before being given to the prisoner. Correspondence deemed inappropriate is never received.

Most *laogaidui* are established in remote, rather inaccessible areas. After days of grueling travel, family members visiting prisoners in such LRCs are usually allowed a visit right away, for as long as one or two hours. In LRCs located in cities or suburbs, periodic times are set when visitors are allowed. Usually one visit per month is allowed—the LRC informs the prisoner that in this month on such-and-such a date visits will be allowed, and then each prisoner must write to his family members and inform them. Often prisoners with poor behavior have their letter and visiting privileges revoked by the public security cadre. Only visits from immediate family members are allowed. Before family members are allowed to see the prisoner, public security cadres give them a report on the prisoner's reform progress and thought reform work. During the visit a public security cadre is present and at times joins the conversation. These visits usually last from twenty–thirty minutes. Those with good reform behavior as well as those whose families are high-level cadres or have connections have more liberal visiting privileges.

The LRCs have always had a policy of allowing a small number of prisoners to return home for visits because this is a very effective tool to encourage prisoners to actively reform and to become more supportive of the government. Prisoners from LRCs in urban areas are usually given a twenty-four-hour leave. Prisoners from LRCs in remote areas under special circumstances—for instance, parents who are sick or dying—can be given leaves of seven to fifteen days.

All packages are first opened and inspected, and any items considered inappropriate are confiscated before the prisoner ever sees them. Food brought by visiting relatives is usually not allowed, or at most 1 kg or so is permissible. There is no such restriction on clothing or other necessities.

Every battalion has an infirmary staffed with two to three "doctors." These doctors are all prisoners or FJP personnel, and the infirmary is established within the LRC itself. These "doctors" can grant prisoners sick leave, but only on the approval of the public security cadre.

Flies, mosquitoes, bedbugs, and lice are very common in the *laogaidui,* and the rate of sickness and disease is very high.

Notes

1. *Faxue jikan* (Legal Quarterly), "Reeducation Through Labor is Our Nation's Unique Public Security System," Southwest Political Science and Law Institute, April, 1983, pp. 29–30.

2. "Contradiction among the people" (*renmin neibu maodun*) is a political term coined by Mao, referring to the nonantagonistic contradictions among the workers, between the intellectuals and the peasants, between the leaders and the people, between the individual and the collective, etc. It is contrasted to "contradictions between the enemy and ourselves" (*diwo maodun*), which refers to the basically antagonistic struggle between the exploiting classes (i.e., the capitalists, landlords, rich peasants, etc.) and the people [translator's note].

3. Suppress Bandits and Oppose Hegemonists, 1950–1951, was a mopping up of various regional political forces conducted by the Communists on a national scale, especially in the Northwest, Southwest, and Central Southern regions.

4. Movement to Suppress Counter-Revolutionaries, 1950–1951, was a violent suppression conducted by the Communists on a national scale, directed against hostile movements and remaining nationalist military and government personnel.

5. Three Anti's, Five Anti's began in December of 1951, ended in late 1952; the Three Anti's were anti-corruption, anti-waste and anti-bureaucracy; the Five Anti's were anti-graft, anti-tax evasion, anti-embezzlement, anti-theft of public property, and anti-economic espionage. The objects of attack were public officials and especially private enterprises. After this movement the CCP not only obtained a great deal of wealth but also gained control of the national economy.

6. Collectivization of Agriculture was a large-scale development conducted in 1952 that gathered together the lands originally distributed to the peasants during the Agrarian Revolution and organized them into collectives.

7. Public and Private Joint Ownership started in 1953. Private enterprises were reorganized under the principles of "national capitalism," in which capitalists' prices were fixed, their compensation paid by the government in installments, and all enterprises came under the control of CCP cadres.

8. Liquidate Counter-Revolutionaries occurred in 1955 and resulted in the purging of approximately 400,000 people.

9. An Examination of the Hunan Peasant Movement," in *Maozedong xuanji* (The Selected Works of Mao Zedong), vol. 1, Beijing: People's Press, 1967, p. 14.

10. "Lean to one side" refers to the policy formulated by Mao in 1949, which stated that the Communist revolution in China was part of the larger international revolution; the Chinese people, therefore, in international relations should favor and develop ties with their partners in the international socialist revolution (i.e., the Soviet Union and other Communist nations) and oppose the forces of international imperialism (i.e., the United States and Great Britain). This slogan was used to justify seeking and receiving Soviet aid.

11. The Anti-Rightists Movement, May, 1957–May, 1958, was a political movement aimed at capitalist-class rightists in which close to 1 million intellectuals were purged.

12. See Note 2.

13. "On the Correct Handling of the Problem of Internal Contradictions Among the People," in *Mao Zedong xuanji* (The Selected Works of Mao Zedong), vol. 5, Beijing: People's Press, 1977, p. 289.

14. Ibid., p. 364.

15. Ibid., p. 365.

16. Ibid., p. 364.

17. Ibid., p. 371.

18. Ibid., p. 370.

19. Laogai gongzuo (Labor Reform Work), Beijing: CCP internal document, 1983, p. 1.

20. Ibid.

21. Ibid.

22. "Maozedong: Wenhuibao de zechanjieji fangshang yingdang pipan" (Mao Zedong: Report on the Proper Criticism of Our Capitalist-Class Objects), Beijing: *People's Daily*, July 1, 1957.

23. *Dengxiaoping wenxuan: Duiyu qicao "Guanyu jianguo yilai dang de ruogan lishi wenti de jueyi" de yijian* (Selected Literary Works of Deng Xiaoping: Thoughts Concerning the Drafting of "Resolutions Regarding Several Historical Problems in the Establishment of the Nation and the Future of the Party"), Beijing: People's Press, p. 447.

24. The punishments for rightists were split into five levels of severity (based upon the author's recollection of announcements made by various levels of CCP organs in February of 1958): (1) "extreme rightists" were given a rightist "hat" (i.e., label), removed from their jobs and sent to a life term of RTL; (2) "serious

rightists" were given a rightist hat, removed from their jobs, and sent to life terms of laboring under supervision in villages or mines with bare sustenance pay; (3) Many rightists were given rightist hats, allowed to keep their jobs, but sent to work under supervision in villages or mines with reduced salaries for one to three years; (4) "common rightists" were given rightist hats and transferred to another work unit to remain on probation and receive a reduced salary for one to three years; and (5) "petty rightists" were given a rightist hat but were not punished.

Punishment for student rightists followed along the same lines, with only four levels (the second and third being combined into one). Being expelled from school took the place of being removed from one's job, academic probation replaced job probation, and withdrawal of scholarships took the place of reduced salaries.

25. Laojiao gongzuo (Reeducation Through Labor Work), Beijing: CCP internal document, 1983, p. 15.

26. The Peng Dehuai Rightist Anti-Party Clique was a group of dissenters (Peng Dehuai, chief of the Defense Department, acted as their spokesman) who fiercely attacked the Three Red Banners Movement and as a result were castigated by Mao and purged in August of 1959 [translator's note].

27. Gonganbu guanyu dangqian gongan gongzuo shige juti zhengce wenti de buchong guiding (Public Security Bureau Supplementary Regulations Concerning Ten Recent Practical Policy Problems in Public Security Work), approved by the CCP in March of 1961. This document proposed that the RTL system be cut back and restructured as well as made important changes and supplementary regulations concerning the focus of RTL, subjects of detention, examination process, and length of RTL terms.

28. "Cow sheds" refers to the rather primitive labor reform camps with harsh living conditions that were set up during the Cultural Revolution to house counter-revolutionaries.

29. "May 7 cadre schools" were labor camps for CCP cadres "sent down to the countryside" in accordance with the May 7 Directive issued by Mao on May 7, 1966. Mao felt this was "an excellent education opportunity" for urban cadres; it was also an effective method for removing political opponents within the party.

30. The author has been unable to locate the text of this document.

31. Guowuyuan guanyu zhuanfa gonganbu "Laodong jiaoyang shixing banfa" de tongzhi (National Assembly Notification Concerning the Promulgation of Public Security Bureau's Experimental Methods in Reeducation Through Labor), issued 1982, National Document No. 17. This document in all consists of 11 chapters, with 69 articles: Chapter 1: General Principles; Ch. 2: RTL Facilities; Ch. 3: Detention Criterion; Ch. 4: Administrative Management; Ch. 5: Educational Reform; Ch. 6: Labor Production; Ch. 7: Living Conditions; Ch. 8: Correspondence and Personal Visits; Ch. 9: Examination, Rewards and Punishments; Ch. 10: Release and Assignments; Ch. 11: Cadres.

32. Laodong jiaoyang (Reeducation Through Labor), article 1: "RTL detention actions should be instituted against the following types of people: (1) those unable to hold a regular job, hoodlums, petty thieves, swindlers, violators of public order, and stubborn incorrigibles; (2) petty criminals, minor counter-revolutionaries, anti-socialist reactionaries, and those dismissed by their organizational, collective,

entrepreneurial or academic work units and who possess no means of livelihood; (3) those in organizational, collective, entrepreneurial or academic work units who are able to labor but who consistently shirk their labor responsibilities, break rules, disrupt public order, or are subjected to dismissal and thus have no means of livelihood; (4) those who do not obey work allocation or job transfer orders, or those who ignore production procedures, incessantly make trouble, ignore civic responsibilities, and prove to be incorrigibly unreformable."

33. Laodong jiaoyang shixing banfa (Experimental Methods for Reeducation Through Labor), article 10: Nationally Published Document No. 17, January 21, 1982. This document states, "RTL detention procedures should be instituted against the following types of people:

(1) petty criminals, counter-revolutionaries not worth prosecuting, and anti-party, anti-socialist elements; (2) those who associate with murderers, robbers, rapists and arsonists, but are not themselves worth prosecuting; (3) hoodlums, prostitutes, thieves, swindlers and other criminals who are repeat offenders but not worth prosecuting; (4) rioters, fight instigators and other trouble makers that disturb the public peace but are not worth prosecuting; (5) those with jobs who consistently shirk labor responsibilities, break rules and cause incessant trouble, disrupting production procedures, work procedures, research procedures or the order of daily life, and ignore civic responsibilities, reasonable advice and all restraints; (6) those who encourage others to violate the law but are not worth prosecuting."

34. "Sexiang jiben yuanze" (Four Basic Principles), in *Selected Works of Deng Xiaoping,* Beijing: People's Press, 1986.

35. Constitution of the People's Republic of China, published in 1954.

36. Quanguo renmin daibiao dahui changwu weiyuanhui guanyu chuli taopao huozhe chongxin fanzui de laogaifan he laojiao renyuan de jueding (Resolutions of the Standing Committee of the National People's Congress Concerning the Disciplining of Escapees and Repeat Offenders Among CLR and RTL Subjects, passed by the Fifth Plenary Session of the standing committee of the Nineteenth National People's Congress, June 10, 1981).

37. *Laodong jiaoyang shixing banfa* (Experimental Methods in Reeducation Through Labor), Chapter 11, National Document No. 17, January 21, 1982.

38. Laojiao gongzuo (RTL Work), p. 19, Beijing: CCP internal document, 1983.

39. Laodong jiaoyang buchong guiding (Supplementary Regulations for Reeducation Through Labor), article 3, note No. 1, 1971.

40. RTL Work, pp. 19–20.

41. Ibid., p. 64.

4

Forced Job Placement *(Jiuye)*

The following phrase appears in *The First Half of My Life,* the memoirs of Pu Yi, the last emperor of China: "Without the Communist Party, without criminal reform policies, I would not be the true person I am today." Pu Yi, his memoirs, and this phrase are frequently referred to in the prolabor reform propaganda of Public Security and the Judicial Bureau. The Communists claim that Pu Yi underwent successful "reform through labor," and became a "new socialist man." If this is so, if reactionary counter-revolutionaries are all successfully "reformed," then why do we not see more examples of reform like Pu Yi? If FJP policies state that political counter-revolutionaries all must be subject to FJP after their terms expire, why was Pu Yi not forced to remain within the *laogaidui*? Why was he allowed to return to Beijing and given work in the Research Institute of Culture and History? Why is it that those who committed offenses much less serious than Pu Yi were executed? If CCP labor reform policies are so effective, why are those who have completed their terms forced to remain in the *laogaidui*? Are FJP policies really public welfare measures for those who would have difficulty returning to work in society?

The True Nature of Forced Job Placement

Those subjected to FJP are referred to as "job placement personnel" (*jiuye renyuan*). They are one of the "three types of personnel" (*sanlei renyuan*).

The term "job placement personnel" does not refer to those in the general population who are out of work and are thus given employment. In the PRC, this term has a special meaning. Job placement personnel after serving their terms are not accorded the same freedoms and rights of an ordinary citizen. They are forced to "continue reform" in labor reform enterprises (*laogai qiye*) run by the public security and judicial bureaus. They are deprived of the right to choose their own jobs or their own lifestyles. Their political standing in society is totally different from that of ordinary citizens.

At present, there have only been three publicly issued documents dealing with FJP: (1) Temporary Disciplinary Methods for Releasing and Job Placement of Labor Reform Prisoners Who Have Completed Their Terms, September 7, 1954; (2) Resolutions Regarding the Disciplining of Escapees or Repeat Offenders Among Labor Reform Prisoners and Reeducation Through Labor Personnel, June 9, 1981; (3) Announcement Concerning the Release of Some Temporarily Detained Reeducation Through Labor Personnel Who Have Completed Their Terms, December 9, 1983.

Labor Reform Regulations of the People's Republic of China was announced on September 7, 1954; Temporary Disciplinary Methods for Releasing and Job Placement of Labor Reform Prisoners Who Have Completed Their Terms was announced at the same time. So as soon as labor reform arrest and sentencing policies went into effect, the handling of convicts after the expiration of their terms was already arranged.

The purpose of FJP policies is obvious: "To fully implement labor reform policies and ensure public security." FJP policies "are organized in accordance with article 62 of the People's Republic of China Labor Reform Regulations."[1] It is thus rather apparent that FJP is part of, or an extension of, labor reform. FJP's purpose is to uphold the dictatorial regime and maintain public order; it is not a typical job placement or public welfare service.

Looking at it from a political angle, the CCP, faithful to Marxist doctrine, maintains that class struggle will be present on a long-term basis and feels that thought reform is also a long-term process. The CCP is very clear on at least one point: It is absolutely impossible for those who have undergone CLR or RTL—these anti-socialist class enemies who have experienced hell on earth in the *laogaidui*—to accept the Communist regime. These people are probably even more dangerous to the regime than before they were arrested. Because these people have achieved a much clearer understanding of the true nature of the dictatorship, their opposition to the regime can only be strengthened. For this reason it is necessary for the Communist regime to carry through labor reform policies to the end, employing FJP to keep these people, who they refer to as "unreformables," under control within the LRC system. At the same time, within the *laogaidui* it is necessary from a managerial and disciplinary point of view to have a group of people who have been prisoners, and are familiar with criminals, to serve as an important tool for public security police in the managing of production, daily life, and political control.

Looking at it from an economic perspective, *jiuye* personnel constitute an indispensable component of labor reform production. Prisoners who are totally deprived of all freedom are suitable only for simple, primitive handicraft production. This type of work force is inefficient and unproductive. Over forty years, the scale of labor reform production has steadily increased and is now beginning to modernize and become automated. Labor reform production has become a very important force in the socialist modernization of mainland China. Modern management methods and production techniques require a reasonably stable work force with a certain degree of freedom. For this reason FJP personnel are essential. Presently, those industrial LRCs with slightly more advanced technologies have a correspondingly higher proportion of FJP personnel. Conversely, labor reform farms, road construction teams, etc.—those work units that involve only simple physical labor—have a correspondingly lower proportion of *jiuye* personnel.

For example, an official in the Shanghai Municipality Judicial Bureau gave a "moving speech" to Shanghai prisoners who were being sentenced to CLR, noting that during the "legal construction" (*fazhi jianshe*) in June of 1984, "Our Huadong Electric Welder Factory (LRC-29-07) was run by Forced Job Placement personnel . . . we have made a regulation stating that any who during the course of their prison terms express genuine remorse for their crimes can remain in Shanghai for job placement . . . presently, prisoners from Anhui or Subei who display good behavior or who have completed their sentences and who, upon returning to Shanghai . . . have difficulty finding a job, are given job placement by our labor reform bureau."[2] From this we can see that

- Huadong Electric Welder Factory is one of the many LRCs run by Shanghai Municipality's labor reform bureau.
- Since this LRC is in the city of Shanghai itself, prisoners obviously hope to be placed there after serving their terms, especially those who have family in Shanghai. Those wishing to be placed in Shanghai must meet the LRC's condition of "expressing true remorse." From this we can see the political function of Huadong Electric Welder Factory.

Another point of interest is that Huadong Electric Welder Factory is one of the Shanghai Municipality Labor Reform Bureau's major sources of income. In 1986 this factory's overall production reached 35 million *yuan,* tax revenues submitted to the government 14.76 million *yuan.* It is the only factory in China that produces the HZA12-400 narrow-aperture pulsating air automatic welding machine.

The Development of Forced Job Placement

In December of 1953 the Second Plenary Session of the National Labor Reform Work Congress decided[3] "with regard to criminals who completed their terms, a 'keep more, release less' [*duoliu shaofang*] principle should be adopted, to the point where 70 percent are kept and 30 percent released. With regard to counter-revolutionaries, habitual thieves should be kept. Most common criminals and counter-revolutionaries serving terms of under two years, however, should be released. Those criminals who are being held far from their place of origin, except under special circumstances, should not be released."[4]

In 1964, the Sixth Plenary National Labor Reform Congress, "Several Problems Regarding Strengthening Labor Reform" noted,

> Usually serious counter-revolutionaries and hardened common criminals have become accustomed to crime; with the exception of a few who have shown exemplary reformed behavior, they should all remain in the LRC for job placement after the expiration of their terms. Offenders from working-class families and most common criminals should, in principle, be allowed to return home after completion of their terms. With regard to criminals who have completed their terms, a "Keep Four, Release Four" [*seliu, sebuliu*] system should be employed. "Keep Four" refers to those who have not reformed; those homeless or unemployed; those whose homes lie in border areas or on the coast; and those whose homes lie adjacent to counties or large cities on the coast or borders. "Release Four" refers to those who have reformed; those whose homes are in the countryside; those who have no longer have the potential for counter-revolutionary activity; etc.[5]

What types of people are released back to society after serving *laogai* or *laojiao* terms?

- Important figures who can serve as "political examples," such as former emperor of Manchuria, Pu Yi, or high-level nationalist general, Du Liming
- CCP cadres or their children
- Minor criminals and a portion of those who served terms of under two years
- Those old and infirm prisoners who have lost the ability to labor, whose *laogaidui* is not willing to support them, and who have family in the countryside

As far as the author has been able to determine, during the 1950s and 1960s almost 95 percent of CLR and RTL subjects were forced into job placement within the *laogaidui* after completing their terms. This is due in part to the fact that during the 1950s and 1960s, "the revolutionary scene was changing very rapidly, with one movement after another, and wave after wave of class struggle." The general populace had good reason to be nervous—how much more so those who were "objects of the dictatorship?" There was no way for these people to be assimilated by society. Another consideration was that the LRC greatly needed these underpaid, obedient production tools. The number of FJP personnel thus snowballed, increasing daily. Under the direction of provincial-level labor reform organs, certain old or infirm subjects who had lost the ability to labor and had relatives in the countryside could depend upon being allowed to leave. This was FJP personnel's only chance to leave the *laogaidui*.

In 1981, the Eighth Plenary National Labor Reform Congress passed a few new resolutions. Those who since the 1950s and 1960s had constituted the largest proportion of *laogaidui* prisoners—the former nationalist soldiers and officials, landlords and rich peasants (most of whom were labeled historical counter-revolutionaries or active counter-revolutionaries), counter-revolutionary rightists, post-1960 "thought offenders," and counter-revolutionaries purged during the Cultural Revolution—had by the 1980s generally disappeared; had grown old, sick, weak or crippled, thus losing the potential for criminal activity; or had been politically rehabilitated and released. This includes FJP personnel, who by the 1980s had largely been released and allowed to return to society, resulting in a significant decrease in size and change in constitution of the FJP system. This congress established new FJP regulations, reiterating,

Forced Job Placement is a type of compulsory administrative measure, is designed to assist in job placement, and also serves the function of continuing the reform process. Its purpose is to prevent released convicts from committing repeat offenses and endangering public welfare. There are two main categories of FJP personnel:

(1) Those who by law must be subjected to job placement. In accordance with "Resolutions Regarding the Disciplining of Escapees and Repeat Offenders Among Convicted Labor Reform Convicts and Reeducation Through Labor Personnel," passed by the 5th Plenary Session of the 19th National Congress Standing Committee, any prisoner committing an offense after escaping from an LRC or after being previously released from an LRC must remain for job placement after serving his term (excepting those who display exemplary reformed behavior).

(2) Those prisoners who have not been reformed will generally be subjected to job placement. This category consists mainly of the following types of convicts: serious counter-revolutionaries, instigators, clique leaders, thieves, hoodlums, robbers, etc., who are accustomed to a life of crime, who during their period of incarceration have shown no clear signs of repentance and

possibly pose a threat to society; those who hold fast to their reactionary viewpoint; those who oppose party leaders and the socialist system, slander the party line, goals and policies, display an incorrigible and extreme attitude and seem unreformable; those serious offenders who refuse to acknowledge their guilt or submit to the law, who consistently cause trouble, seriously disrupt the reform process, have a bad influence on the other prisoners and who seem unreformable; those who consistently violate the rules, form gangs, engage in fights or playing tricks on other prisoners, plan disruptive outbursts or display other illegal behavior, and who have received repeated warnings, demerits, solitary confinements or increased sentences and yet display no clear signs of repentance; those who regularly refuse to labor or attempt to disrupt production and who seem unreformable.[6]

Most of those "who display good reform behavior" have a possibility of leaving the *laogaidui;* however, there are no time frames or specific conditions set.

The first type described above is numerically not very important; the more important type is the second. This type is sentenced to *jiuye* the day his CLR or RTL term expires. Among CLR prisoners, approximately 50 percent are subsequently subjected to FJP; among RTL personnel, the number is closer to 20–30 percent (Recently a new type of FJP personnel has appeared among RTL subjects—if one, when being sentenced to RTL, has the condition "urban household registration cancelled" added, one is sent to an LRC in Qinghai, Xinjiang, etc., and after completing one's term must remain in that LRC for forced job placement).

Regardless of governmental policies, the situation has always been one of "They go in but don't come out"—the number of FJP personnel has thus increased steadily. Assuming every year 400,000–600,000 people are subjected to *jiuye,* then in the ten years since 1980, 4–6 million FJP personnel have accumulated. Including the FJP personnel already present in the *laogaidui,* the total number can be estimated at something like 8–10 million.

Early on, in the 1950s, there were 100,000–200,000 people who had political, historical, or class background problems but had not actually committed any sort of offense and had never been arrested or convicted, but who nonetheless were subjected to FJP in the *laogaidui.* An example is the author of *Prisoner of Mao,* Bao Ruowang, who was suspect because of his foreign lineage and background. The level of freedom and personal rights allowed these people can be gleaned from a reading of *Prisoner of Mao.* These types of people were obviously not treated as common workers, but their position was also not that of CLR or RTL subjects. In any case, this type of FJP personnel has already disappeared.

Since 1980 there has been a significant change in FJP policy. A large number of FJP personnel were released to return to society. In addition, with regard to those completing their *laogai* or *laojiao* terms, a policy of keeping few and releasing most (*shaoliu duofang*) was implemented. In early 1983, however, the release of prisoners back to society was temporarily halted because of class struggle and political expediency; FJP policies were revised and the number of FJP personnel began to increase again. Further research is needed to determine the exact nature of the present situation.

Actual Conditions of Forced Job Placement

FJP personnel are organized into squadrons, general brigades, battalions, etc. Each level has public security police directors. Each battalion has a mass training team to which personnel with poor ideological behavior are sent. Battalions also have solitary confinement facilities.

All FJP personnel live within the *laogaidui* under this military system of organization. If FJP personnel have family, they can be allocated housing within the confines of the LRC. Family members can also engage in labor and receive a definite salary.

It is not possible for FJP personnel to choose their jobs, transfer, or move their place of residence.

The salary of FJP personnel is 60–70 percent that of a general worker. They also have use of the LRC infirmary and receive workman's compensation and benefits from their labor reform enterprise. The standard of these services within the LRC system are obviously not up to the level of those in society at large.

Two weeks a year *jiuye* personnel are given paid leave to visit relatives. However, because they have no worker or identification registration cards, in order to return home they must receive a family visitation certificate from their LRC. This type of certificate does not specify the enterprise name, only that it was issued by XX Provincial or Municipal No. XX Labor Reform Detachment. Thus, in using this sort of certificate in the PRC to buy tickets or find hotel rooms or rentals one is rather likely to meet with some strange looks and difficulties. Upon arriving in one's hometown, one must appear at the local public security branch to give a report and receive supervision and instruction. Upon returning to one's LRC, one must report to the appropriate public security branch. Those who do not report back in time are treated as escaped convicts. Their *laogaidui* notifies the appropriate public security agency, which then apprehends the subject and returns him to his LRC, where he is subsequently forced to undergo self-criticism, solitary confinement, or even forced to "do another stint"—that is, serve another *laogai* or *laojiao* term.

Sick-leave pay is 50 percent of regular pay. Salary is issued monthly to each individual. The LRCs employ internal meal cards that are used at their cafeterias; FJP personnel eat together in these cafeterias.

FJP personnel are not sent to work under armed escort, but their work is directed by public security cadres, and production arrangements are directly under the control of Public Security. There are definite labor quotas, and records are kept of each individual's performance. The work day is at least eight hours long, six days a week.

Correspondence is not openly subjected to examination, but all letters pass through the hands of public security police.

Jiuye personnel also engage in political study sessions similar to those of *laojiao* subjects.

The family members of FJP personnel are welcome to come and live within the *laogaidui*. However, this does not apply to those camps located in urban areas; moreover, family members who wish to live within the *laogaidui* must have urban, not rural, household registration cards because FJP personnel and the LRCs are registered as urban households. In the PRC it is extremely difficult to have a rural household registration changed to an urban one. Only if the LRC is located in a wasteland area, such as the Xinjiang region or Qinghai Province, will rural household registration holders be welcome, because of the need to encourage immigration to these areas.

Very few family members come to live in the *laogaidui;* those that do generally fall into the following categories:

1. In cases where there are strong feelings between a husband and wife, and they are willing to sacrifice and struggle together, the spouse often comes to live within the *laogaidui,* especially if in their original home the spouse is likely to meet with discrimination or attack for being related to a criminal.
2. During the Cultural Revolution, some cities expelled the families of criminals and forced them to move to the *laogaidui.*
3. Many peasant women from poor regions, fleeing famine and poverty and with no other choice (such as the large groups of Szechuan Provence women fleeing famine in the 1970s), marry FJP personnel. For instance, FJP personnel in Shanxi Province labor reform coal mines (Guzhung Coal Mine, Wangzhung Coal Mine, Jinpupushan Coal Mine) have the possibility of finding wives from among the peasant women in the surrounding mountain regions.
4. Sometimes the spouse is also an FJP worker, in which case they are transferred to the same *laogaidui.*

Jiuye personnel are required every year to participate in "mass criticism meetings," "fiercely attack criminal activities meetings," "punishment and reward meetings," etc., during which some personnel are arrested and sentenced to terms. Whenever society at large is in the throes of a political movement, among the *jiuye* personnel population there is always necessarily a large number who are suppressed and arrested.

Recently the authorities have been attempting to conceal the true nature of FJP policies. For instance, the term "three types of personnel," used for thirty years, is now no longer in use, being replaced by "two types of personnel," "double labor work," "double labor production," etc. Another point to note is that for various productive or social reasons some workers and technical personnel from society at large have been introduced to the *laogaidui*. These people's political and social status is equivalent to that of public security police, but they are not police, nor are they prisoners. They thus constitute a gray area between the two. The *laogaidui* have also recently instituted a few policies that allow for the reinstatement of "those with good behavior" to the status of regular workers. However, the overnight transformation of these former prisoners into workers with all the political and economic benefits of public security police would seem rather strange, to say the least.

Recently the CCP has been actively striving to "socialize" these types of labor reform enterprises, with the purpose of decreasing the amount of public attention on this sort of slave labor and also to increase the possibility of these enterprises' products entering the international market. After the publicity regarding the Dynasty wine incident, the French company Remy Martin announced that they were previously unaware of the use of convict labor in grape production; moreover, based upon information provided by their Chinese partners, the use of convict labor to produce grapes had already stopped in 1986.

The questions, however, are Who is the Chinese partner in this joint venture? What type of labor force is used in the winery? If the use of convict labor has been stopped, what about *jiuye* labor?

The CCP has always been rather fast and loose in its handling of FJP personnel. Here is an example:

Xinxiang Incident

In 1965, the cadres of the Xinjiang Production Construction Army arranged for the cadres of the Beijing Municipality Labor Reform Bureau to announce a new policy to the *jiuye* personnel under their jurisdiction: "Everyone is welcome to join the Xinjiang Production Construction Army and become a glorious land reclamation warrior in the construction of our nation's border regions. Those who are interested should apply, priority being given to younger people. 'Internal contradictions among the people' offenders and political counter-revolutionaries are acceptable, and female *jiuye* personnel are especially welcomed. All those who are accepted will be released from the *laogaidui,* become a part of the army, be issued uniforms, and be accorded treatment appropriate for land reclamation warriors." At that time 5,000–6,000 applied, and most of those accepted were juvenile offenders and common criminals, though a few counter-revolutionary rightists were also accepted. On the day of departure the various *laogaidui* had a huge sending-off ceremony where each person was given a glorious red flower and four days of dry rations, the uniforms to be issued once they reached Xinjiang. It was difficult for people to choose between remaining in the Beijing *laogaidui* as FJP personnel or leaving their homes and loved ones to go work in the desert border regions as land reclamation troops. Many chose the latter option, willing to leave their homes to obtain a little more freedom. All those who were accepted gathered at Beijing's Yongdingmen Station (all Beijing region *laogaidui* prisoners are transferred from this train station). The first specially chartered train carried 1,500 people; as the train left the station, it was noticed that at the end were added two carriages of armed guards. Not long after leaving the Beijing region, these armed guards fanned out through the train, informing everyone that their movements were to be confined to their own carriage. "How is it that glorious land reclamation warriors have become criminals under armed guard?" everyone angrily demanded of the cadres and police, but no answer was given. The situation gradually deteriorated. The train only stopped at small, remote stations, and the occupants were not allowed to disembark. When the train stopped in Henan Province, Xinxiang City to obtain water, the FJP personnel finally forced their way out of the train in anger, capturing the guards' guns and demanding that the cadres return them to Beijing, refusing to continue to Xinjiang. The cadres claimed they did not have the authority to make such a decision and said they had to contact Beijing for instructions. After a few hours of stalemate airplanes suddenly appeared, and the crack troops of the First Paratrooper Unit stationed in nearby Kaifeng Municipality descended from the sky, surrounding the area and using guns and bayonets to force everyone back on the train. The train was forced to continue, the major instigators one by one being bound and arrested. Once in Xinjiang, everyone was forced off the train, the first order of business being the immediate execution of seventeen instigators. This was referred to as "firm suppression." This incident occurred twenty-five years ago; the author has a few friends who to this day are still in the wasteland of Xinjiang. There are also some who felt that life in the Beijing *laogaidui* is better than life in the Production Construction Army of Xinjiang and thus escaped back to Beijing to commit crimes, be given a CLR or RTL sentence, and then be subjected to *jiuye* in the Beijing LRC. This way, at least, they were back in their hometown.

Notes

1. Laodong gaizao zuifan xingman shifang ji anzhi jiuye zhanxing chuli banfa (Temporary Disciplinary Methods for the Release and Job Placement of Labor Reform Convicts Who Have Completed Their Terms), article 1 in Collection of the Public Security Regulations of the People's Republic of China, 1950–1979, Beijing: Legal Press, 1980.

2. Shanghai Municipality has LRCs established in Anhui Province, Jiangxi Province, Jiangsu Province, and even Xinjiang and Qinghai Provinces.

3. Note that Temporary Methods in Forced Job Placement was not announced by the CCP government until September 7, 1954.

4. Laodong gaizao zuifan de lilun yu shijian (Labor Reform Criminals: Theory and Practice), Beijing: Legal Press, 1987, p. 39. This is the reason criminals sentenced from Beijing, Shanghai, Tianjin, etc. want desperately to find a way to serve their terms in *laogaidui* or prisons in their own city. Once one is transferred to a remote *laogaidui,* there is no chance of returning to one's hometown. For this reason criminals in urban LRCs, except for special political cases—such as Jiang Qing, Mao's wife, who could not be transferred to an outside prison—are those who have "demonstrated excellent politically reformed behavior," gained the trust of public security police, and thus obtained this special "status." This state of affairs naturally produces a great deal of lies, betrayals, and scheming.

5. Ibid., p. 40.

6. Ibid., p. 41.

5

Labor Reform
Under Deng Xiaoping

After Deng Xiaoping came to power, and especially after 1983, there was a definite effort to change labor reform policies.

By 1978, Mao Zedong, Lin Biao, and the Gang of Four had all disappeared from the political scene, leaving a situation in which "there was no faith in socialism, no faith in Marxism or Maoism, and no faith in the CCP leadership." These three crises in faith (*sanxin weiji*) extended even into the inner recesses of the Party itself. With the economy on the verge of collapse, moral values disintegrating, and an inadequate ideology, all levels and aspects of society were in danger. This collective political, economic, societal, ideological, and moral crisis caused the Communist regime's rulers to seriously reconsider their past policies.

Deng Xiaoping's "four basic principles" (*jiben yuanze*) were challenged publicly; under the directions of CCP leaders China began developing in a totally new direction.

In 1957 Mao Zedong only needed to issue a few directives and enlist the help of Deng Xiaoping and Peng Jen to mobilize the propaganda machines and Party organizations in order to have close to a million intellectuals attacked as counter-revolutionary rightists and made objects of the dictatorship. During the 1986–1987 democracy demonstrations that swept the nation, protesters openly proclaimed anti-dictatorship, profreedom, prodemocracy slogans—a far cry from the minor offenses of 1957's rightists—and yet the government did not dare to arrest a single student. Spokespeople and leaders of the movement such as Fang Lizhi, Liu Binying, and Wang Ruowang professed political and ideological beliefs directly opposed to those of the government, and yet all Deng Xiaoping dared to do was label them bad elements and remove them from the Party—he did not dare to have them sent off to *laogaidui*.

By May of 1989 the situation developed to the point where tens of thousands of students and workers occupied the symbolic center of the

Communist regime—Tiananmen Square—in a democracy movement that lasted over fifty days. The regime responded with the only method it understands—force—and the Tiananmen movement was crushed with tanks and soldiers. This knee-jerk response reveals clearly the essentially weak nature of the regime and indicates that it may not be long before a turning point is reached.

Recent Developments in Labor Reform

It should be noted that Deng Xiaoping, more than any other CCP leader, understands the historical currents in China. He recognizes that the regime is paying for the thirty years of injustice it imposed upon the country and that if the CCP wishes to remain in power it must compromise and reform. This is the origin of his *Four Basic Principles,* which not only ensures the future political, economic, and cultural rule of the CCP but also includes legal and public security reforms. Support of these principles necessarily implies support of the LRC system.

With regard to public security, law, and the LRC system, the Communist regime must deal with a few new situations.

A Defunct Original Legal System

Since 1949 the Communist regime has created several constitutions and legal systems whose general quality and completeness we will not discuss for the time being. What matters is that the rights specified in these documents have been completely ignored by the regime. Such figures as National Chairman—the "Second Venerated"—Liu Shaoqi or CCP Politburo member and Political Legal Commission Director Peng Jen have had their basic rights and freedom stripped from them at will— how much more so do the rights and freedom of the common people seem as insubstantial as smoke? The Communists themselves realize that "incessant political movements seriously interfered with judicial work . . . the old method of large-scale violent mass struggles seriously eroded the judicial system."[1] Moreover, the old laws and policies are not adaptable to the present situation.

Significant Changes in the Structure of Society

Events after 1978—the "rehabilitation" of several million "wrongly accused" people; the reinstatement of hundreds of thousands of counter-revolutionary rightists; the re-evaluation of millions of historical counter-revolutionaries; the desire to resolve the problem of tens of millions of cadres and young intellectuals "sent down to the countryside"; the purging of the Gang of Four; etc.—all reflect various types of social contradictions and the changing structure of society.

For thirty years the Communists have used class struggle and class contradiction to define the border between criminal and noncriminal actions. They often ignored distinctions between politics and civil and criminal law, resulting in a confused and disorderly judicial system.

Change in the Subjects of Labor Reform

CCP legal specialists feel that ". . . over the course of the past thirty years, the class relation and class struggle situation in our country has undergone profound changes. With a change in work emphasis brought about by this new era, there has been a change in the nature of the subjects of Labor Reform."[2] "The major object of supervised reform has already changed from counter-revolutionaries with exploiting-class origins to common criminals."[3] Of those criminals in custody in 1987, 78 percent were under thirty-five years of age; 52 percent had at most a high school education; 49 percent had committed economically motivated crimes; and 32 percent had committed crimes against morality.[4]

Necessity of Labor Reform Production to Adapt to Deng Xiaoping's New Era of Economic Reform

It is necessary for LRP to increase its economic efficiency. The CCP, which has always considered labor reform an important productive force, must adopt new policies. The CCP has thus formulated new guiding principles with regard to labor reform policy.

Deng Xiaoping still holds to the Leninist line with regard to class struggle and legal theory: "Law is a political measure, a type of policy"[5]; "law should follow and serve politics, embodying political needs, protecting political actions, and preserving political stability."[6]

Deng has stated that "In a socialist society there will still be counter-revolutionaries, hostile elements, various types of criminals who disrupt the socialist order and other bad elements, corrupt thieves and robbers, and new exploiting opportunists; moreover, this type of phenomenon is impossible to eliminate totally on a long-term basis. Although their struggle is not the same as historical inter-class struggle (it is impossible for them to openly constitute a public class), it should still be regarded as a special type of class struggle, or perhaps as a special type of class struggle that can still remain under the conditions of a socialist society. It is still necessary for us to exercise the power of the dictatorship over these people. If we do not subject them to the dictatorship, then it will be impossible to have democratic socialism. This type of struggle is domestic and also sometimes international—these two aspects are inseparable."[7] He also noted,"Under the present conditions, using the suppressive force of our nation to attack and disintegrate all types of counter-revolutionary bad elements, anti-party anti-socialist elements and serious criminal offenders in order to preserve public security is entirely in accord with the demands of the people and with the demands of socialist modernization construction."[8] These two comments form the basis of present labor reform policy.

With regard to law and policy, starting in 1980 the CCP in the short space of two or three years publicly announced Penal Laws, Supplementary Regulations Concerning Reeducation Through Labor, Resolutions Regarding the Disciplining of Escapees or Repeat Offenders Among CLR and RTL Subjects, and Announcement Concerning the Release of Some Temporarily Detained Personnel Who Have Completed Their Terms. At the same time, the CCP internally released A System of Contractual Responsibility Between Management and Production (*goanjiao, shengchan shuang chengbao zeren zhi*), Three Extension Policies (*sange yanshen zhengce*), Detailed (Experimental) Regulations Regarding Prison and Labor Reform Camp Management Work (*jianyu, laogaidui goanjiao gongzuo xize [shixing]*), Management Methods for Labor Reform Enterprises (*laogai qiye goanli banfa*), Management Methods for Forced Job Placement Personnel (*liuchang jiuye renyuan goanli banfa*), Experimental Methods in Reeducation Through Labor, etc. They even made improvements to and strengthened documents published in the 1950s such as Labor Reform Regulations, Temporary Disciplinary Methods for the Release and Job Placement of Labor Reform Criminals, and Reeducation Through Labor Regulations.

By 1983, the CCP had completed basic changes in the judicial and LRC system. "*Laogai* and *laojiao* were originally under the jurisdiction of Public Security organs; after returning to the jurisdiction of the Judicial organs, the nature of the work and work responsibilities remains the same. . . . Public Security, the Courts, the Procurate and the Judicial [*laogai, laojiao*] are all organs of the dictatorship of the proletariat, and in their collective duty to struggle against criminals they are given different responsibilities, just as different processes of a job are split among different segments of an assembly line."[9]

Even after the completion of the reforms, the labor reform process is still under the supervision and leadership of the various levels of CCP political directors.

Recent Changes in Labor Reform Policy

Changes in Jurisdiction

In 1983, CCPCC decided to move the LRC system from under the Public Security Bureau's jurisdiction and place it under the jurisdiction of the Judicial Bureau. The LRCs' public security police were renamed

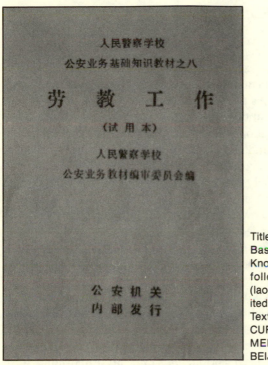

人民警察学校
公安业务基础知识教材之八

劳　教　工　作

（试 用 本）

人民警察学校
公安业务教材编审委员会编

公 安 机 关
内 部 发 行

Title page of People's Police School Basic Public Security Professional Knowledge Textbook #7, reading as follows: LABOR REFORM WORK (laogai gongzuo) (TRIAL DRAFT) Edited by Public Security Professional Textbook Committee; PUBLIC SECURITY ORGAN INTERNAL DOCUMENT; QUNZHONG PRESS; 1983 BEIJING.

labor reform work police, but their pay and uniforms remained exactly the same.

In the last ten years, there were thirty-two labor reform work police schools established in twenty-six provinces and autonomous regions; in addition, the central Labor Reform Management Cadre Academy was established, the main purpose of which was to train police for the LRC. Because of the economic and political importance of the LRC, CCP legal specialists created a labor reform organ that was independent of the Judicial Bureau and on an equal level as other bureaus—the National Labor Reform Bureau (*Guojia laogai zongju*), which was under direct control of the State Council.[10]

Deng Xiaoping criticized the Labor Reform Bureau for "... a consistent lack of strict administrative laws concerning levels of command or a system of personal responsibility, and a lack of regulations that would clearly define the scope of responsibilities of each organ and each individual."[11] Therefore, a system was established in which the professional responsibilities of each bureau and each level of police were clearly demarcated.

The Expansion and Development of Laojiao

Forced Labor. Since 1961 there has been a policy referred to as "forced labor" (*qiangzhi laodong*), which sent those suspected by the government of being petty criminals or vagabonds to special camps for forced labor. Forced labor had specific terms (usually one to three years) and was employed mainly in large cities and their suburbs. On February 29, 1980, the CCP State Council announced that forced labor was to be included in RTL policies and forced labor policies eliminated. Since that time, the number of RTL personnel and the number of RTL sites has increased dramatically. For example, Tiantanghe Farm in Beijing Municipality's Nanyuan District was originally a forced labor farm; now it is Tuantanghe Reeducation Through Labor Camp (LRC-03-13). Forced labor was originally a level below *laojiao;* now it is included in *laojiao*. Obviously the scope of RTL has thus expanded greatly.

The Use of Reeducation Through Labor in the Military. On August 14, 1987, The People's Liberation Army (PLA) General Political Department and the Public Security Bureau jointly announced the application within the PLA of Experimental Methods in Reeducation Through Labor. It seems that although there is already a system of military law, the Communist authorities have decided to subject some soldiers to *laojiao* because of a problem with "unauthorized absences." This problem is not serious enough to warrant military legal action, but PLA administrators have found it impossible to control without the use of RTL. Even more important is the recent appearance of "anti-party, anti-socialism elements" among the lower-grade officers and soldiers. Currents of public opinion in society at large are reflected in the army, causing dissension and discord. Because the PLA is the base of the regime's power, this problem is cause for much concern, and RTL is the most appropriate solution.

Expanding the Scope of Reeducation Through Labor. In 1979 when the National People's Congress announced and promulgated Supplementary Reeducation Through Labor Regulations, it was legislated that "RTL facilities should accept those from mid-size and large municipalities who are in need of Reeducation Through Labor." However, in 1980 CCPCC approved a resolution stating that "Reeducation Through Labor can also be applied to those from the countryside who wander into cities, major railways or mines and commit offenses." This internal notice superseded any publicly announced law. This decision was reaffirmed in Experimental Methods in Reeducation Through Labor (CCP internal document), released on January 21, 1982. All this aside, it is even more important to note that the RTL policies approved by the National People's Congress in 1954 and 1979 limited the types of people who could be subjected to

RTL to four types; however, Experimental Methods in Reeducation Through Labor expanded RTL to encompass six types, adding the new categories of "anti-party and anti-socialism elements."[12] In mainland China it is very easy to be classified as an anti-party or anti-socialism element. Serious offenders of this type are sentenced to *laogai;* minor offenders to *laojiao.*

Managing of Labor Reform Production on Economic Principles

Creation of Managerial Bureaus. It is legislated that all *laogaidui* and labor reform enterprises are under the direct management of provincial, autonomous regional, and special municipal labor reform work management bureaus (*laodong gaizao goanli gongzuo ju*). The major responsibilities of these bureaus are to (1) organize and specify long-term planning, annual production, basic construction, financing and resources for each region's labor reform production; (2) appoint and dismiss labor reform enterprise leaders and cadres, establish production awards and penalties, and organize allocation of the labor force; (3) act as intermediaries between labor reform enterprises and outside agencies; and (4) supervise all labor reform enterprises.

In managing production, the Labor Reform Bureau has established several mutually independent types of entrepreneurial companies. These companies have a board of directors, who are appointed by the Labor Reform Bureau chief or assistant chief. Presently existing companies include

- Shanghai's Shenjiang General Entrepreneurial Company
- Beijing's Xin Xin Industry and Commerce Company
- Jiangsu's Shicheng Managerial Company
- Zhejiang's Xinxing Entrepreneurial Development Company
- Jiangxi's Jianxin Entrepreneurial and Technological Development Company
- Fujian's Minxin Supply and Marketing Company
- Xinlian Trade Supply and Marketing Company (located in Fujian Province, Xiamen Municipality, a conglomeration of twelve LRCs nationwide).

These companies organize and direct local labor reform production as well as take care of financial matters. They also very often establish relations with foreign companies. Shanghai's Shenjiang General Entrepreneurial Company has already discussed such matters as importation of technology and joint ventures with American, Japanese, and West

German companies. Shanghai's Pingban Glass Factory (LRC-29-01) has already imported a glass fiber production line through this company.

Increasing the Autonomy of Labor Reform Enterprises. Labor reform enterprises are similar to the normal state-run enterprises in many ways.

- Authority to manage personnel. Various levels of Party Committee cadres, from the department level on down, have the authority to dismiss and hire employees (except for county- or collective-level cadres, who receive orders from the provincial, autonomous regional, or special municipal labor reform bureaus), and the various labor reform enterprises have the authority to hire technical personnel, retain prisoners who have completed their terms, and decide bonuses and penalties for cadres and workers.
- Authority to direct production. Those serving under the Party Committee—the prison warden, detachment chief (or factory chief), and political director—each have their own responsibilities. The prison warden and detachment chief (factory chief) are responsible for prison management, production management, and general administration; the political director is responsible for political ideological work with the police and professionals and for educational and reform work with the prisoners.
- Authority to establish institutions. Labor reform enterprises have the authority to establish and disband institutions under their jurisdiction and have the power to decide upon small-scale construction matters.
- Authority to manage wages. Labor reform enterprises have the authority to decide their work unit's bonuses, floating wages, and welfare benefits as well as the right to give raises to police and professionals.

Commercial Development of Labor Reform Production. The CCP is now in the process of commercializing labor reform enterprises. Agricultural enterprises (farms) are now beginning to develop secondary industries to meet domestic and international commercial needs. For example,

- Beijing Qinghe Farm (LRC-03-12) is developing the culturing of prawns.
- Beijing Tuanhe Farm (LRC-03-13) is engaged in a joint venture with Hong Kong to produce fresh flowers.
- Yunnan Province has conducted a complete reorganization of its twenty-two labor reform farms, allocating five to specialize in sugarcane, two to specialize in tea, two to specialize in fruit trees, one to specialize in pseudoginseng, and the others to specialize in grain.

- Inner Mongolia Autonomous Region has converted former agricultural farms to livestock raising and then unified these ranches in order to develop ranching and livestock processing industries.

Industrial labor reform enterprises have begun emphasizing producing products to meet the commercial needs of the domestic and international market. In the past, Fujian Province's labor reform enterprises were mainly involved in preparing for war against the nationalist government in Taiwan and so were little developed. Recently, Fujian has become a major center for attracting investors from Taiwan. Its labor reform enterprises have also become very active, producing cafeteria chopsticks, athletic shoes, and clothing that has begun entering the international market. Qinghai Province, because it is landlocked and thus has little contact with the outside world, is in the process of acquiring a "window" in Guangdong Province, entering in a joint venture with Juhai Municipality's Fruit & Vegetable Company to market its labor reform products.

The implementation of "a system of contractual responsibility" has also had a large impact upon the manner in which the *laogaidui* are run.

The New Pattern of Labor Reform Production

In 1980, the labor reform system began to institute a system of top-down financial responsibility as well as experimented with "a system of dual contractual responsibility between discipline[13] and production" (*Goanjiao, shengchan shuang chengbao zeren zhi*). At the National CLR and RTL Work Conference held in July of 1984, it was demanded that "economic effectiveness must be increased, deficits made up and surpluses increased"; a nationwide application in labor reform facilities of a system of dual contractual responsibility between discipline and production (abbreviated "dual responsibility system" [*shuangbao zhi*]) was also called for.

Contents and Purpose of the Dual Responsibility System

This policy is based upon a system of split responsibility that has been traditional in the *laogaidui*—political reform of prisoners and financial performance—with individual indexes of achievement for each.

The disciplinary and educational indexes consist of the rate of escape and recapture of prisoners, rate of uncovering and solving cases, rate of unnatural deaths, the crime rate and rate of repeat offenses within the LRC, as well as rate of improvement in cultural and technological knowledge and the rate of outstanding labor efforts.

The production indexes consist of LRC production value, production totals, production quality, cost of production, consumption, profits, and similar economic and technological indicators. Because of the special nature of labor reform enterprises—labor personnel constantly changing, inability to select quality of labor force, limits on the conditions, time, and location of labor—the various economic departments' standards for these indexes for labor reform enterprises are 20 percent below those of similar enterprises in society at large.

The responsibility to meet standards in these two types of indexes is delegated on down the levels of authority, to the battalions, general brigades, squads, and even individuals. There are specific demands on both public security police and prisoners to meet these two types of standards.

A certain definite proportion of labor reform enterprises' profits are submitted to the government in the form of taxes and fees. The remaining profits can be allocated at will by the enterprise. This money is usually allocated in accordance with the "3-3-4 system" (*sansanse zhi*): 30 percent to expand production (or invest in technology); 30 percent to improve living conditions (improving the housing of public security police, establishing schools and child care centers, etc.); and 40 percent for bonuses (most of which goes to public security police, not to prisoners). The material quality of life of public security police is directly linked to the profits of the LRC, and their quality of work directly affects the level of profits. Prisoners receive no material benefits; they are violently compelled to work, and the only benefit received for "good behavior" is a reduced sentence.

With the promulgation of the dual responsibility system, control in the *laogaidui* became even more strict, and the compulsory nature of forced labor intensified greatly. The example related below is of a type unprecedented in the history of the *laogaidui*.

On February 8, 1989, in Xinjiang Autonomous Region's Dumoxiuka area on the southern border of the Takalamagan Desert, among the prisoners of Xinjiang Productive Construction Regiment, Third Division, No. 5 Labor Reform Company, were six that had been transferred from Hunan Province: Duan Jiancheng, Liu Shanbao, Yiu Rueiyang, Deng Weixin, Ou Shixiong, and Xu Zhiping (serving terms of 20, 20, 17, 15, 10, and 9 years, respectively). These six announced that ". . . there are a few characters here who are getting a little out of hand, sucking up to the authorities to get special privileges, and even betraying the rest of us. . . . This year the detachment began this Dual Responsibility thing, and things have gotten a little tight around here, getting hard to get along, so we might as well kill off a few extra people." They used knives, hammers, and axes to kill six "reform activist" prisoners and also held for ransom two prison guards (one of whom was later killed), planning to escape that evening at dusk. However, some of the other prisoners alerted the police, and the prison was surrounded by armed policemen. Aid was requested from the Beijing Judicial Ministry, Xinjiang Autonomous Regional Government and Public Security Bureau, Xinjiang Armed Police Brigade, Xinjiang Productive Construction Regiment, and Xinjiang Military District Command, who transferred a few hundred armed policemen, vehicles, and helicopters, to the scene under the direction of Judicial Ministry Chief Cai Cheng and his assistant Jin Jian, who suppressed the riot. Of the six riot instigators, one was beaten to death, two committed suicide, and three were arrested and later executed. The whole ordeal lasted eighteen hours (please refer to "Record of Western Region Prison Riots," in *Law and Life.* Beijing: Legal Press, September 1989, pp. 22–23). This example reflects a few important points:

- Prisoners native to more centrally located provinces who are transferred to Xinjiang (or Qinghai), far away from their families and native villages, are easily incited to commit desperate acts.
- Each division in Xinjiang Productive Construction Regiment has established its own LRCs. These camps house mainly serious offenders; these prisoners, condemned to spend the rest of their lives laboring in the desert, will often in desperation band together in a group.
- The first to be killed by the rioters were their fellow prisoners. Under LRC preferential treatment policy some prisoners rise to become tools of the prison, engaging in surveillance, compulsion, beating, and betraying their fellow prisoners, and so came to be especially hated.

Labor reform enterprises—their dictatorial nature aside—as a production unit share the common failings of all socialist government-run enterprises: low production efficiency, high production costs, no personal responsibility, no creativity, inefficient economically, as well as the problems of the "iron rice bowl" and "the common rice bowl,"[14] etc.

The purpose of the dual responsibility system is to harness two types of positive professional spirit—that of the public security police and that of the prisoners—in order to produce even more material wealth for the regime.

Beginning in 1984, labor reform enterprises instituted a system of detachment chief (prison warden) responsibility, which unifies responsibility, authority, and benefit into one management system and employs material incentives and bonuses to encourage work rather than the political criterion used in the past. This was all done to increase the effectiveness of forced labor in the PRC's socialist economy.

Effectiveness of the Dual Responsibility System

Under the auspices of the dual responsibility system, various LRCs have independently established regulations and methods to meet the two index standards, increase their production development, and thus obtain actual material benefits. The CCP's few media sources have attested to the success so far of this system. Some examples:

- According to a Zhejiang Province Judicial Bureau report, after the entire province began to institute the dual responsibility system in 1985, it greatly improved the work attitudes of both public security police and convicts (including RTL and FJP personnel). Its effects: The rate of repeat offenses and escapes decreased; labor reform industrial production for the first half of 1985 was 57 percent greater than for the first half of 1984, and profits were 35.8 percent greater; and the constant deficit suffered by the labor reform agricultural work units also decreased greatly.
- After Hebei Province's labor reform work units began instituting the dual responsibility system in 1984, industrial production increased 40 percent over 1983, profits increased 60 percent, there was an obvious improvement in prison morale, and the rate of prisoner escapes was the lowest ever.[15]
- Henan Province has fifty-three labor reform farms, with over 60,000 *mu* of land under cultivation. In the past, these farms had many problems with escapes and large deficits. After instituting the new system in 1982, the escape rate decreased from 5 percent in 1980 to 0.34 percent in 1984; production increased greatly, resulting in a summer yield of over 20 million *jin* of grain in 1984, an increase of 38 percent over the entire year's harvest in 1978; industrial production also increased greatly, reaching 100 million *yuan* in 1982, a 52.7 percent increase over 1978; lastly, from a 770,000 *yuan* deficit in 1978, Henan LRC enterprises by 1983 had a 1.55 million *yuan* surplus.[16]
- Laiyang Labor Reform Detachment (LRC-21-23, Shandong Province, Yantai Municipality) after instituting the dual responsibility system in 1984 experienced the following benefits: from 1984–1987, the crime rate in the camp went from 0.7 percent to 0.18 percent; the rate of cases uncovered went from 0.23 percent to 0.06 percent; and the rate of appeals went from 1.3 percent to 0.05 percent.[17] Over the course of five years, this LRC's production, profits, and foreign exchange earnings increased by 28.5, 48.3, and 43 percent respectively; two product lines were named the best in the province or department; and two product lines were sold to over twenty East Asian and Western European countries, as well as the United States.[18]

In the past ten years, under the guidance of Deng Xiaoping's economic reforms, labor reform production has also instituted major reforms. A notable one is the commercialization of labor reform products. Another is the encouragement of the export of labor reform enterprises' products, even to the point of encouraging joint ventures with foreign capitalists. The Dynasty brand wine mentioned previously is one example. It is said that the Volvo-Chinter automobile offer is another (see Appendix 4).

There were major changes in the three categories of labor reform production. The first was in water conservancy, railroad construction, development of wasteland, construction, etc.—all of which were very important in the 1950s. There is no way to measure this type of work in monetary terms. This type of slave labor is very primitive, simple physical labor requiring no capital investment or technology. In the past ten years this type of work has declined greatly, although it is presently more prevalent in such provinces as Qinghai and Xinjiang.

The second category is agricultural production. Because the production value of agriculture is rather low, prisoners forced to engage in such labor can usually only barely provide for their own LRC's operating expenses. These expenses include the upkeep of public security police (salary, equipment, uniforms, living allowance, housing, etc.). Therefore, agricultural labor reform enterprises are usually in the red—over the past ten years agricultural camps have been pressed to reduce these deficits and increase surpluses. Besides adopting the dual responsibility system,[19] the LRCs have taken measures including making grains the major crop and changing the production structure to allow for the development of processing industries such as dairies, brick factories, distilleries, woodworking mills, ranches, etc. By 1987, two out of five labor reform farms had gotten out of the red and were making profits, and the proportion of production from processing industries went from 47 percent to 60 percent. The CCP praised two model examples, Jiangxi Province's Zhuhu Pharmaceutical Factory (LRC-09-09) and a factory established by Shanghai Municipality in Anhui province, No. 2 Labor Reform Brigade's Baimaolin Valve Factory (LRC-29-11), whose annual production exceeded 30 million *yuan,* from which the government earned 6 million *yuan* annually in tax revenues.[20]

Presently agriculture is still the mainstay of the *laogaidui.* One reason is the ability to accommodate many prisoners and the relative ease in forcing them to labor. Also, agricultural products are still the Communists' main export item, and the proportion of agricultural products produced by the LRC—such as rice, cotton, tea, fruit, pigs, etc.—is not small. According to a report, the amount of foreign exchange earned by the LRC's three traditionally most important export items—fruit, tea, and pigs—increased 50 percent from 1984 to 1987.[21]

The third category is industrial production, which in the past ten years has been heavily pushed by the Communists. According to a report, in the seven years between 1977 and 1983, the average annual level of labor reform industrial production was 2.58 billion *yuan* (compared to only 0.2 billion *yuan* in 1952).[22] Already twenty-four *laogaidui* have attained the standards of level-two national enterprises, and many LRC products are well known domestically and internationally (see Appendix 5). According to a report, the LRCs produce close to eighty types of export products, and over 40 percent of the total LRC agricultural production is exported. Recent important export products have included electrical appliances, industrial chemicals, and partially processed agricultural products.[23]

During the past five or six years, the Communist Party has been pushing a new type of educational system in the LRC. This type of education has two main components: In the area of political ideology and law it involves force-feeding of socialist ideology and CCP legal knowledge and in the area of culture and technology it involves the cultural and technological training of prisoners. Although the concept of turning labor reform brigades, prisons, and RTL facilities into schools was mentioned by Mao Zedong to American reporter Edgar Snow back in the 1960s, at that time it had not yet been systematically implemented. It was Deng Xiaoping who systematized it and turned it into government policy, with the result that today certain LRCs that have successfully implemented this system of education have earned a third official name: XX Province (or Municipality) XX School. For example, Shandong Province Shengjian Motorcycle Engine Factory (LRC-21-05) is also known as Shandong Province Tai Shan Yuxin ("Cultivate the New") School.

Lingering Problems

Deng Xiaoping inherited Mao Zedong's labor reform system, necessary for "upholding the four basic principles." The two main purposes of the LRC—violent suppression and production by slaves—have not changed. Deng Xiaoping's policy reforms have, however, included reforms in the LRC system; after ten years, what is the present situation?

Problems Resulting from Changes in Forced Job Placement Policy

Forced job placement policies have actually not been abolished. In 1980 the Communists approved a policy under which FJP personnel who had spent years in the LRC and "display good behavior, support the leaders of the Chinese Communist Party and the socialist system, respect the law, actively labor, and have a definite work skill" could be reclassified as workers; these "workers," however, continued to remain within the confines of labor reform enterprises. In the past ten years the Communist Party has made efforts to replace the term *three types of personnel* with the term *double labor personnel,* thus obscuring the existence of FJP. These efforts have not had much effect on public opinion. Can it be said that these former prisoners—still laboring in their original LRC, under their original public security guards—have any sort of political or personal status of equality? Can it really be said that the element of compulsion has disappeared?

After FJP policies were reformed, however, a large number of *jiuye* personnel were returned to society. How many? Using Heilongjiang Province, Harbin Municipality, as an example: In the three years from 1986–1988, 5,062 former CLR and RTL subjects were returned to society; it is estimated that in the future an average of 2,000 such people will be returned to society every year. A CCP specialist has revealed that after 1988 200,000–300,000 *jiuye* personnel annually were released.[24] This number does not include those who had been serving RTL sentences, who, according to statistics, should number between 200,000 and 300,000. Taking these numbers together, we can say that at least 400,000–600,000 former FJP personnel were returned annually to society. In a society whose every aspect—from politics to public opinion, economics to daily life—is strictly controlled, this presents something of a problem, a problem unlike any encountered in the past thirty years. Recently the PRC's economy has taken a turn for the worse; the number of people "waiting for work" has increased steadily, and society has had to deal with a transient labor force of 5–8 million. The hundreds of thousands who emerge from the *laogaidui* each year find it extremely difficult to get along. In the countryside most of the land is already "contracted"; no land remains to be allocated. Although the village industries are developing rapidly, this does not mean there will be a place for former FJP personnel because many peasants are vying to get in on the action. Former FJP personnel who return to the cities are very rarely able to return to their original work unit. Each unit has a quota for hiring, and the number of people on the waiting list is always larger than the number of available spaces. Additionally, it is very difficult to obtain an urban household registration card. For a politically disadvantaged former FJP worker, the problems of hiring quotas and urban registration are extremely difficult to overcome without "connections" (*goanxi*) or going through "the back door" (*houmen*).[25] However, if these people were allowed to roam at will, it would certainly have an effect on public order. Therefore, in the past few years the government has been forced to issue administrative orders requiring various enterprises to do their best to settle these former *jiuye* personnel.

Many former *jiuye* personnel have become independent businesspeople (*geti hu*). Recently, "independent businesspeople" have become something of a distinct type, a political class like the capitalists or landlords of the 1950s and 1960s, distinct from the political classes of workers or cadres. In a society dedicated to preserving the leadership of the Communist Party and socialism, these people are in a very difficult position. Moreover, their numbers are increasing annually.

After the reforms in FJP policy, another problem that appeared was repeat offenses by released FJP personnel. The China Legal Report of October 17, 1987, reported that before 1983 the rate of repeat offenses was from 7–8 percent; after 1983, it was 6 percent. "However, examination of several areas has shown that rates of over 10 percent are not unusual."[26] For example, of the 5,062 former prisoners released in Harbin Municipality from 1986–1988, 682 (13.5 percent) committed repeat offenses.[27] Those who served short-term sentences are more likely to commit repeat offenses. The CCP Judicial Bureau Crime Prevention and Labor Reform Research Institute made an examination of releases in Guangdong in 1982 and found that among those who had served terms of under three years the repeat offense rate was 14.84 percent; the rate in Shanghai Municipality in 1984 was 15.2 percent, in 1986 26.2 percent; the overall rate for Wuhan Municipality's five districts was 25 percent in 1982.[28] Although these repeat offenders after completing their new RTL or CLR sentences will never leave the LRC again, the rising crime rate and deteriorating political situation of the past ten years has been a major headache for the Communist regime; its only course of action is to again increase the proportion of those subject to *jiuye,* thus once again adding to the growing snowball of *jiuye* personnel.

Problems Caused by Expansion
of Reeducation Through Labor

After the scope of RTL expanded (to include "anti-party and anti-socialism elements," military, and country dwellers who committed offenses in cities or along rail lines) there was an increase in the number of RTL prisoners. However, over 90 percent of these people were juveniles, a significant portion of whom were also the sons of Party cadres. This has had something of an effect upon RTL production: these juveniles have no education and are not accustomed to hard labor; moreover, because the limit on *laojiao* terms is three years (compared with ten, twenty, or even life terms for *laogai*), and after the term is expired only a small number are retained as FJP personnel, this has created a situation where RTL's production force is unstable and its technical ability severely limited. It is thus difficult to make advances in production. This makes *laojiao* not only unprofitable but actually a drain upon the regime—exactly what the government does *not* have in mind. Recently the government has attempted to improve the situation by relying on large numbers of FJP personnel to support *laojiao* production.

Because RTL is an administrative measure, how is it that it can "limit" a citizen's freedom for up to three years? Moreover, RTL regulations only list a few types of people that may be subject to *laojiao;* they do not specify in detail what type of behavior or words are cause for *laojiao* or what criterion are considered in deciding the length of an RTL term. This type of policy, which is defined only by the political needs of the CCP and exercised at will by Public Security, is starting to be legitimately questioned.

Problems Caused by Changes in Managerial Techniques

All prisons and detachment facilities (except juvenile offender camps) have begun implementing entrepreneurial management techniques, including the dual responsibility system. These LRC enterprises undoubtedly benefit the regime economically; however, there still exist quite a few problems:

Harsh Realities of the Free Market. During the 1950s and 1960s labor reform enterprise products were all bought and sold by the government in a noncompetitive market. All raw materials and equipment were allocated by the government. With an underpaid, compelled labor force of criminals, the profits of labor reform enterprises were rather large. Now, however, labor reform enterprises must cope with a competitive market system and are facing many problems with acquisition of raw materials, product marketing, production cost analysis, equipment modernization, improving technological skill, and developing new products. For example, Shanxi Province's Fenhe Automotive Factory (No. 3 Provincial Prison, LRC-01-07) before 1985 was very profitable due to excellent sales, was one of the economic mainstays of the Shanxi Province Labor Reform Bureau, and was used to offset losses by other provincial labor reform work units. In the past few years, however, because it has been unable to obtain government funding for technological improvements, it has been unable to retool its production line and is still producing 1950s-style Liberation brand trucks. At the same time, other automotive factories have begun marketing new products, causing Fenhe truck sales to plummet. This has had an influence not only on this single enterprise but on the entire province's labor reform bureau. In this new competitive market system many LRCs, especially those in remote regions with poor access and outdated technology, have had difficulty adapting.

Emphasis on Profits at the Expense of Reform. The basis of the entrepreneurial management system is the detachment chief (prison chief) personal responsibility system. Presently every *laogaidui,* besides submitting a specified amount of tax revenues to the government, is also responsible for dealing with all operating expenses: public security police salaries, living allowances, medical costs, uniforms, retirement benefits, housing, children's education, and infirmary, as well as prisoners' termination pay, clothes, food, etc. Each work unit is responsible for its own expenses. Thus, the "enterprise" aspect of labor reform enterprises has taken precedent over labor reform itself. In order to cope with these production problems *laogaidui* are employing many methods, the bottom line of which is "earn money." Methods used to motivate prisoners and *jiuye* personnel include giving reduced sentences, holidays, and small bonuses, as well as increasingly employing violence and extending working hours (do criminals have the right to protest?). In industrial camps every day the quality and quantity of the output of each prisoner is examined and recorded, with rewards and penalties being issued for meeting or failing to meet quotas. In agricultural camps, a portion of the fields, orchards, or pastures are assigned to a squad of prisoners. Bonuses are also employed to motivate public security police. Of the two indexes of the dual responsibility system, the production index is referred to as the "hard" index, while the discipline and education index is referred to as "soft." The production index is "hard" for two reasons: First, production and technology, products and profits, are things that can be measured; second, the material benefit of each public security officer is directly tied to this index. The discipline and education index is "soft" because as long as not too many prisoners escape and there are no unnatural deaths, nothing else is really important. "Reform" sort of falls by the wayside, causing a definite problem with "quality of reform."

This emphasis on profits at the expense of reform can be illustrated by the three examples provided below, incidents the like of which the LRCs have never experienced before in thirty years:

1. Unsupervised contracts: A certain camp, in order to "create income," instituted a policy of "unsupervised contracts" (*tuogoan chengbao*). This policy allowed prisoners to leave the supervision of the camp as long as they continued to submit money to the camp in accordance with their individual production index. As long as prisoners met their production index and submitted money to the camp, that was all that mattered. (This was very much in keeping with Deng Xiaoping's statement that he did not care if a cat was black or white, as long as it caught mice.) In April of 1988 153 prisoners from this LRC began "urban contracts" (that is, they left the camp and entered the city); only nineteen were kept in the camp for "supervision." At the same time, in order to reduce expenses,

thirty-two prisoners (16.8 percent of the total prisoner population) were given "outside medical leave" (i.e., allowed to return home). One of the unsupervised contract prisoners traveled to Wuhan, Nanjing, and other cities on a lark, having his sworn brothers submit his "contract money" on schedule; moreover, because he "fulfilled his contract well," his camp twice applied for a reduced sentence in his behalf.[29]

2. Using laborers for cadres: Jiangcheng Prison (an alias; its real name is probably Anhui Province Wuhu Municipal Prison) confined repeat offenders. It was not very successful financially and had accumulated a debt of a few million *yuan*. In 1984, the newly appointed prison commissioner (surnamed Fu) implemented the dual responsibility system, calling a meeting of the entire prison, public security cadres and prisoners, and informing them that under this new, rational system, cadres could receive rewards and prisoners could have their sentences reduced.

In the cotton goods workshop there was a prisoner named Shi Zheng (serving a twelve-year sentence), who suggested that he could utilize his old contacts in Maanshan Municipality to obtain steel and several thousand *yuan* in capital to establish a production line to produce nails. Because of a dearth of nails on the market, Shi Zheng claimed great profits could be made.

Prison commissioner Fu took Shi Zheng to Maanshan Municipality under the auspices of "using laborers for cadres" (*yilao daigan*).[30] Fu felt that in order to improve the prison's economic situation, it would be best not to use the prison name—a corporation name would be more convenient for doing business. Thus, with the permission of the prison's Party commissioner, Fu established the "Yangze River Trading Company," making himself manager and Shi Zheng assistant manager and purchasing agent. Moreover, the company seal and 220,000 yuan were turned over to Shi, the money to be used for any necessary bribes.

Shi decided that not only could they buy steel to produce nails but they could turn the steel over and resell it at a profit. Through the introduction of a businessman named Li, they traveled to Shanghai to meet with a Hong Kong businessman named Fang, planning to obtain U.S. $2 million at an exchange rate of 1:4.60, plus a 0.1 *yuan* "processing fee" for every *yuan* exchanged. Shi informed Fu that they could exchange this U.S. $2 million on the Canton black market at a rate of 1:5.40, thus making a profit of 1.4 million *yuan*. Fu then immediately entered negotiations with Fang (incidentally paying 6,000 *yuan* and HK $3,000 in bribes), dispatching Shi to Canton to assess the black market situation. Fu felt that with 1.4 million *yuan* his prison could thrown off its debts, become entrepreneurially successful, and perhaps become the nation's most progressive model labor reform enterprise. This would not only mean a hefty paycheck for Fu, but becoming such a successful reformer would also have immense political benefits. After Shi reached Canton, he announced that he had signed contracts with many businessmen, with the potential for great profits; Fu greatly encouraged him, improving his living conditions in Canton and furthermore promising that if business went smoothly Shi would receive a 5,000 *yuan* bonus and have his sentence reduced by six years. Shi spent his time wining, dining, and womanizing in Canton; when the prison sent a public security cadre named Hu to check up on him, Shi gave Hu 1,645 *yuan* and HK $400 from public funds for "traveling expenses." Furthermore, Shi suggested that as he was to be going to Tianjin to deal with some U.S. $2 million in cash, it would be safer and more convenient if Hu loaned him his police uniform and gun. Hu agreed (Shi had a picture taken of himself in police uniform in Canton). Thus prisoner Shi went to Beijing, Tianjin, and Dalian wearing a police uniform and carrying a gun.

A subsequent CCP decision made it illegal to deal in foreign currency, spoiling Shi's plan. The prison's Party commissioner had Shi brought back to prison, and after the true nature of what had transpired was revealed he had an additional twelve-year sentence added on for bribery, hooliganism, and corruption. Hu was prosecuted on criminal charges, and Commissioner Fu committed suicide, shooting himself in the head.[31]

Another example of using laborers for cadres is the case of Chen Zhengsu, originally the factory chief of Hueinan Machine Tool Factory. CCP Party member Chen Zhengsu was sentenced to six years in Hueinan Municipal Labor Reform detachment for corruption. Because Chen was a middle-level cadre, he had many connections in the Party and government. Therefore, in the *laogaidui* he was not confined with the other prisoners but lived apart with his own kitchen. In order to increase the LRC's profits, Chen was allowed to collaborate with others on the outside and open a hardware factory, a store, and a business capital supply organization. During the course of his term Chen earned 20,000 *yuan;* moreover, because of his "success" his term was reduced twice.[32]

3. Increased Corruption: Incidences of corruption and physical abuses by *laogaidui* public security cadres have become more and more serious. Except for certain urban prisons that have definite limits imposed upon them, the public funds and products of *laogaidui* all over the country are subject to open corruption at all levels. LRC coal, lumber, electrical appliances, office supplies, grain, meat, fruit, vegetables, vehicles, and construction materials are openly and recklessly expropriated by any who need them. The use of prisoners and *jiuye* personnel to perform personal services for cadres has also been traditional in the LRC system. Most prisoners are very willing to perform these sorts of services because this indicates that they have the trust of the public security cadres; moreover, eventual paybacks of one sort or another are inevitable. Incidents of

prisoners bribing cadres in order to have their families live with them, obtain home sick leave, reduced sentences, family visits, gifts of food for family members, etc. have become so common that it would be impossible to control them. For example, in Hunan Province's No. 7 Labor Reform Detachment, three public security cadres—Luo Guiyuan, Liao Shoubao, and Cai Kang—accepted 200,000 *yuan* from the family members of Chen Wenxiong, who was sentenced to death by Hunan Province's Hengyang Municipal People's Court for counterfeiting name chops (a signature seal or stamp) and robbery. On April 14, 1989, Chen was released from his handcuffs, given a police uniform, smuggled out of the prison and handed over to family members, who helped him escape. Chen Wenxiong was recaptured in Chengdu, Szechuan Province, and executed. The three public security cadres were arrested.[33] This type of incident is something that could never have occurred in the first thirty years of labor reform.

Entering the International Market

LRCs are not only encouraged to improve their products but are also encouraged to enter the competitive international market and export their products like other enterprises. An enterprise that can earn foreign exchange is considered a reform success. The CCP is not content merely with the LRC's traditional export items—rice, fruit, tea, meat, cotton, etc.—but has established provincial labor reform trade companies to not only market labor reform products but also "to fully exploit the advantages of the labor reform work units in the open cities along the coast and in the special economic zones by establishing joint ventures with foreign companies," as well as "actively exploiting foreign capital to import technology and equipment."[34] This is an important recent trend in CCP labor reform policy. The failure of the Volvo-Chinter deal does not mean that this policy has not had its successes; on the contrary, this policy has been rather successful. For example, America's Washington State Potato Growers Association has supplied the Beijing Labor Reform Bureau with potato processing equipment and has entered into a joint potato product venture; Liaoning Province's Linyuan Automotive Company (LRC-27-23) has made a deal with Japan's Isuzu to import parts for 500 automobiles, have them assembled, and export the finished cars; and Shandong Province's Qingdao Municipality has established a machine factory and imported silk rolling machines from the French technological company Escofier. Labor reform bureaus from provinces in the interior have established relations with coastal enterprises.

The international community has begun to take notice of the LRCs and labor reform products (forced labor products). Sino-American trade in 1989 reached U.S. $19 billion; the Chinese side of the trade picture includes not a few labor reform products (processed and half-processed). In some of these joint ventures and trade relationships it is possible that the foreign partner does not understand the actual situation; in others, financial profit is all that is considered. For many years the United States, Great Britain, and other countries have had laws forbidding the import of forced labor products, but implementation of these laws is often hindered by considerations of political and economic expediency. It is also possible that the CCP transfers all *laogai* and *laojiao* subjects from these enterprises, employing only *jiuye* personnel and claiming that they are regular workers, thus confusing the situation.

It is also possible for foreign capital financiers or joint venture enterprises to act as brokers, obtaining labor reform products or products processed by labor reform enterprises and then turning around and exporting them. It is possible that parts utilized in the American joint venture Jeep factory in Beijing or that cotton or cloth utilized in the Levi Strauss products are labor reform products. Imported foreign technology is utilized by labor reform enterprises and also possibly used in national defense industries. For example, Liaoning Province's Wafangdian Labor Reform Detachment (LRC-27-12, also called Wafangdian Machine Tool Factory) was responsible for constructing China's first intercontinental ballistic missile base; Yunan Province's Ejinmase Agricultural Machine Factory (LRC-11-01, also No. 1 Provincial Prison) produces sprayers for the CCP's anti-chemical warfare corps. These few examples are only the tip of the iceberg.

Labor reform products are sold on the international market through one of the following processes:

1. Passing through CCP provincial import and export trading companies—for example, Yingteh Black Tea is marketed by Guangdong Province's Tea Import and Export Company
2. Exporting by a foreign representative—for instance, Dynasty wine is marketed in America by Nanyang Trading Company, Inc., Palo Alto, CA. Hubei Province's Xiangyang Machine Tool Factory's (LRC-19-27) B6050 Shaping machine is exported via Hong Kong's Datong Company, Dazhong Dynamics Company, and Singapore's Machinery Company, Ltd. These types of companies (including Belgium's Chinter Company) are generally run by Chinese, and some may be invested in and controlled by the CCP;
3. Dealing with foreign businesspeople directly. This type of transaction has recently become somewhat rare.

The LRC economy has over forty years become an integral part of the PRC's national economy. Therefore, when reforms are attempted in the economy as a whole, labor reform enterprises must also change. The political and economic influences of these changes on the LRC system have been very significant.

In the thirty years from 1953–1983, the LRCs have submitted a total of 13 billion *yuan* in tax revenues to the government, offsetting the nation's entire investment in the LRC organs as well as paying for all operating expenses—prisoners, police, and facility costs . . . all are provided by the LRC themselves.[35] So the LRC are thus able to suppress class enemies, maintain the dictatorship, and also provide economic benefits. Is this not one of the CCP's great achievements?

Notes

1. "Sefa tizhi gaige chutan" (Preliminary Examination of Possible Judicial System Reforms), *Fa Xue,* Legal Studies, Shanghai: March 1988, p. 1.

2. "Zhiding laodong gaizao fa shi jiaqiang laogai gongzuo de zhongyao cuoshi" (Formulating Labor Reform Law Is an Important Measure in the Strengthening of Labor Reform Work), *Fazhi jianshe* (Law and Order), Beijing: April 1985, p. 14.

3. A statement by Wang Zhongfang of the Chinese Legal Society, *People's Daily,* November 17, 1986.

4. Law and Order, January 1987, p. 24.

5. *Lenin's Complete Works,* vol. 23, Beijing: People's Press, p. 40.

6. "Preliminary Examination of Possible Judicial System Reforms," p. 2.

7. *Selected Works of Deng Xiaoping,* Beijing: p. 155.

8. Ibid., p. 333.

9. "Qiantan jiansuo jianchazhong de jiangoan yu peihe" (Elementary Notes on Supervision and Coordination of Prosecutions in Prisons), Law and Order, January 1988, p. 26, Beijing: Legal Press.

10. Li Kangtai and Han Yusheng, *Woguo laodong gaizao lifa de yiju ji qi neirong chutan* (Preliminary Discussion of the Basis and Content of Our Nation's Labor Reform Law), Beijing: China People's University report, 1987, pp. 6-121.

11. *Selected Works of Deng Xiaoping,* p. 188.

12. Laodong gaizao zuifan de lilun yu shijian (Labor Reform Criminals: Theory and Practice) Beijing: Legal Press, 1987, p. 42.

13. Translator's note: The term *goanjiao,* here rendered "discipline," is somewhat difficult to translate into a single English word. *Goan,* the first character of the term, means to manage or take care of; *jiao,* the second character, means to educate. Thus, *goanjiao* means to take care of and educate, as well as subject to discipline.

14. "The iron rice bowl" (*tie woanfan*) means a very secure job; it often refers to the tendency of people in a bureaucracy or in a socialist system to resist any changes or reforms that would affect their position. "Common rice bowl" (*daguofan*) refers to the socialist system, in which everyone is fed, in effect, from one

big rice bowl, regardless of ability or level of work, which tends to reduce motivation.

15. Laodong gaizao zuifan de lilun yu shijian (Labor Reform Criminals: Theory and Practice), Beijing: Legal Press, 1987, p. 27.

16. Ibid.

17. Because in the *laogaidui* appeal has historically been seen as evidence of a prisoner "not acknowledging guilt," "making trouble," and "resisting reform," it is considered an index of the quality of the reform process. The author was in the *laogaidui* for nineteen years and came into contact with countless prisoners, yet only heard of one prisoner who ever made an appeal. It was concluded that this prisoner was guilty of "not acknowledging guilt" and "resisting reform," and he was subsequently criticized, beaten, and subjected to an even longer sentence. In the past ten years, however, it seems there has been a large increase in the number of prisoners daring to make appeals.

18. *Legal Daily,* Beijing: October 28, 1989.

19. The detachment political director, Si Wimin of Xinjiang's Kuche Labor Reform Detachment was fined 80 *yuan* in 1985 because his camp did not meet certain index standards. The Deputy Warden Li Guanlei was fined 60 *yuan,* and a few cadres were also fined. In 1986 the situation began to change, the prisoner escape rate declined 75 percent, and the camp pulled itself out of the red.

20. *Legal Daily,* Beijing: November 10, 1987, p. 2.

21. Labor Reform Criminals: Theory and Practice, p. 266.

22. Ibid., p. 270.

23. Ibid., p. 270.

24. Xu Qiancheng, *Laogai gongzuo yao shiying gaige de xuyao* (Labor Reform Work Should Adapt to the Necessities of Reform), China People's Police Academy Report, Beijing: Philosophical Society Press, March 1988, p. 26.

25. *Goanxi* ("connections") has always been an important means of getting things done in the PRC—this is as true today as it was in the old days of imperial bureaucracy. Many things in the PRC are difficult, if not impossible, to accomplish without the proper *goanxi.* "Going through the back door" (*zou houmen*) refers to getting things done in a perhaps not entirely legal manner through the use of *goanxi.*

26. Xu Qiancheng, p. 25.

27. *Law and Order,* June 14, 1990, p. 32.

28. Xu Qiancheng, p. 25.

29. Ibid., p. 26.

30. In communist society, workers and cadres are two different classes, but in certain circumstances it is policy to allow workers to take on the function of cadres—this is called "using workers for cadres" (*yigong daigan*). There is no policy allowing *laogaidui* prisoners to function as cadres—Fu's "using laborers for cadres" is entirely his own invention.

31. *Minzhu yu fazhi* (Democracy and Law), Shanghai: Democracy and Law Association, September 1987, pp. 26–28.

32. China News Agency dispatches, November 18, 1989.

33. *People's Daily,* fourth edition, Beijing: May 12, 1989.

34. Labor Reform Criminals: Theory and Practice, p. 237.

35. Ibid., p. 267.

Afterword

After the draft of this book was completed in December 1990, I continued to receive a steady stream of new materials, especially during the summer of 1991. During that summer, I returned twice to mainland China, covering 15 thousand kilometers over the course of forty days, investigating over twenty LRCs, and in various ways meeting with many Public Security police and ordinary people as well as CLR, RTL, and FJP personnel still in the LRCs. In this way much valuable information was obtained, including film, photographs, audio tapes, written notes, and various types of documents. Because the book at this point was already set for printing, there was some difficulty involved in making additions or revisions, and for this reason much of this new information cannot be included in the book.

I wish to take advantage of the opportunity presented by the publication of this book to briefly sketch some new impressions.

1. Over the past ten years, the Communist Party has instituted many new LRC policies and measures (most of which were not made public). Although there are definite differences between general LRC conditions in recent years and those of the thirty previous years (1949–1979), the LRCs are still a central part of the Communist Party's control structure, and over forty years their political function has not changed. On this point the Communist Party has been very firm.

2. The question of the actual number of LRCs and their total population is one that could only be answered by the Communist authorities, yet it is precisely this information that they refuse to divulge to the international community. After my recent trip to mainland China, it is my impression that the numbers given in the book regarding number of LRCs and the size of LRC populations are possibly a bit higher than is actually the case today. However, as has been noted, the number of LRCs and their populations is variable—large fluctuations result whenever the Communist Party initiates a political crackdown or relaxes restrictions. In the past ten years, every province and municipality has experienced the transferal of responsibility for managing LRCs from the Public Security Bureau to local governments. Examples include Beijing municipality's Yanqing Steel Factory, Xihongshan Iron Mine, and Yingmen Iron Mine;

Qinghai Province's Qinghai Lake Farm, Delinghe Farm, and Geermu Farm; and Hebei Province's Lutai Farm. This sort of transfer of responsibility has the effect of nominally decreasing the number of LRCs and their populations while at the same time establishing new LRCs, such as Shandong Province's Daizhuang Coal Mine.

3. The number of political offenders in the LRCs has decreased sharply and now stands at approximately 10 percent of the total population. Moreover, in accordance with CCP regulations, each province, municipality, and autonomous region has established specialized LRCs (prisons) for political prisoners, such as Beijing municipality's #2 Prison (also known as Taicheng Prison), Gansu Province's #1 Prison (also known as Lanzhou Door Factory), and Qinghai's #1 Prison (also known as Gandu Farm).

4. Over the past ten years the effectiveness of thought reform and political education has decreased dramatically, mirroring the general collapse of faith in socialism and Mao Zedong Thought in the society at large. Thus, the use of violence in the LCRs has increased in order to compensate for the decreased effectiveness of thought control. The report by *Guangming Daily* (a Communist Party organ) reporter Zai Qingzeng of his several months of imprisonment after the June 4 Tiananmen incident does not reflect the actual conditions existing in the LRCs, no doubt due to the favored treatment he enjoyed as a result of his special status.

5. The Forced Job Placement policies concerning prisoners who have completed their CLR or RTL terms has not been abandoned but has been decreased somewhat in scope. The Communist Party has instituted several new regulations that specify in detail the types of people that should be subjected to FJP. At the same time there has been some reshuffling of the FJP personnel that have multiplied over the past thirty years, some portion of whom have been returned to their original hometowns or have left those LRCs that have been turned over to local government management. This has resulted in a large decrease in the number of FJP personnel present in the LRCs. Another portion of FJP personnel has been "rehabilitated" as regular workers, but in name only "enjoy" the same political rights as Public Security police or the general public.

6. The modernization and commercialization of LRC production has accelerated the trend of selling LRC products on the international market. Under the guidance of relevant Communist Party policies, the use of forced labor to provide wealth has been a major task for many LRCs.

I feel that it is necessary to gather and examine materials regarding large-scale persecution of various types of political prisoners and the human rights abuses committed in the LRCs over the previous thirty years as well as to investigate more carefully the economic function of and actual conditions prevailing in the LRCs over the past ten years of Communist Party control. These two areas of study spring from the same source, and their investigation is in substance one task.

Appendix 1: Information on 990 Labor Reform Camps

To date, I have collected information about 990 labor reform camps. This is between one-fourth to one-sixth of the total number of labor reform camps in the People's Republic of China by my reckoning.

What follows are their names and locations and the numbers of prisoners in them. Their locations are marked on Map A1.1, an administrative map of the PRC.

Some explanations: According to CCP policy, every labor reform camp is given two names. The first name designates the camp as a labor reform camp, a name to be used only by the public security system and the judiciary—such as Shanxi Province No. 13 Labor Reform Detachment, Tuanhe Reeducation Through Labor Camp, Xinjiang No. 3 Prison. The second name designates the camp as an enterprise and is for public use—such as Qinghe Farm, Hunan Heavy Truck Factory, or Yanfankuo Coal Mine. The labor reform camps included here are sometimes listed only by their internal name, sometimes only by their enterprise name. It should be noted that there may be a few cases where the same camp is listed under different names. However, all the names here have been verified.

The majority of the labor reform camps listed here have been located (see Table A1.1), but a large number can only be classified as "uncertain" at this moment and need further research.

The number of prisoners in a given labor reform camp usually varies with political changes. In general, we can classify labor reform camps into five categories according to number of prisoners:

A. Under 3,000
B. Between 3,000 and under 5,000
C. Between 5,000 and under 10,000
D. Above 10,000
Unknown

As for the number of camps in certain provinces, autonomous regions, and direct municipalities where communications are more frequent and information is easier to obtain, such as Guangdong Province, Shanxi Province and Beijing Municipality, the numbers given here are closer to the actual figures. The figures given here for the number of camps in more isolated places, such as Henan,

MAP A1.1 Labor Reform Camps Distribution Map, People's Republic of China (first number is LRC code number; second number is number of LRC)

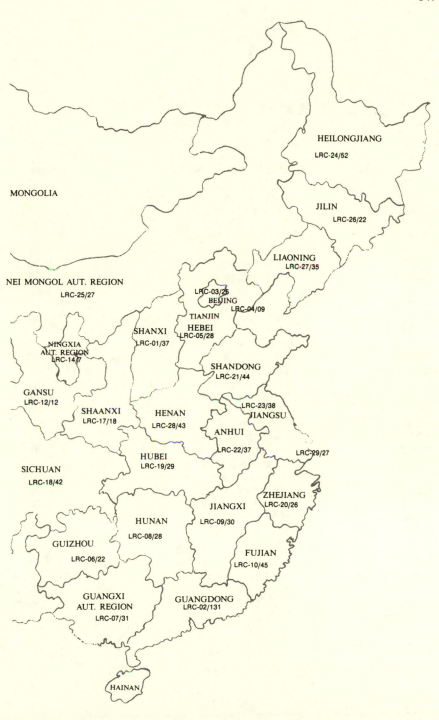

MONGOLIA

HEILONGJIANG
LRC-24/52

JILIN
LRC-26/22

LIAONING
LRC-27/35

NEI MONGOL AUT. REGION
LRC-25/27

LRC-03/25
BEIJING
LRC-04/09

TIANJIN

SHANXI
LRC-01/37

HEBEI
LRC-05/28

NINGXIA
AUT. REGION
LRC-14/7

SHANDONG
LRC-21/44

GANSU
LRC-12/12

SHAANXI
LRC-17/18

HENAN
LRC-28/43

LRC-23/38
JIANGSU

ANHUI
LRC-22/37

LRC-29/27

SICHUAN
LRC-18/42

HUBEI
LRC-19/29

ZHEJIANG
LRC-20/26

HUNAN
LRC-08/28

JIANGXI
LRC-09/30

GUIZHOU
LRC-06/22

FUJIAN
LRC-10/45

GUANGXI
AUT. REGION
LRC-07/31

GUANGDONG
LRC-02/131

HAINAN

TABLE A1.1 Labor Reform Camps of the People's Republic of China

Code no.	Province/Municipality	No. of LRC
LRC-01	Shanxi province	37
LRC-02	Guangdong province (incl. Hainan province)	131
LRC-03	Beijing municipality	25
LRC-04	Tianjin municipality	9
LRC-05	Hebei province	28
LRC-06	Guizhou province	22
LRC-07	Guangxi Aut. Region	31
LRC-08	Hunan province	28
LRC-09	Jiangxi province	30
LRC-10	Fujian province	45
LRC-11	Yunnan province	66
LRC-12	Gansu province	12
LRC-13	Xizhang Aut. region	12
LRC-14	Ningxia Aut. region	7
LRC-15	Xinjiang Aut. region	29
LRC-16	Qinghai province	38
LRC-17	Shaanxi province	18
LRC-18	Sichuan province	42
LRC-19	Hubei province	29
LRC-20	Zhejiang province	26
LRC-21	Shandong province	44
LRC-22	Anhui province	37
LRC-23	Jiangsu province	38
LRC-24	Heilongjiang province	52
LRC-25	Nei Mongol Aut. region	27
LRC-26	Jilin province	22
LRC-27	Liaoning province	35
LRC-28	Henan province	43
LRC-29	Shanghai municipality	27
	Total	990

Note that abbreviations given here appear in the listings that follow.
LRC: Labor Reform Camp; LRD: Labor Reform Disciplinary Production Detachment; RTL: Reeducation Through Labor Camp; JOD: Juvenile Offender Discipline Camp; FJP: Forced Job Placement Camp; [W]: Female Prisoners; D.: District; C.: City; Co.: County; Pr.: Autonomous Prefecture; T.: Town.

Szechuan and Qinghai Provinces and Xinjiang Autonomous Region, are probably much smaller than the actual figures.

Some labor reform camps originally located in highly isolated and underdeveloped regions, such as Xinjiang Autonomous Region, Heilongjiang Province, Qinghai Province and the north of Jiangsu Province have been moved to new locations after the original sites were opened up to cultivation. However, only prisoners undergoing CLR and RTL were relocated. Those who completed their sentences were not allowed to leave. These so-called FJP personnel and their families were forced to stay and work at the original labor reform sites, hence transforming them into immigration settlements. These settlements are no longer controlled by Public Security or the judiciary but by the local governments. However, their organization and management still differ from those of ordinary enterprises. This kind of "quasi-labor reform camp" is very common but is not included in this book.

Only a small number of "quasi-military" labor reform camps, such as the Xinjiang Productive Regiment, are included in this book. Every infantry division of the Xinjiang Productive Regiment, such as Farm 1 Division, Farm 3 Division, Farm 8 Division, and Factory 2 Division, has its own "military court" and labor reform branch and is not under the direct control of the Public Security Department and the judiciary.

The conditions of the prisoners in military prisons are not covered by this book.

There must be a vast number of short-term prisoners held in detention centers. According to CCP's regulations, there should be about 4,000 detention centers in the whole country. These detention centers are not listed here.

I am continuing to search and collect information, such as name, location, population, and production of the labor reform camps, to correct and substantiate the list.

152

Code No: LRC-01
LRC Distribution of Shanxi Province

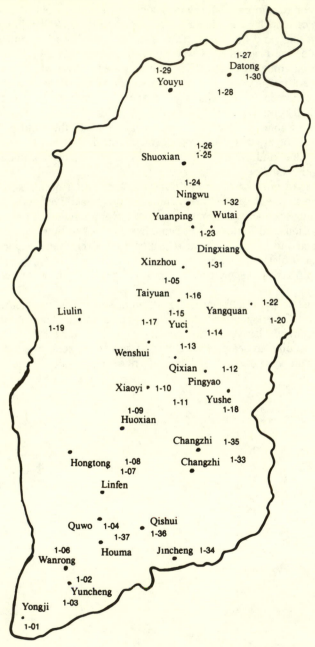

1. Shanxi Province (LRC-01) **Collected Number: 37**

No.	Name of LRC	Location	Number	Remarks
1-01	Wuxinghu Farm	Yongji Co.	B	
1-02	Dongcun Farm (RTL+LRD)	Yuncheng Co.	D	
1-03	Yuncheng RTL	Yuncheng Co.	B	
1-04	Quwo Farm	Quwo Co.	Unknown	
1-05	Taiyuan Brickyard (Provincial No. 6 LRD)	Taiyuan C.	2,000	
1-06	Jiedian Farm	Wanrong Co.	Unknown	
1-07	Fenhe Automobile Factory (Provincial No. 3 prison)	Linfen C.	B	Produced Fenhe truck
1-08	Hongtong RTL	Hongtong Co.	Unknown	
1-09	Wangzhuang Coal Mine (Provincial No. 4 LRD)	East of Huoxian Co.	2,000	Produced 200,000 ton coal/yr
1-10	Xiaoyi RTL	Xiaoyi Co.	A	Produced matches
1-11	Pingyao JOD	Pingyao Co.	A	
1-12	Qixian Textile Factory (Provincial No. 2 prison)	Qixian Co.	B	
1-13	Dongshe Coal Mine	Wenshui Co.	A	
1-14	Yuci Chemical Plant (Provincial No. 4 Prison)	Yuci Co.	A [W]	Produced toothpaste, cosmetics. Sewing.
1-15	Xiyu Coal Mine (LRD+FJP) (Provincial No. 3 LRD)	W. of Taiyuan C.	8,000	Produced 1,200,000 ton coal/yr
1-16	Provincial No. 1 Prison	Taiyuan C.	3,000	
1-17	Taiyuan Wind Dynamic Tools Factory	Taiyuan C.	2,000	
1-18	Nanguan Coal Mine	Yushe Co.	Unknown	
1-19	Liulin Coal Mine	Liulin Co.	Unknown	
1-20	Yangquan RTL	Yangquan C.	A	
1-21	Yinying Coal Mine (LRD+FJP)	North of Yangquan C.	8,000	Produced 1,200,000 ton coal/yr
1-22	Guzhuang Coal Mine (FJP)	Northern Suburbs of Yangquan C.	8,000	Produced 1,200,000 ton coal/yr
1-23	Yuanping Farm	Yuanping Co.	10,000	
1-24	Yangfangkou Coal Mine	Ningwu Co.	A	Produced 1,200,000 ton coal/yr
1-25	Shentou Coal Mine	Shuoxian Co.	B	Produced 1,500,000 ton coal/yr
1-26	Shuoxian Farm	Shuoxian Co.	Unknown	
1-27	Pingwang Coal Mine	S. of Datong C.	B	
1-28	Provincial No. 6 Prison	Datong C.	A[W]	
1-29	Dongchuan Forestry Center	Youyu Co.	Unknown	
1-30	Datong RTL	Datong C.	A	
1-31	Dingxiang Brickyard	Dingxiang Co.	A	
1-32	Wutai Farm	Wutai Co.	B	
1-33	Provincial No. 5 Prison	Changzhi Co.	B	
1-34	Jinpushan Coal Mine	Jincheng Co.	D	
1-35	Changzhi Machinery Repair Factory	Changzhi C.	B	
1-36	Yuanli Farm	Yangcheng Co.	B	
1-37	Provincial No. 13 LRD	Qishui Co.	Unknown	

154

Code No: LRC-02
LRC Distribution of Guangdong Province
(including Hainan Province)

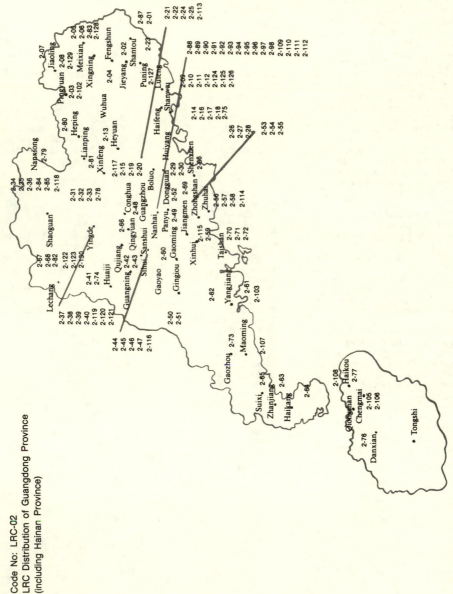

2. Guangdong Province (LRC-02) (incl. Hainan province*)　　　　　　　　**Collected Number: 131**

No.	Name of LRC	Location	Number	Remarks
2-01	Shantou Prison	Shantou C.	Unknown	
2-02	Baitaxu Farm	N.W. of Jieyang C.	A	
2-03	Zhanghang Wolfram Mine	Qiling, Xingning Co.	B	
2-04	Wuhua LRD	Tunmiao, the south gate of Wuhua Co.	A	
2-05	Jianshan Iron Mine	E. of Meixian Co.	B	
2-06	Jinxin Farm	Meixian Co.	A	
2-07	Jiaoling Manganese Mine	Jiaoling Co.	3,000	
2-08	Pingyuan LRD	27 km. n. of Pingyuan Co.	3,000	
2-09	Dawen LRD	Haifeng Co. Meilong	Unknown	
2-10	Nantang Farm (Lufeng LRD)	Nantang T. of Lufeng Co.	800	
2-11	Longtan Tin Mine	Longtan, Lufeng Co.	5,000	
2-12	Chishiwang LRD	Haifeng Co.	B	
2-13	Heyuan LRD	Dongpu, Heyuan Co.	500	Farming, stock raising, brick making
2-14	Lianghuaxu LRD	Jilong mountain area n. of Huiyang Co..	A	
2-15	Tonghu Farm (Tonghu LRD)	Shi'aoxu, Boluo Co.	1,000	Rice, sugarcane, vegetables. Established in 1983.
2-16	Yan'ao Farm (Yan'ao LRD)	Yan'aocun, e. suburbs of Huiyang Co.	Unknown	
2-17	Zhangmutou RTL	N. of Zhangmutou, Huiyang Co.	Unknown	
2-18	Xiapu LRD	W. of Huizhou, Huiyang Co.	Unknown	
2-19	Shi'ao Farm	Shi'aoxu, Boluo Co.	2,000[W]	There are several hundred ha. cultivated land.
2-20	Provincial JOD	Boluo Co.	Unknown	
2-21	Tanshawei LRD	Tanshawei, Conghua Co.	B	
2-22	Shilong LRD	Conghua Co.	A	
2-23	Puning LRD	Danan mountain area e. of Puning Co.	A	
2-24	Provincial No. 6 LRD	Yangcun, Conghua Co.	B	
2-25	Huangzhulang LRD	Zhulangfeng, Conghua Co.	A	
2-26	Dayouwei Farm	Dalang, Dongguan Co.	1,000	Farming, spinning and weaving, iron-smelting.
2-27	Longgangzai RTL	Tangtousha, Dongguan Co.	A	
2-28	Dawangcun LRD	Songgang, Dongguan Co.	Unknown	
2-29	Bao'an RTL	Hengjiang, Bao'an Co.	1,000[W]	Five hundred ha. cultivated land, farming.
2-30	Satoucun LRD	Nantou, Bao'an Co.	A	
2-31	Lishi LRD	Lishi, Qujiang Co.	1,000	
2-32	Huanggang LRD	E. of Qujiang Co.	Unknown	
2-33	Qujiang LRD	S.W. mountain area of Qujiang Co.	A	
2-34	Maba Farm	Maba, Shaoguan C.	1,000	
2-35	Dongheba LRD	Dongheba, Shaoguan C.	B	
2-36	Tianluochong Iron Mine	Shaoguan C.	5,000	

2. Guangdong Province (LRC-02) (incl. Hainan province*)

2-37	Shengtian Sulphur-Iron Mine (LRD+RTL+FJP)	Dongguapu, Yingde Co.	10,500	Four branch mines, produced sulphur-iron ore.
2-38	Provincial No. 2 LRD	Mashixu, Yingde Co.	Unknown	
2-39	Shihuipu LRD	Yingde Co.	A	
2-40	Hetou LRD	Hetou, Yingde Co.	B	
2-41	Provincial No. 1 Prison	Wentang, Huaiji Co.	C	
2-42	Dahuang LRD (LRD+FJP)	Sihui Co.	120,000	Area: 25 sq. km. Farming, stock raising.
2-43	Jiwangtang LRD	5 Km. n.e. of Sihui Co.	3,000	Plants coarse crop and raises stock.
2-44	Baoyue RTL	Xinan T., Sanshui Co.	A	
2-45	Xinsheng Coal Mine	S.W. of Sanshui Co.	A	
2-46	Hengshengwo Farm (Sanshui LRD)	3 Km. e. of Huangtan, Sanshui Co.	700[W]	Farming.
2-47	Jitipu Farm	Nanba, Sanshui Co.	Unknown	
2-48	Chini Stone Material Works	Xinhua T. Huaxian Co.	1,000	Exploits stone materials.
2-49	Shunde LRD	Rongqi T. Shunde Co.	A	
2-50	Rongshan RTL	Rongshan, Shunde Co.	A	
2-51	Xingtan LRD	Xingtan, Shunde Co.	Unknown	
2-52	Guanshan Xijiang Manganese Mine	N. of Xijiaoshan Nanhai Co.	1,000	Area: 25 sq. km. Farming.
2-53	Shiqi zhejiao LRD	W. of Shiqi Zhongshan Co.	B	
2-54	Jianfeng RTL	Doumenwan, Zhongshan Co.	1,000	
2-55	Provincial No. 2 Prison	Shaxi, Zhongshan Co.	1,000	
2-56	Fenghuangshan RTL	Fenghuang mountain area in Zhuhai Co.	A	
2-57	Tangjiawan LRD	Tangjiawan, Zhuhai Co.	Unknown	
2-58	Shanchang RTL	Zhuhai Co.	A	
2-59	Yangmei LRD	Yangmeixu, Gaohe Co.	B	
2-60	Baitu LRD	Baitu, Gaoyao Co.	B	
2-61	Provincial No. 3 LRD	Heshan, Yangjiang Co.	1,000	
2-62	Yangchun RTL	Yangchun Co.	A	Farming and mining.
2-63	Zhanjiang LRD	Chikan, Zhanjiang C.	A	
2-64	Guangdong 138 LRD	Tiaofeng, Leizhou peninsula	D[W]	Embankment.
2-65	Suixi LRD	Yuezhen T., Suixi Co.	B	
2-66	Shanhe Sulphur-iron Mine	Qingyuan Co.	C	
2-67	Guangbei LRD	Xiaojinping, Jiuhua mountain area in Lechang Co.	D	
2-68	Tiantou Coal Mine	Tiantou, Lechang Co.	B	
2-69	Shawan RTL	Shawan, Panyu Co.	Unknown	
2-70	Gudoushan LRD	Duxie, Taishan Co.	A	
2-71	Shangchuandao RTL	Shangchuandao, Taishan Co.	B	
2-72	Zhenshanwang RTL	Taishan Co.	A	
2-73	Datiandingshan LRD	Datiandingshan, Gaozhou Co.	B	
2-74	Hekou LRD	Hekouxu, Huaiji Co.	D	
2-75	Maan JOD	Maan, Hiuyang Co.	300	
2-76*	Nada LRD	Nada, Danxian Co.	A	

2. Guangdong Province (LRC-02) (incl. Hainan province*)　　　　　　　　　　　　　　**Collected Number: 131**

2-77*	Sanmenpo LRD	Dongshan, Qiongshan Co.	A
2-78	Guitou LRD	Guitouxu, Qujiang Co.	B
2-79	Guangbei Tree Farm	Nanxiong Co.	1,000
2-80	Shangbei LRD	Shangbeiling, Heping Co.	B
2-81	Yuangangling Farm	Baijuehan, Xinfeng Co.	B
2-82	Luojiadu Coal Mine (Luojiadu LRD, LRD+RTL+FJP)	Tiantou, Lechang Co.	36,000	Area: 30 sq. km. Three coal mines and one battery factory. Farming.
2-83	Meizhou Prison	Meixian Co.	A
2-84	Shaoguan Prison	Shaoguan C.	A
2-85	Shaoguan LRD	Shaoguan C.	Unknown
2-86	Shenzhen LRD	Shenzhen C.	Unknown
2-87	Shantou LRD	Shantou C.	Unknown
2-88	Guangzhou Marble Mine	Baiyun mountain, Guangzhou C.	A	Exploited stone material.
2-89	Mashong RTL	Xicun, Guangzhou C.	A
2-90	Xicun Xinsheng Farm	Fuzhou street, Guangzhou C.	A	Farming, brick making.
2-91	Guangzhou Xinsheng No. 1 Factory (No. 1 LRD)	Nanshitou, Guangzhou C.	2,000	There are five branch factories: Huanan chemical plant; Xinsheng flashlight plant; Xinsheng battery plant, which produced White-Elephant battery; Xinsheng steel-melting factory; Xinsheng brickyard.
2-92	Baihedong Paper Mill	S. bank of Zhujiang river, Guangzhou C.	1,000
2-93	Shahe Farm	Shahe, Guangzhou C.	1,000	Attached machinery factory.
2-94	Chuiluotian Stone Material Works (RTL)	S. of Liuqi river Guangzhou C.	B
2-95	No. 1 Prison of Guangzhou C.	Huanghua street, Guangzhou C.	1,200[W]	Produced machinery, bricks. Escorted 100 convicts to Xinjiang in October 1989. Makes shoes for export.
2-96	Chatou Farm (Chatou RTL)	Guangzhou C.	1,000	Planted fruit trees.
2-97	Yagang RTL	Shijing, Yagang n. suburbs of Guangzhou C.	Unknown
2-98	Jiufu RTL	20 km. s.w. of Jiufu Guangzhou C.	Unknown
2-99	Renhua Farm	Unknown	D
2-100	Liantang LRD	Unknown	D
2-101	Longtouying LRD	Unknown	C
2-102	Huanghuai LRD	Huanghuai mountain, Xingning Co.	Unknown
2-103	Yayi Tree Farm	Yayi, Baisha Co.	C
2-104	Dongjin LRD	Unknown	D

2. Guangdong Province (LRC-02) (incl. Hainan province*)   Collected Number: 131

2-105* Chengmai LRD	N.W. of Chengmai Co.	Unknown	
2-106* Anding LRD	Chengmai Co.	B	
2-107 Maoming RTL	Maoming C.	Unknown	
2-108* Qionghai Prison	Haikou C.	Unknown	
2-109 Guangzhou Dongkeng RTL	Guangzhou C.	Unknown	
2-110 Xicun Meihua Farm	Xicun, Guangzhou C.	300[W]	Farming, stock raising, handicraft.
2-111 Liyao Brickyard	S. suburbs of Guangzhou C.	3,000	Brick making
2-112 Xinsheng No. 3 Factory	Xincun, Guangzhou C.	3,500	Produced machinery, building material, spinning, and weaving.
2-113 Xinsheng No. 2 Factory (mining equipment factory)	N.W. of Conghua Co.	Unknown	Produced sulphur.
2-114 Qianshan Stone Material Works	Qianshan T. of Zhuhai Co.	1,000	Exploited stone material.
2-115 Xinhui Farm	E. of Xinhui Co.	A	Farming.
2-116 Sanshui Farm	N. of Sanshui Co.	B	Area: 5,000 ha. Planted sugarcane, rice.
2-117 Jizi Farm	Boluo Co.	700	
2-118 Huanggang Brickyard	E. Shaoguan C.	1,000	Brick making.
2-119 Sanou Farm (incl. 11 branch farms)	Sanou, Yingde Co.	35,000	Area: 12 sq. km. Farming and sideline production. Planted sugarcane, peanuts, tea.
2-120 Xinsheng United Enterprise (Provincial No. 7 LRD) (LRD+RTL+FJP)	N. suburbs of Yingde Co.	30,000	Four branch farms. Farming, tea (Yingteh black tea exported). Sugar factory, lime factory, tea-processing factory, machinery factory (produces tea-making equipment), chemical factory.
2-121 Makou Farm (RTL)	Makou, Yingde Co.	5,000	Area: 500 sq. km. Six workshops, mines 500,000–700,000 ton ore. Steel-melting, sulphur-melting, farming, and sideline production.
2-122 Provincial No. 2 LR General Brigade	Pingshishui T. Lechang Co.	3,100	Farming, construction, weaving.
2-123 Yuebei Mine (RTL)	Yongjiqiao, Lechang Co.	1,000	Produced gypsum, 100 ton/mo.
2-124 Chianqiao Brickyard	Chianqiao, Haifeng Co.	Unknown	
2-125 Haifeng Prison	N. suburbs of Haifeng Co.	Unknown	
2-126 Yuandun Farm (RTL)	W. Haifeng Co.	1,000	Produced fruits.
2-127 Lufeng Prison	Hetouling, Lufeng Co.	300	

2. Guangdong Province (LRC-02) (incl. Hainan province*) **Collected Number: 131**

2-128	Meixian No. 4 Construction Zone	Meixian Co.	12,000	Total 12 battalions, No. 1–No. 5 battalions, mining; No. 6–No.12 battalions construct railway from Fuxing to Meixian Co.
2-129	Pingyuan Farm	10 km. s.w. of Pingyuan Co.	2,000	Farming, mining, lumbering.
2-130	Pingshi Prison	Lechang Co.	Unknown	Tea farm and factory.
2-131	Wujiang LRD	Northern part of Guangdong	Unknown	There is a Dongshan battalion, which controls two women's companies and one men's company. Planted tea.

160

Code No: LRC-03
LRC Distribution of Beijing City
Code No: LRC-04
LRC Distribution of Tianjin City
Code No: LRC-05
LRC Distribution of Hebei Province

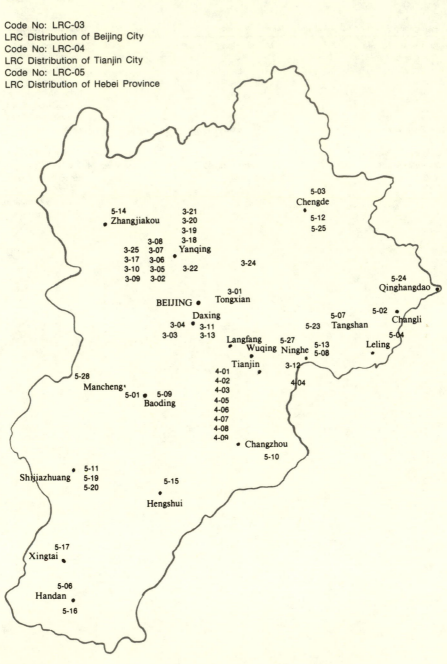

No.	Name of LRC	Location	Number	Remarks
3-01	Tongxian Hardware Factory	Doudian, Tongxian Co.	1,000	
3-02	Qinghe Chemical Factory	Chaoyang D. Beijing	Unknown	
3-03	Scientific Experiment Instrument Factory (FJP)	Xuanwu D. Beijing	1,000	
3-04	Liangxiang Elevator Factory (RTL+FJP)	Fengtai D. Beijing	2,500	Largest elevator factory in China.
3-05	Xindu Conditioning Equipment Factory (FJP)	Out of Deshengmen, Beijing	1,500	The conditioning equipment of People's Hall in Beijing was supplied by this factory.
3-06	Liuhai prison	Xicheng D. Beijing	Unknown	
3-07	No. 3 Prison	Xicheng D. Beijing	3,000	
3-08	No. 2 Prison	Gongdelin, out of Deshengmeng, Beijing	3,000	
3-09	No. 1 Prison	Zixing Rd. Xuanwu D. Beijing	3,000[W]	Includes Beijing Knitting Factory, which produced 3 million pair Jinshuangma nylon socks/yr.; supplied domestic market and exports.
3-10	Beijing JOD	Chaoyang D. Beijing	1,000	
3-11	Tuanhe Farm	Huangcun, Daxing Co. Beijing	8,000	In 1960s, it included No. 1 battalion (LRD), No. 2 battalion (RTL+FJP), No. 3 battalion (JOD). Included 867 ha. cultivated land, in which there were 330 ha. grapes and 87 ha. fruit trees. Produced 1,015 ton grapes and exported to Hongkong and Japan. Now it supplies the Sino-French wine factory that produces "Dynasty" wine.
3-12	Qinghe Farm (Beijing No. 1 LRD)	Ninghe Co. Tianjin municipality	60,000– 80,000	Established in 1950. There are more than 20 agricultural and industrial units; the Qinghe machinery factory produced vehicle batteries; the farm produced artifically bred prawns (1 million lbs/yr.); forage; assembly of TV. Total output value: 100 million/yr.

3. Beijing Municipality   Collected Number: 25

3-13	Tiantanghe Farm (RTL)	Nanyuan, Daxing Co. Beijing	3,000	
3-14	Tao'erhe Farm	Baichengzi, Jilin Prov.	10,000	
3-15	Yinhe Farm (FJP)	Keshan Co. Heilongjiang Prov.	10,000	
3-16	Xingkaihu Farm (FJP)	Mishan Co. Heilongjiang Prov.	20,000	
3-17	Direct Current Motor Factory (JOD)	Xindian, Chaoyang D. Beijing	1,000	May be same camp as 3-10.
3-18	Yingmen Iron Mine	Yanqing Co. Beijing	1,000	May have been passed on to local enterprise.
3-19	Xihongshan Iron Mine	Yanqing Co. Beijing	1,000	May have been passed on to local enterprise.
3-20	Yanqing Steel-iron Factory	Kangzhuang, Yanqing Co. Beijing	3,000	May have been passed on to local enterprise.
3-21	Yanqing brickyard	Yanqing Co. Beijing	1,000	Handicapped and psychotic convicts.
3-22	Qingcheng Prison	Changping Co. Beijing	3,000	Most are political convicts.
3-23	Shuanghe Farm	Northeast of China	Unknown	
3-24	Shunyi Brickyard	Shunyi Co. Beijing	2,000	
3-25	Beiyuan Chemical Factory	Dewaitucheng, Beijing	1,000	May be same camp as 3-02. Produced chemical materials.

Beijing LRC enterprises are cooperating with foreigners to develop aquatic product breeding, auto repairs, toilet tissue workshop, potato food factory (cooperating with the Washington State Potato Growers Association in the United States).

4. Tianjin Municipality (LRC-04)   Collected Number: 9

No.	Name of LRC	Location	Number	Remarks
4-01	Tianjin No. 3 LRD	Tianjin C.	Unknown	
4-02	Tianjin No. 4 LRD	Tianjin C.	Unknown	
4-03	Xitou LRD	Western Suburbs of Tianjin C.	D	
4-04	Xinhe Farm	Eastern Suburbs of Tianjin C.	Unknown	
4-05	Banqiao Farm (RTL)	S.E. of Tianjin C.	B	
4-06	Tianjin JOD	Tianjin C.	Unknown	
4-07	Liqizhuang Farm	Liqizhuang, in s.w. of Tianjin C.	C	
4-08	Tianjin C. No. 2 Prison	Tianjin C.	Unknown	
4-09	Tianjin No. 1 LRD	Tianjin C.	Unknown	

No.	Name of LRC	Location	Number	Remarks
5-01	Provincial No. 1 Prison (machinery factory)	Baoding C.	5,000	Produced Model AB-1 infrared ray alarm equipment, Model JZJ-50 welding machine, electronic controller, and tool machine.
5-02	Jieshishan LRD	Jieshishan, Changli Co.	Unknown	
5-03	Chengde RTL	Chengde C.	A	
5-04	Zhaogezhuang Farm	Zhaogezhuang, Changli Co.	C	
5-05	No. 1 LR General Brigade	Unknown	D	
5-06	Handan RTL	Handan C.	A	
5-07	Kanping RTL	Tangshan C.	B	Three industrial products for export.
5-08	Lutai Salt Works	Lutai Co.	5,000	
5-09	Baoding RTL	Baoding C.	Unknown	
5-10	Changzhou RTL	Changzhou C.	B	
5-11	Shijiazhuang RTL	Shijiazhuang C.	D	
5-12	Hongsong Farm	Hongsong T., Chengde C.	B	
5-13	Hangu RTL	Hangu C.	C	
5-14	Zhangjiakou RTL	Zhangjiakou C.	A	
5-15	XX LRD	Hengshui Co.	B	
5-16	Pengcheng Coal Mine	Ci Co.	5,000	
5-17	Guanzhuang Farm	Xingtai C.	Unknown	
5-18	No. 3 LR General Brigade (textile mill)	Unknown	Unknown	No. 9 company produced and exported 30,000 sheets in 1988.
5-19	Shijiazhuang JOD	Shijiazhuang	Unknown	Profits 110,000 yuan in 1984; profits 270,000 yuan/1985; profits 470,000 yuan/1986; profits 570,000 yuan/1987.
5-20	Provincial No. 4 Prison	Shijiazhuang C.	Unknown	
5-21	No. 7 LR General Brigade	Unknown	Unknown	
5-22	Provincial No. 2 Prison	Unknown	Unknown	
5-23	Tangshan JOD	Tangshan	Unknown	
5-24	Qinghuangdao RTL	Qinghangdao C.	Unknown	
5-25	Provincial No. 5 Prison	Chengde C.	Unknown	
5-26	No. 2 LR General Brigade	Unknown	Unknown	Established in 1960. Grew cotton.
5-27	Lutai Farm	Lutai Co.	D	Profits 1 million yuan/1986. Grew mushrooms; wood processing, food processing; produces crystal glass, cement prefabricate component.
5-28	Mancheng LRD	Mancheng C.	Unknown	Dealt with building material, printing, plastics making, spinning, auto repairing. Output value 18 million yuan/1988, profits 4 million yuan. There is 16 million yuan fixed capital. Produced 5,000 ton carbonate of potassium, exported to many countries.

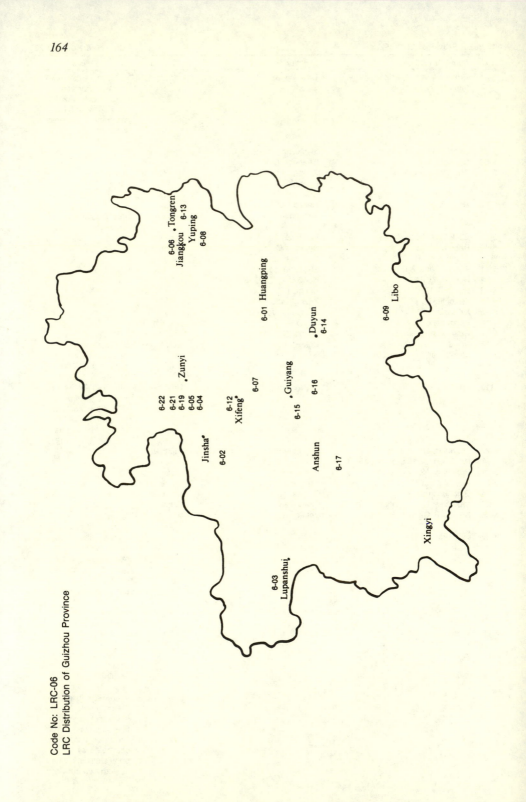

164

Code No: LRC-06
LRC Distribution of Guizhou Province

6-06 · Tongren 6-13
Jiangkou Yuping
6-08

6-01 Huangping

Libo
6-09

Duyun
6-14

Zunyi

6-07

Guiyang

6-22
6-21
6-19
6-05
6-04

6-16

6-12
Xifeng

6-15

Jinsha
6-02

Anshun
6-17

Xingyi

6-03
Lupanshui

6. Guizhou Province (LRC-06)   **Collected Number: 22**

No.	Name of LRC	Location	Number	Remarks
6-01	Huangping LRD	Huangping Co.	C	
6-02	Jinsha Farm	Jinsha Co.	Unknown	
6-03	Weining LRD	Weining Aut. Co.	D	
6-04	Zunyi Coal Mine	Lijiawan, Zunyi C.	C	
6-05	Zunyi RTL	Zunyi C.	Unknown	
6-06	Jiangkou LRD	Jiangkou Co.	B	
6-07	Xifeng LRD	Xifeng C.	C	
6-08	Yuping LRD	Yuping Co.	C	
6-09	Chaoyang Lead Mine	Chaoyang T., in Libo Co.	D	Produced lead
6-10	Wangwu LRD	Unknown	Unknown	
6-11	Jinxi Coal Mine	Unknown	B	
6-12	Chaoyang LRD	Yongjing T. in Xifeng C.	D	
6-13	Tongren LRD	Tongren Co.	B	
6-14	Duyun RTL	Duyun C.	B	
6-15	Provincial No. 1 Prison	Guiyang C.	Unknown	
6-16	Guiyang RTL	Guiyang C.	Unknown	
6-17	Anshun RTL	Anshun C.	B	
6-18	Provincial No. 9 LRD	Unknown	Unknown	
6-19	Zunyi Prison	Zunyi C.	B	Processing machinery.
6-20	Jiaozishan Coal Mine (Jiaozishan LRD)	Unknown	Unknown	
6-21	XX Phosphate Fertilizer Factory	Zunyi C.	Unknown	
6-22	XX Brickyard	Zunyi C.	Unknown	

166

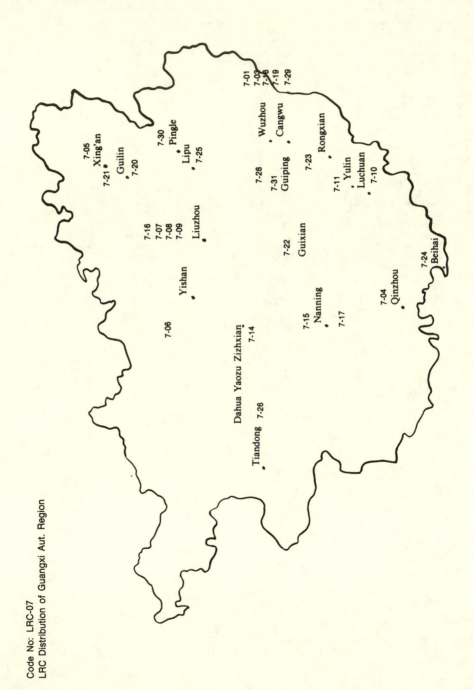

Code No: LRC-07
LRC Distribution of Guangxi Aut. Region

7. Guangxi Zhuang Autonomous Region (LRC-07)   **Collected Number: 31**

No.	Name of LRC	Location	Number	Remarks
7-01	Chishui LRD	Chishui, Wuzhou C.	C	
7-02	Luoyangshan Forestry Center	Fuwang, Pubei Co.	D	
7-03	Wuzhou RTL	Wuzhou C.	B	
7-04	Qinzhou Manganese Mine	Qinzhou C.	D	
7-05	Zhenbao Iron Mine No. 3 Prison of Guilin C.	Xing'an Co.	D	
7-06	Xiangbei LRD	Xiangbei, Yishan Co.	C	
7-07	Shatang LRD	Shatang, Liuzhou C.	1,000	
7-08	Xinxing LRD	Liuzhou C.	Unknown	
7-09	Liuzhou RTL	Liuzhou C.	B	
7-10	Wushi Tin Mine	Luchuan Co.	5,000	
7-11	Liufangshan Tin Mine	Yulin Co.	1,000	
7-12	Yingshan Prison (machinery factory)	Unknown	B	Included cement factory.
7-13	Lutang Farm	Unknown	Unknown	
7-14	Provincial No. 5 LRD	Dahua Aut. Co.	D	Included at least 7 battalions.
7-15	Zhegugang Farm (incl. two branch farms)	5 km. n.w. of Nanning C.	81,000	6,666 ha. in area; dealt with farming and stock raising.
7-16	Shipaiping Farm (FJP)	Shipaiping, Liuzhou C.	1,000	Planted sugarcane.
7-17	Nanning RTL	Nanning C.	B	Produced cement.
7-18	Wuzhou Manufactory (prison of Wuzhou C.)	Fuminfang, Wuzhou C.	3,000[W]	Produced cement, brick, paper, tool machine.
7-19	Xinsheng No. 2 Cement Factory	Beishan Garden, Wuzhou C.	500	Produced cement
7-20	Bao'an Farm (Bao'an RTL)	Yanshan, Guilin C.	1,000[W]	Included brick factory; reclaims wasteland; dealt with farming
7-21	Guilin C. Prison	Guilin C.	A	
7-22	Xijiang Farm	Guixian Co.	5,000	
7-23	Pingpo LRD	7 km. n.w. of Rongxian Co.	D	
7-24	Beihai RTL	Beihai C.	A	
7-25	Dumo RTL	Dumo T., Lipu Co.	B	
7-26	Tiandong Farm	Maling, Tiandong Co.	Unknown	Dealt in farming and stock raising.
7-27	Provincial No. 9 LRD	Unknown	Unknown	
7-28	Liaoping Farm	Guiping Co.	Unknown	Included sugar mill.
7-29	Cangwu Farm	Cangwu Co.	Unknown	Produced brick.
7-30	Pingle Farm	S. of Pingle Co.	Unknown	Area is about 30 sq. km. Planted poppies, opium, peanuts, and rice.
7-31	Shipai Farm (incl. FJP)	20 km. s.w. of Guiping Co.	2,100[W]	Included 7 branch farms; cultivated land: 200 ha.; grew rice, grains, and medicinal materials. Afforest.

168

Code No: LRC-08
LRC Distribution of Hunan Province

Jinshi
8-25
8-26
Huarong
8-04
8-13
Yueyang

Changde
8-06

8-19
Yiyang

8-09
8-03 8-08
8-01

Ningxiang
8-17
Changsha

8-14
Xiangtan
Zhuzhou

8-21
Lengshuijiang

8-05
Liling

Huaihua
8-28

8-15
Hengshan
8-23

8-20
Shaoyang

8-10
Hengyang
8-16
8-24

8-18
Chaling

Leiyang

8-22
Chenxian

8. Hunan Province (LRC-08)

No.	Name of LRC	Location	Number	Remarks
8-01	Provincial No. 1 Prison	Changsha C.	B	
8-02	Heavy Truck Plant (Provincial No. 2 Prison)	Unknown	Unknown	
8-03	Xinsheng Cement Factory	Wanggongtang, e. of Changsha C.	B	
8-04	Luojiazhou Farm	Luojiazhou, Huarong Co.	1,000	
8-05	Lukou RTL	Lukou, Zhuzhou C.	1,000	
8-06	Changde LRD	Changde C.	Unknown	
8-07	Muyun LRD (along Xiangjiang river)	Unknown	1,000	
8-08	Xinkaipu RTL	Changsha C.	Unknown	Produced JJ-1A(S) high/low pressure switch; PHZ-1 direct current set.
8-09	Changsha LRD	Changsha C.	1,000	
8-10	No. 5 LRD (Hengyang LRD)	Hengyang C.	D	
8-11	Chenglong Farm	Unknown	Unknown	
8-12	Hongqiao LRD	Unknown	Unknown	
8-13	Yueyang Farm	Yueyang C.	5,000	
8-14	Xiangtan LRD	Xiangtan C.	3,000	
8-15	Hengshan Wolfram Mine	Hengshan Co.	B	
8-16	Hengshan RTL	Hengshan Co.	C	
8-17	Ningxiang Farm	Ningxiang Co.	D	
8-18	Chaling Farm	Chaling C.	C	
8-19	Yiyang RTL	Yiyang C.	B	
8-20	Shaoyang Prison	Shaoyang C.	B	
8-21	Lengshuijiang RTL	Lengshuijiang C.	C	
8-22	Chenxian LRD	Chenxian Co.	C	
8-23	Liling Coal Mine	Liling Co.	5,000	
8-24	Xinmin Auto Parts Factory	Hengyang C.	Unknown	Produced auto parts.
8-25	Qingtan Farm	Jinshi C.	Unknown	
8-26	Huarong Prison	Huarong Co.	C	
8-27	Longxi Prison	Unknown	Unknown	
8-28	Provincial No. 8 LRD	Huaihua Co.	Unknown	

Code No: LRC-09
LRC Distribution of Jiangxi Province

9. Jiangxi Province (LRC-09) **Collected Number: 30**

No.	Name of LRC	Location	Number	Remarks
9-01	Furong Farm	Furong T. Pengzhe Co.	D	Included spinning factory, machinery factory.
9-02	Jiujiang RTL	Jiujiang C.	B	
9-03	Xihuashan Wolfram Mine	Unknown	C	
9-04	Pingxiang Coal Mine	Pingxiang C.	D	
9-05	Nanchang LRD	Nanchang C.	B	
9-06	Shangrao LRD	Shangrao C.	C	
9-07	Chengxin Farm	Nanchang C.	10,000	
9-08	Xinyu Iron Mine	Fengyi Co.	D	Xinyu iron and steel company established in 1958. Convicts came from Shanghai.
9-09	Zhuhu Pharmaceutical Factory	Boyang Co.	D	Farming and pharmacy. Output value at least 300 million yuan and profits 6 million yuan yearly.
9-10	Jianggang Farm	Nanchang C.	D	
9-11	Huangxi LRD	Nanchang C.	B	
9-12	Boyang Farm	Boyang Co.	D	
9-13	Changzhou Farm	Changtouling, Nanchang C.	Unknown	
9-14	Jingde LRD	N. of Jindezhen C.	D	
9-15	Jing'an LRD	Jiulingshan, n.w. of Jing'an Co.	1,000	
9-16	Provincial No. 1 RTL	Unknown	Unknown	
9-17	Jinxian Farm	Qilixu, n.w. of Jinxian Co.	C	
9-18	Guixi LRD	Guixi Co.	Unknown	
9-19	Ruichang Farm	Ruichang Co.	Unknown	
9-20	Ji'an RTL	Ji'an C.	C	
9-21	Gangzhou RTL	Gangzhou C.	C	
9-22	Ruijin LRD	Ruijin C.	Unknown	
9-23	Fuzhou RTL	Fuzhou C.	A	
9-24	Provincial No. 1 LRD	Unknown	D	Included at least 12 battalions.
9-25	Provincial No. 5 LRD	Unknown	Unknown	
9-26	Provincial No. 2 LRD	Unknown	Unknown	
9-27	Binghu Farm	Unknown	Unknown	
9-28	Provincial No. 4 LRD	Unknown	Unknown	
9-29	Provincial No. 2 Prison	Unknown	Unknown	
9-30	Henghu Farm	50 km. n.w. of Nanchang C.	C	

Code No: LRC-10
LRC Distribution of Fujian Province

10-40
Pucheng

•Mingxi
10-37   10-41
Chong'an
•Zhenghe
10-38
Jianyang   10-39   Taining
•10-06
10-43   Fu'an 10-27
•10-26
Jian'ou
10-13

Taining   10-31
•Nanping
10-09

10-10   10-11
10-05   •Minhou   •Liancheng
10-30   10-34   10-20   10-16
10-35   Sanming   Longxi   Fuzhou 10-15
10-32 Qingliu   10-18   Changle
Ninghua   10-04

•Fuqing
10-25

10-33
10-24
10-23
10-07   10-14
Anxi 10-08
Longyan   Nan'an 10-29
10-03   Jinjiang
10-01   10-02   Tong'an 10-17
Yongding   10-22   10-28
Zhangzhou   Xiamen
10-21
10-12
10-19

10. Fujian Province (LRC-10)   **Collected Number: 45**

No.	Name of LRC	Location	Number	Remarks
10-01	Fengren Farm	Fengren, Yongding Co.	B	
10-02	Shizhong LRD	Shizhong T., Longyan Co.	B	
10-03	Longyan Coal Mine	Longyan Co.	C	
10-04	Changle LRD	Yingqian, Changle Co.	B	
10-05	Rongxin Machine Tool Factory (Provincial No. 3 Prison)	Baisha T. Minhou Co.	1,100	Five companies. Produced planers, grinders. Farming and stock raising, construction. Output value was 8.65 million yuan in 1988.
10-06	Provincial No. 2 Prison	Jianyang Co.	600	Six companies. Dealt with construction, wood-bamboo processing, chemical products, farming, stock raising.
10-07	Plastics Factory (Provincial No. 1 Prison)	Longyan Co.	3,000	Produced cement, plastics.
10-08	Anxi Coal Mine	Anxi Co.	10,000	
10-09	Gekou Farm	Taining Co.	1,000	66 ha. cultivated land. Produced 250 ton rice, 50 ton soya bean, 15 ton peanuts in 1962.
10-10	Baisha Farm (Minhou LRD)	Baisha T. Minhou Co.	500[W]	Produced shoes.
10-11	Wangfeng Farm	Liancheng Co.	D	
10-12	Xiaokengtou RTL	N.E. of train station in Zhangzhou C.	A	
10-13	Yangzhe Coal Mine	Jian'ou Co.	5,000	
10-14	Fude Iron Factory	Fude, Anxi Co.	A	
10-15	Fuzhou LRD	Xinjing, Fuzhou C.	A	
10-16	Fuzhou RTL	Fuzhou C.	B	
10-17	Quanzhou Farm	Honglai, Jinjiang Co.	B	
10-18	Taixi LRD	Taixixu, Longxi Co.	B	
10-19	Zhangzhou LRD	Zhangzhou C.	B	
10-20	Minqing LRD	Houshan, Minqing Co.	B	
10-21	Jiangtou Saltern	Junhai, Xiamen C.	B	
10-22	Zhuba Farm	Sazhuba, Tong'an Co.	A	
10-23	Longmen Farm	Longmenkou, Longyan Co.	A	
10-24	Longyan Wolfram Mine	Yanshi, Longyan Co.	B	
10-25	Fuqing Farm	Xindongzhang, Fuqing Co.	C	
10-26	Baidu Farm	Baidu, Fu'an Co.	B	
10-27	Zhengqing Livestock Farm	Yangxitou, Fu'an Co.	C	
10-28	Nan'an Farm	Zuocuo, Nan'an Co.	B	
10-29	Daluling LRD	Dongluo, Nan'an Co.	B	
10-30	Sanming RTL	Sanming C.	A	
10-31	Nanping RTL	Nanping C.	A	
10-32	Xinken Farm (Qingliu LRD)	Qingliu Co.	2,000[W]	
10-33	Qingchaomeng Farm (Longyan LRD)	Longmenkou, Longyan Co.	2,000	
10-34	Provincial No. 4 Prison	Honglai T. Jinjiang Co.	700	
10-35	Liangshangang Farm (Ninghua LRD)	Ninghua Co.	900	
10-36	Dazhouhou Brickyard (Yong'an LRD)	Yong'an Co.	C	Six battalions.
10-37	Huangtu Farm (Chong'an LRD)	Huangtuxiang, Chong'an Co.	2,500	Two battalions. Attached brickyard, hydoelectric station. Grew rice, vegetables, fruit, tea.
10-38	Dongping Farm (Zhenghe LRD)	Dongping, Zhenghe Co.	Unknown	
10-39	Maiqiao Farm (Taining LRD)	Maiqiao, Taining Co.	Unknown	
10-40	Yongping Farm (Pucheng LRD)	Yongping, Pucheng Co.	Unknown	
10-41	Louqian Farm (Mingxi LRD)	Louqian, Mingxi Co.	Unknown	
10-42	Liangbu Farm (Jianyang LRD)	Liangbu, Jianyang Co.	800	
10-43	Mashan Farm (Longxi LRD)	Chengxixu, Longxi Co.	Unknown	
10-44	Provincial No. 1 JOD	Unknown	Unknown	
10-45	Provincial No. 2 JOD	Unknown	Unknown	

Provincial LRC established a "Minxing Supply & Sell Co." and joint-venture with out-provincial 12 LRC Enterprises and established a "Xinglian Trading Co." Both of them got the certificate for export business from the State Council.

Code No: LRC-11
LRC Distribution of Yunnan Province

11-59
Lijiang Naxi

Jianchuan
11-40   •   11-26 • Huizhe
             11-23   11-61
                          Dongchuan
                          11-27
                 11-24
               • Yuanmou
          11-57   11-41   11-10   11-60
        • Dali • Yao'an   11-62   Qujing
11-32   • Songming
11-33 •Baoshan   11-22   11-15
11-34   11-21 Chuxiong Kunming • Luliang
11-36 Changning   Anning
Yingjiang 11-52 Shidian 11-35   11-04
11-42 •   11-39   11-01
        11-38   11-37 Yunxian   11-48 Yuxi 11-03
11-43 11-44   11-53 11-17   11-49   11-06
Ruili •   11-25   11-56   11-07
11-02   11-08
                 Linchang   • Xinping 11-09
               11-31 11-54   11-13
                      11-55   11-64   11-20
        Shuangjiang   11-14   11-45
                                    • Kaiyuan   11-46
                  11-28   11-47
        Pu'er   11-63   Gejiu • Mengzhi   11-50
                           11-19 11-18

                    • Jinghong
            Menghai
            11-30 11-29   11-05

No.	Name of LRC	Location	Number	Remarks
11-01	Jinmasi Agricultural Equipment Factory (Provincial No. 1 Prison)	Jinmasi, Kunming C.	2,000	Produced sprayers for army.
11-02	Ruili Prison	Ruili C.	B	
11-03	Jinma Synthetical Processing Factory	Kunming C.	B	
11-04	Guangming Phosphatic Manure Factory (Provincial No. 3 Prison)	Anning Co.	B	
11-05	Mengla Prison	Mengla Co.	100	
11-06	Kunming Machinery Factory (Provincial No. 2 Prison)	Linjiayuan, suburbs of Kunming C.	2,000	
11-07	Kunming Jute Mill	Kunming C.	2,000	
11-08	Youxi Farm	Kunming C.	1,200	
11-09	Xiaoshiba Farm	E. of Kunming C.	D	Included machinery factory, auto-repairing factory, construction department.
11-10	Siying Coal Mine	Songming Co.	1,000	
11-11	Tongka Sanqi Pharmaceutical Factory	Unknown	Unknown	
11-12	Yangjie Farm	Unknown	Unknown	
11-13	Dapuji LRD	Kunming C.	5,000	
11-14	Xiaolongtan Coal Mine	Kaiyuan Co. [W]	4,000	Produced 20,000 ton coal/mo., exported to North Vietnam.
11-15	Luliang LRD	Luliang Co.	C	
11-16	Xiaguan LRD	Unknown	6,000	Dealt with construction.
11-17	Xinchengba Farm	N. of Yunxian Co.	26,000	Grew rice.
11-18	Chaoba Farm	50 km. n. of Mengzhi Co.	20,000	Manufactured agricultural equipment.
11-19	Gejiu RTL	Gejiu C.	B	
11-20	Dabanqiao Farm	E. suburbs of Kunming C.	3,000	
11-21	Huangliuba LRD	Chuxiong Co.	10,000	
11-22	Zaniuba Farm	15 km. e. of Chuxiong Co.	6,000	
11-23	Dayingnong LRD	10 km. n. of Jianchuan Co.	10,000	Exploited aluminium-tin mine.
11-24	Xinming Farm	Yuanmou Co.	1,000	
11-25	Panhe Farm	15 km. s. of Yunxian Co.	3,000	Grew rice.
11-26	Huizhe Farm (Post Box: Hiuizhe No. 201)	Huizhe Co.	900[W]	Grew rice, fruit, and vegetables; food processing factory.
11-27	Wulong Coal Mine (Post Box: Dongchuan No. 403)	17 km. s. of Dongchuan C.	3,000	Attached machinery factory.
11-28	Simao LRD	Pu'er Co.	C	
11-29	Cheli Farm	Manshai, Hongjing Co.	3,500	Four branch farms. Farming and planting rubber trees.
11-30	Provincial No. 41 LRD (Liming Farm)	Menghai Co.	D	
11-31	Mengku Farm	Mengku T., Shuangjiang Co.	5,100[W]	Four branch battalions. Grew rice, tea, coffee, and sugarcane. Attached sugar factory, brewhouse, brickyard.

11-32 "Wujiu" Mercury Factory (FJP+LRD)	S. of Puluo D., Baoshan Co.	200	Exploited mercury mine and processing. Products transported to Kunming C. by truck.
11-33 Weihongzhou Farm	Baoshan Co.	C	
11-34 Baoshan Machinery Factory (LRD+FJP)	Baoshan Co.	500	Produced auto parts, steel parts, diesel engine, tractor.
11-35 Xinguang Farm (Provincial No. 2 LR Battalion)	Changning Co.	1,200	Planted industrial crops, in addition to stock raising. Included sugar factory, paper factory, wood-processing factory, brewhouse, brickyard. Output value 600,000 yuan/yr.
11-36 No. 7 Construction Battalion (Baoshan LRD)	Minqiang street, Baoshan Co.	1,000	
11-37 Puluo Lead Factory	Changning Co.	B	
11-38 Shidian Lead Factory	Shidian Co.	10,000	
11-39 Anning RTL	Anning Co.	C	
11-40 Lashiba LRD	Lashiba, Bijiang Co.	1,200[W]	Dealt with farming, stock raising, exploiting stone material, machinery processing.
11-41 Chaohai Farm	Yao'an Co.	C	
11-42 Xiaopingyuan LRD	Xiaopingyuan, Yingjiang Co.	Unknown	
11-43 Nongguan Farm	Longchuan Co.	C	
11-44 Wandian Farm	Dianba, Shidian Co.	1,600	Farming. Included five factories: sugar factory, oil-extracting factory, agricultural tool factory, machinery factory, electric plant.
11-45 Xishan RTL	Xishan, Kunming C.	200	
11-46 Xishan Stone Mining Works	Xishan, Kunming C.	2,000	
11-47 Hongxing Farm (Guangming Farm)	Changpo, w. suburbs of Kunming C.	Unknown	
11-48 Anning Bajie Farm	Bajie, Anning Co.	A	
11-49 Anning JOD	Anning Co.	200	
11-50 Kunming Machinery Farm	Kunming C.	800	
11-51 Simao Farm	Simao Pr.	11,000[W]	Area: 80 sq. km. Included nine battalions. Dealt with farming, pottery and porcelain making, agricultural tools, and wood processing.
11-52 Baoshan Food Processing Factory	Wandian, Baoshan C.	600	

11-53 Changning Farm	Wandingba, Changning Co.	8,000	Included nine battalions and farm-products–processing factory, steel-smelting factory.
11-54 Mianning Farm	E. of Linchang Co.	3,000	Constructed building. Attached auto-repairing factory, brickyard, wood- and machinery-processing factory.
11-55 Maqunti Farm	Xujiapu, n. of Linchang Co.	3,000	Farming
11-56 Huaning Farm	Yuxi Co.	1,500	
11-57 Baiyan Lead Factory	Dali Bai Aut. D.	1,000	
11-58 Mojiang RTL	Unknown	Unknown	
11-59 Dayan Farm	Dayan T. Lijiang Naxi Aut. Co.	1,000	
11-60 Fuyuan Iron Factory	Qujing Co.	600	
11-61 Huizhe Lead Mine	Huizhe Co.	1,000	
11-62 Jializhe Farm	Songming Co.	1,000	
11-63 Puwen Farm (LRD+FJP)	S. of Puwen Co.	9,000	Grew rice, coarse grain, sugarcane, tea, coffee, and rubber trees. Now plants sugarcane, mainly to supply Puwen sugar factory. There are a sugar factory, coal mine, and hydroelectric station.
11-64 Mosi Subropics Zone Gardening Farm (No. 3 RTL)	Mosi D. in Xinping Co.	Unknown	
11-65 Niujing Farm	N. of Baochuan Co.	10,000	Four branch farms. Farming and manufacture of agricultural tools.
11-66 Menghua Iron Factory	Menghua Co.	30,000	Exploited iron mine.

Code No: LRC-12 (portion)
LRC Distribution of Gansu Province
Code No: LRC-14
LRC Distribution of Ningxia Aut. Region

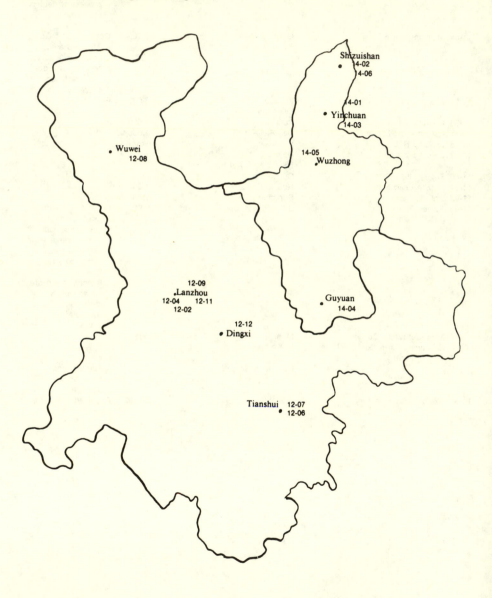

Shizuishan
14-02
14-06

14-01
Yinchuan
14-03

14-05
Wuzhong

Wuwei
12-08

12-09
Lanzhou
12-04   12-11
12-02

12-12
Dingxi

Guyuan
14-04

Tianshui   12-07
12-06

12. Gansu Province (LRC-12) Collected Number: 12

No.	Name of LRC	Location	Number	Remarks
12-01	Jiuquan Farm	Jiuquan C.	D	
12-02	Provincial RTL	Lanzhou C.	C	
12-03	Provincial No. 7 LRD (Farm)	Unknown	Unknown	
12-04	Santan Farm	Lanzhou C.	B	
12-05	Wudaping Farm	Unknown	Unknown	
12-06	Tianshui RTL	Tianshui C.	A	
12-07	Tianshui LRD	Tianshui C.	C	
12-08	Wuwei LRD	Wuwei C.	D	
12-09	Provincial No. 1 Prison (Lanzhou Valve Factory)	Lanzhou C.	B	
12-10	Yumen Prison	Yumen C.	A	
12-11	Provincial No. 2 LRD (Lanzhou Truck Plant)	Lanzhou C.	Unknown	
12-12	Dingxi Crane Factory	Dingxi C.	Unknown	

14. Ningxia Hui Autonomous Region (LRC-14) Collected Number: 7

No.	Name of LRC	Location	Number	Remarks
14-01	Provincial No. 1 Prison	Yinchuan C.	1,000	Produced fans, clothes, shoes. Reaped profits 800,000 yuan/1986.
14-02	Shizuishan C. RTL	Shizuishan C.	Unknown	
14-03	Xincheng RTL	Yinchuan C.	B	
14-04	Guyuan Prison	Guyuan Co.	A	
14-05	Wuzhong Farm	Wuzhong Co.	1,000	
14-06	Ningxia No. 1 RTL	Shizuishan C.	Unknown	Produced TV parts.
14-07	Hui'an Farm	Unknown	Unknown	

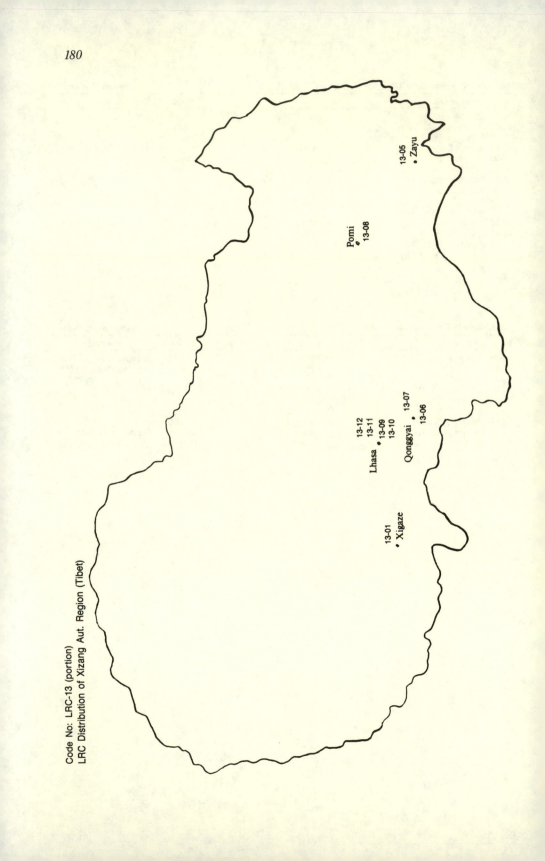

180

Code No: LRC-13 (portion)
LRC Distribution of Xizang Aut. Region (Tibet)

Zayu
13-05

Pomi
13-08

13-07
Qonggyai
13-06

13-12
13-11
13-09
Lhasa
13-10

13-01
Xigaze

13. Xizang Autonomous Region (Tibet) (LRC-13)

Collected Number: 12

No.	Name of LRC	Location	Number	Remarks
13-01	Xigaze Prison	Xigaze C.	100	
13-02	Engeli Prison	Unknown	Unknown	
13-03	Gaergang Prison	Unknown	Unknown	
13-04	Geermu Farm	Gar Co.	Unknown	
13-05	Zayu Farm	Zayu Co.	Unknown	
13-06	Qonggyai Farm	Qonggyai Co.	Unknown	
13-07	Zetang Prison	Zetang Co.	A	
13-08	Yigong Farm	Pomi Co.	Unknown	
13-09	Fuduolang Farm	Lhasa C.	A	
13-10	Garza Prison	4 km. e. of Lhasa C.	400[W]	
13-11	Shengyebo Prison	8 km. n.e. of Lhasa C.	2,000	
13-12	Penglapuzi Prison	12 km. n.e. of Lhasa C.	700	

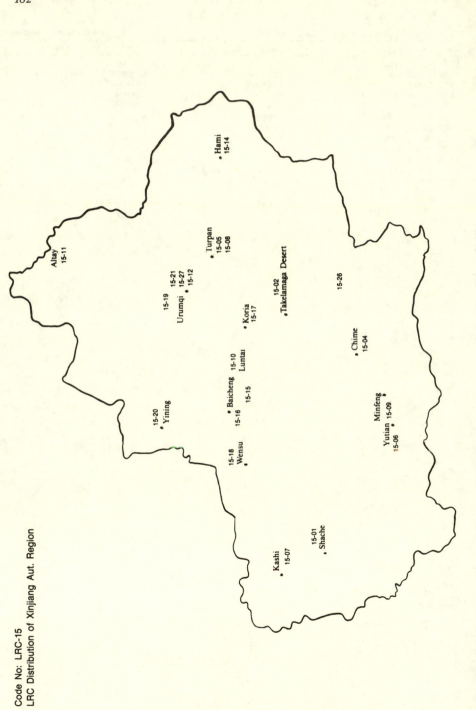

Code No: LRC-15
LRC Distribution of Xinjiang Aut. Region

15. Xinjiang Uygur Autonomous Region (LRC-15)   **Collected Number: 29**

No.	Name of LRC	Location	Number	Remarks
15-01	Shache LRD	Shache Co.	B	
15-02	Pailou Farm	Takelamaga desert	Unknown	
15-03	No. 3 LRD of Xingjiang P & C M.C., N. 8th Division	Unknown	B	
15-04	G. 2nd Division of Xingjiang P & C M.C.	Chime Co.	D	
15-05	G. 1st Division of Xingjiang P & C M.C.	Turpan Co.	D	
15-06	Yutian LRD	Yutian Co.	D	
15-07	Kashiker LRD	Kashi Co.	D	
15-08	Turpan LRD	Turpan Co.	D	
15-09	Nanjiang LRD	Minfeng Co.	1,000	
15-10	Luntai LRD	Luntai Co.	50,000	
15-11	Altay Gold Mine	Altay C.	25,000	
15-12	Urumqi Construction Brigade	Urumqi C.	3,400	
15-13	Puli Uranium Mine	Unknown	1,000	
15-14	Hami LRD	Hami Co.	D	
15-15	Kuqa LRD	Kuqa Co.	10,000	
15-16	Baicheng LRD	Baicheng Co.	11,000	
15-17	Koria LRD	Koria Co.	22,000	
15-18	Wensu LRD	Wensu Co.	23,000	
15-19	Shawan LRD	Shanwan Co.	D	
15-20	Yining prison	Yining C.	Unknown	
15-21	Xinjiang No. 3 Machine Tool factory (No. 3 Prison)	Urumqi C.	2,000	Built the stage equipment of the Xingjiang People's Hall.
15-22	Talimu LRD	Unknown	Unknown	
15-23	No. 1 LRD of N. 8th Division, Xingjiang P & C M.C.	Unknown	Unknown	
15-24	LRD of N. 10th Division, Xingjiang P & C M.C.	Unknown	Unknown	
15-25	LRD of N. 3rd Division, Xingjiang P & C M.C.	Unknown	Unknown	
15-26	Kalakale Farm	Takelamagan desert	Unknown	
15-27	Xinjiang No. 1 Prison	Urumqi C.	Unknown	
15-28	Xiabahu Farm	Unknown	Unknown	
15-29	Kueitunhong Coal Mine	Kueitun C.	Unknown	Produced coal.

Xingjiang P & C M.C.—Xingjiang Production and Construction Military Corp.
N. 3rd division—The No. 3 Agricultural Division
G. 2nd division—The No. 2 Industrial Division

184

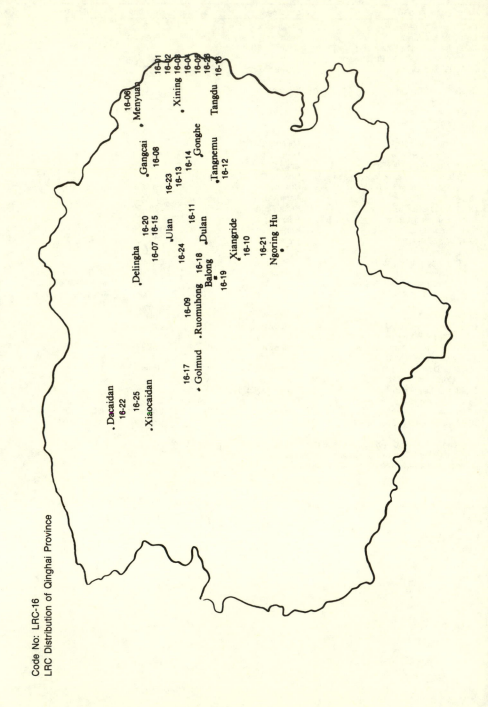

Code No: LRC-16
LRC Distribution of Qinghai Province

16. Qinghai Province (LRC-16)   **Collected Number: 25**

No.	Name of LRC	Location	Number	Remarks
16-01	Qinghai RTL	Xining C.	C	
16-02	Qinghu Machine Tool Factory (Prov. No. 1 LRD)	Xining C.	B	Hand tools and lathe.
16-03	Qinghai Hide & Garment Works (with Qing-gong Foam Plastic Works and Qinghai Auto Repair Works makes up Prov. No. 2 LRD)	Xining C.	B	Exported furs and leather, $5.2 million/ 1991, $3.5 million/ 1990.
16-04	Qinghai Leather Factory (Prov. No. 3 LRD)	Xining C.	B	
16-04	Qinghai Brick Factory (Prov. No. 4 LRD)	Xining C.	C	
16-05	Qinghai Electric Equipment Plant (Prov. No. 5 LRD)	Xining C.	C	
16-06	Haomen Farm (No. 305 Farm)	15 km. n. suburbs of Menyuan Co.	35,000	Area: 30 sq. km.
16-07	Delingha Farm	E. of Ulan	100,000	Included 15 sections Delingha Steel-iron enterprise, Xiuduowang Coal Mine Co., Qinghai Fishing Co., including 6,000 ha. cultivated land, livestock, wheat, potatoes, vegetables.
16-08	Gangcai Farm (No. 105 Farm)	9 km. s.w. of Gangcai Co.	80,000	Planted rape, wheat.
16-09	Ruomuhong Farm	200 km. w. of Dulan Co.	100,000	Wheat, livestock, bricks.
16-10	Xiangride Farm	10 km. w. of Xiangride T.	100,000	Wheat, livestock, bricks.
16-11	Sishika Farm	Dulan Co.	60,000	Wheat, livestock.
16-12	Tangnemu Farm	120 km. w. of Gonghe Co.	20,000	Included 5 sections.
16-13	Wayuxiangka Farm	200 km. w. of Gonghe Co.	20,000	
16-14	Chachaxiangka Farm	160 km. w. of Gonghe Co.	15,000	
16-15	Bachuang Farm	Ulan Co.	Unknown	
16-16	Gangdu Farm (Prov. No. 1 Prison)	Xunhua Co.	Unknown	
16-17	Ge'ermu Farm	10 km. w. of Ge'ermu C.	Unknown	
16-18	Xiariha Farm	Xiariha T. Dulan Co.	Unknown	
16-19	Balong Farm	Balong T. 40 km.	Unknown	
16-20	Lingbu Farm	S. bank of Bayin River	Unknown	
16-21	Elunhu Farm	N. of Elun lake, s.e. of Xiangride T.	Unknown	
16-22	Dacaidan Farm	N. suburbs of Dacaidan C.	Unknown	
16-23	Caika Farm	N. of Caika lake, Ulan Co.	Unknown	
16-24	Xiligou Farm	Xiliguo T. s. of Ulan Co.	Unknown	
16-25	Xiaocaidan	Xiaocaidan T.	Unknown	

Code No: LRC-17
LRC Distribution of Shaanxi Province

17-09
. Yulin

17-05
Yan'an • Yanchang
17-10

. Huangling
17-16

17-12
Tongchuan

17-11

17-04   • Huayin
• Baoji   • Xianyang
17-03   17-13   17-06
             . Weinan
            . Xi'an   17-07
            17-08

17-15
• Hanzhong   17-01
17-02   . Xixiang

17. Shaanxi Province (LRC-17)   **Collected Number: 18**

No.	Name of LRC	Location	Number	Remarks
17-01	Hankou LRD	Xixiang Co.	D	
17-02	Hanzhong RTL	Hanzhong C.	A	
17-03	Baoji Construction Brigade	Baoji C.	3,000	
17-04	Baoji RTL	Baoji C.	1,500	
17-05	Yanchang LRD	Yanchang Co.	Unknown	
17-06	Huayin LRD	Huayin Co.	10,000	
17-07	Weinan prison	Weinan	Unknown	
17-08	Provincial No. 1 Prison	Xi'an C.	B	
17-09	Yulin LRD	Yilin Co.	C	
17-10	Yan'an LRD	Yan'an C.	B	
17-11	Tongchuan Copper Mine	Tongchuan C.	5,000	
17-12	Tongchuan RTL	Tongchuan C.	B	
17-13	Xianyang RTL	Xianyang C.	A	
17-14	Shaanxi Boiler Factory (Provincial No. 2 Prison)	Unknown	Unknown	Produced industrial boilers.
17-15	Provincial No. 3 Prison	Hanzhong C.	Unknown	
17-16	Provincial No. 9 LRD (Shangzhenzi Farm)	Huangling Co.	Unknown	
17-17	Luyang RTL	Unknown	Unknown[W]	
17-18	Provincial No. 1 LRD	Unknown	Unknown	

188

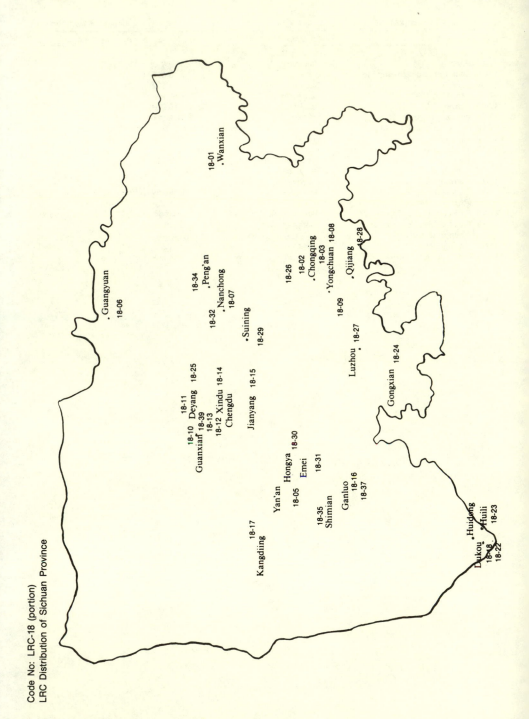

Code No: LRC-18 (portion)
LRC Distribution of Sichuan Province

. Guangyuan
18-06

18-01
. Wanxian

18-34
. Peng'an
18-32 . Nanchong
18-07

. Suining
18-29

18-26
18-02
. Chongqing
18-03
. Yongchuan 18-08
18-09 . Qijiang
18-28

Luzhou
. 18-27

Gongxian 18-24

18-11
18-25
18-10 Deyang
18-39
Guanxian 18-13
18-12 Xindu 18-14
Chengdu

Jianyang 18-15

Yan'an
18-05

Hongya 18-30
. Emei 18-31

18-35 Ganluo
Shimian 18-16
18-37

Kangdiing 18-17

Dukou . Huideng
18-18 . Huili
18-22 18-23

18. Sichuan Province (LRC-18)   Collected Number: 42

No.	Name of LRC	Location	Number	Remarks
18-01	Wanxian Farm	Wanxian Co.	D	
18-02	Geleshan LRD	Chongqing C.	C	
18-03	Huangshan RTL	Chongqing C.	B	
18-04	Garze LRD	Garze Co.	D	
18-05	Ya'an LRD	Yan'an Co.	10,000	
18-06	Rongshan Mine	Guangyuan Co.	11,000	
18-07	Nanchong RTL	Nanchong C.	B	
18-08	Xinsheng Tea Farm	Yongchuan Co.	5,500	
18-09	Sanwu LRD	Yongchuan Co.	D	
18-10	Guanxian Construction Brigade	Guanxian Co.	3,000	
18-11	Deyang Brickyard	Deyang Co.	5,100	
18-12	Shengli Fire-fighting Equipment Factory	Chengdu C.	1,600	
18-13	Chengdu Machinery Factory	Chengdu C.	5,000	
18-14	Xindu LRD	Xindu Co.	C	
18-15	Pingquan Stock Farm	Jianyang Co.	D	
18-16	Shaping Farm	Ebian Co.	Unknown	
18-17	Kangding RTL	Kangding C.	A	
18-18	Dukou RTL	Dukou C.	B	
18-19	Dayan RTL	Unknown	Unknown	Attached a brickyard.
18-20	Dalu LRD	Unknown	Unknown	
18-21	Leimaping LRD	Unknown	Unknown	
18-22	Huili Copper Mine	Huili Co.	D	
18-23	Huidong Aluminium-zinc Mine	Huidong Co.	D	
18-24	Furong Mine	Gongxian Co.	D	
18-25	Deyang Machinery Factory	Deyang Co.	B	
18-26	Xinsheng Gardening Farm	Chongqing C.	A	
18-27	Luzhou LRD	Luzhou C.	B	
18-28	Qijiang LRD	Qijiang C.	C	
18-29	Suining LRD	Suining Co.	A	
18-30	Hongya LRD	Hongya	B	
18-31	Emei LRD	Emei Co.	D	
18-32	Nanchong LRD	Nanchong C.	5,800	
18-33	Shuokezhong Farm	Unknown	Unknown	
18-34	Peng'an 9-1 Factory (Peng'an prison) (Jingping LRD)	Peng'an Co.	2,000	Established in 1970 and began on weaving production. Produced valves in 1973 and produced automobile parts; EQ-14 speed reducer shell, CA10 B-back bridge shell, EQ-140 front wheel shell, EQ-140 rear wheel shell; output value 5,863,000 yuan and profits 367,000 yuan/1987.
18-35	Xinkang Asbestos Factory	Shimian Co.	15,000	Biggest asbestos factory in China.
18-36	Yanyuan Gold Mine	Unknown	Unknown	
18-37	Ganluo Farm	Ganluo Co.	Unknown	
18-38	Yongchuan LR General Brigade	Unknown	D	Included at least six battalions.
18-39	Chengdu JOD	Chengdu C.	A	
18-40	Provincial No. 2 Prison	Unknown	Unknown	
18-41	Rongshan LR General Brigade	Unknown	Unknown	
18-42	Provincial No. 2 Prison	Unknown	Unknown	

190

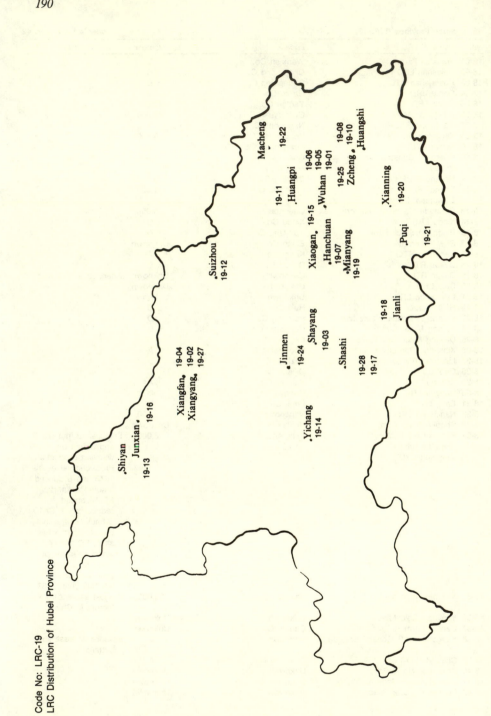

Code No: LRC-19
LRC Distribution of Hubei Province

19. Hubei Province (LRC-19)   Collected Number: 29

No.	Name of LRC	Location	Number	Remarks
19-01	Hewan Branch of Wuhan RTL	Wuhan C.	Unknown	
19-02	Xiangyang Farm	Xiangyang Co.	D	
19-03	Shayang Farm	Shayang T. Jinmen Co.	D	Established in 1952. It is a large farm in agriculture and industry. It included Xinsheng brickyard, stock raising farm, Maliang cement and stone material plant (which produced 88,000 ton cement yearly), Jianghan milk cow company, dairy works, gunnysack works, chemical fiber factory, dyeing and weaving factory, spinning and weaving equipment factory, and auto repairing factory. Exported pigs, fruit, tea, chickens, and milk cows. The industrial output value will be 256 million yuan in 1991.
19-04	Xiangfan RTL	Xiangfan C.	A	
19-05	Wuhan JOD	Xiaoqingshan, Wuhan C.	2,000	
19-06	Provincial No. 2 Prison	Wuhan C.	B	
19-07	Makou Farm	Hanchuan Co.	D	
19-08	Echeng LRD	Echeng Co.	Unknown	
19-09	Jiangbei Farm	Unknown	D	Included 4 branches at least.
19-10	Huangshi RTL	Huangshi C.	Unknown	
19-11	Huangpi Farm	Huangpi Co.	Unknown	
19-12	Liulin Farm	Shuixian Co.	Unknown	
19-13	Shiyan RTL	Shiyan C.	B	
19-14	Yichang RTL	Yichang C.	B	
19-15	X X LRD	Xiaogan Co.	D	
19-16	Danjiang construction brigade	Yunxian Co.	D	
19-17	Shashi Prison	Shashi C.	A	
19-18	Jianli Farm	Jianli Co.	D	
19-19	Mianyang LRD	Mianyang Co.	D	
19-20	Xianning Prison	Xianning C.	Unknown	
19-21	Puqi LRD	Puqi Co.	Unknown	
19-22	Provincial No. 1 LRD	Macheng Co.	5,000	Produced bricks, plastic products, and machinery.
19-23	Xiangbei Farm	Xiangyang Co.	D	Included seven branch farms. Included Xinsheng glass factory, Xinsheng plastic factory, fire-fighting equipment factory, and cement factory, which produced 50,000 ton cement. Total profits 1.3 million yuan/yr.
19-24	Zhangwanhu Farm	Shayang T. Jinmen Co.	Unknown	
19-25	Wuhan Silk Factory (Provincial No. 1 Prison)	Wuhan C.	3,000	
19-26	Exi Prison	Unknown	Unknown	
19-27	Xiangyang Machine Tool Factory	Xiangyang C.	A	
19-28	Jinzhou Prison (Xinsheng Dyeing and Weaving Factory, Provincial No. 3 prison)	East Gate of Jinzhou C.	5,000	The industrial output value was 62.23 million yuan, profits 7.15 million yuan, and 8.49 million US dollars during 1986–1988. Included 3 branch factories that produced textiles, auto parts.
19-29	No. 5 Independent Battalion of Provincial No. LR general brigade	Unknown	Unknown	Produced cotton clothes.

Code No: LRC-20
LRC Distribution of Zhejiang Province

20. Zhejiang Province (LRC-20) **Collected Number: 26**

No.	Name of LRC	Location	Number	Remarks
20-01	Shilifeng Farm	Quxian Co.	D	
20-02	Tangxi LRC	Hangzhou C.	B	
20-03	Provincial No. 1 Prison	Yuhang Co.	B	
20-04	Chaoshi Farm	Hangzhou C.	C	
20-05	Jianqiao Farm	Jianqiao, Hangzhou C.	B	
20-06	Ningbo LRD	Yinxian Co.	A	
20-07	Ningbo RTL	Ningbo C.	B	
20-08	Jiangtang Farm	Jinhua C.	D	
20-09	Xuelinshan LRD	Fenghua Co.	B	
20-10	Yinxian LRD	Yinxian Co.	B	
20-11	Wenzhou Construction Brigade	Oujiang hydropower station in Wenzhou C.	D	
20-12	Weiping Iron Mine	Chun'an Co.	D	
20-13	Sanjia LRD	Huangyan Co.	D	
20-14	Nanhu Tree Farm	Changxing Co. Huzhou C.	C	
20-15	Wenzhou Farm	Wenzhou C.	C	
20-16	Anji Farm	Anji Co.	C	
20-17	Jinhua Farm	Jinhua C.	D	
20-18	Changxing Farm	Changxing Co.	D	
20-19	Provincial No. 4 Prison	Unknown	Unknown	
20-20	Hangzhou No. 2 RTL	Unknown	Unknown	
20-21	Qiaosi LRD	Unknown	Unknown	
20-22	Hangzhou No. 1 LRD	Unknown	Unknown	
20-23	Hangzhou No. 2 LRD	Unknown	Unknown	
20-24	Shaoxing RTL	Shaoxing C.	Unknown	
20-25	Wulin Machinery Factory in Hangzhou	Hangzhou C.	Unknown	The second-class enterprise of China.
20-26	Wuyi Machinery Factory	Unknown	Unknown	The second-class enterprise of China.

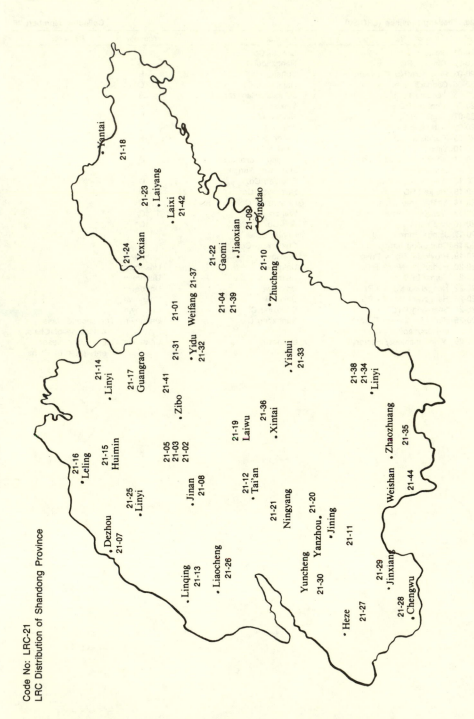

Code No: LRC-21
LRC Distribution of Shandong Province

21. Shandong Province (LRC-21) Collected Number: **44**

No.	Name of LRC	Location	Number	Remarks
21-01	Weibei LRD	Weifang C.	C[W]	Established in 1952; area 4,800 ha. Total output value 13.85 million yuan/1987. Produced paper, silicon-carbon bar, machinery, food cans.
21-02	Provincial No. 1 Prison	Jinan C.	B	
21-03	Jinan No. 8 LRD	Jinan C.	B	
21-04	Zaozhuang RTL	Zaozhuang C.	A	
21-05	Shandong Shengjian Motorcycle Engine Factory	Dangjiazhuang in Jinan C.	3,000	Produced 10,000 Shandong-750 motorcycle/yr.
21-06	Jinan RTL	Jinan C.	Unknown	
21-07	Huanghe Farm	Dezhou C.	Unknown	
21-08	Shandong No. 17 LRD	Jinan C.	A	
21-09	Licun Prison	Qingdao C.	3,000	
21-10	Jiaoxian Farm	Jiaoxian Co.	Unknown	
21-11	Jining RTL	Jining C.	B	
21-12	Tai'an LRD	Tai'an C.	Unknown	
21-13	Linqing LRD	Linqing Co.	B	
21-14	Lijin Farm	Lijin Co.	D	
21-15	Huimin Farm	Huimin Co.	D	
21-16	Leling Farm	Leling Co.	D	
21-17	Beisi Farm	Guangrao Co.	D	
21-18	Qingdao RTL	Qingdao C.	B	
21-19	Laiwu LRD	Laiwu Co.	D	
21-20	Yanzhou Farm	Yanzhou Co.	B	
21-21	Ningyang LRD	Ningyang Co.	B	
21-22	Gaomi LRD	Gaomi Co.	D	
21-23	Laiyang LRD	Yantai C.	3,000	Established in 1984; produced machinery products—two kinds of products exported to West Europe, USA, Southeast Asia. During recent five years, the output value, profit, foreign exchange of export value has been increased by 28.5%, 48.3%, 43%, respectively, every year.
21-24	Yexian LRD	Yexian Co.	D	
21-25	Linyi Farm	Linyi Co.	D	
21-26	Liaocheng LRD	Liaocheng Co.	D	
21-27	Hezhe RTL	Hezhe Co.	B	
21-28	Chengwu Farm	Chengwu Co.	C	
21-29	Jinxiang LRD	Jinxiang Co.	C	
21-30	Yuncheng LRD	Yuncheng Co.	D	

21-31	Shandon No. 1 RTL (Shengjian Basan Factory)	Wangcun Zibo C.	3,371 in 1988	Established in 1958; area 1.06 million sq. m. Produced nitrogen-silicon brick, electrode, machinery, electronic component (supply 75,000 pieces to defense production). The second-class national enterprises.
21-32	Yidu LRD	Yidu Co.	Unknown	
21-33	Yishui LRD	Yishui Co.	Unknown	
21-34	Linyi RTL	Linyi Co.	Unknown	
21-35	Zhaozhuang RTL (mine)	Zhaozhuang C.	C	
21-36	Xintai LRD	Xintai Co.	Unknown	
21-37	Weifang LRD	Weifang C.	5,000	Total output value 30.45 million yuan/ 1986. Produced shaping machine (BC6060), compressor (3L-10/ 8), turbo-generator (QF-3-2), carbon electrode, steel pipe, lathe (DM5440).
21-38	Linyi LRD	Linyi Co.	Unknown	
21-39	Shengjian Machinery Factory (Provincial No. 3 Prison, possibly 21-37 is same one)	W. of Weifang C.	Unknown	Area: 380,000 sq. m. Produced air compressors, chemical fertilizer equipment, spinning and weaving machines, drilling equipment. Some for export. The second class of national enterprise.
21-40	Shandong Liuyi LRD	Unknown	Unknown	The machinery-repair company, produced wood screws, repaired machinery, casting and welding. During Jan. to June in 1988, the profits were 40,000 yuan.
21-41	Qiwu Coal Mine	Zibo C.	Unknown	The Coal Ministry invested 38 million yuan to extend; became a middle-size mine, which produced 600,000 ton coal/yr.

21-42	Beiji Shengjian Graphite Plant	Laixi Co.	8,000	The second class of national enterprise. Produced graphite (14,000 ton/1988), graphite products; total output value 31.62 million yuan; foreign exchange income $4.5 million yuan/1988.
21-43	Provincial JOD	Unknown	Unknown	Sewing and handicraft art
21-44	Daizhuang LRD	Huancheng T.	3,000	Established in 1984. Produced 70,000 ton coal in 1984, 320,000 ton coal in 1989; profits were 8,000,000 yuan.

The CCP's document said there are 30 prisons or LRD, 7 RTL, and 1 JOD of provincial and city level in Shangdong Province (does not include county level).

Code No: LRC-22
LRC Distribution of Anhui Province

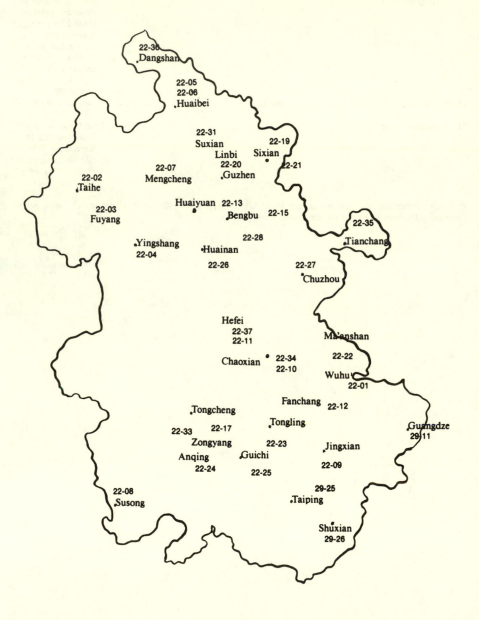

22-36
.Dangshan

22-05
22-06
.Huaibei

22-31
Suxian
Linbi
22-20
.Guzhen

22-19

22-21

Sixian

22-07
Mengcheng

22-02
.Taihe

Huaiyuan
.Bengbu

22-13
22-15

22-03
Fuyang

22-35
.Tianchang

.Yingshang
22-04

.Huainan
22-26

22-28

22-27
.Chuzhou

Hefei
22-37
22-11

Ma'anshan

Chaoxian

22-34
22-10

22-22

Wuhu
22-01

Fanchang

22-12

.Tongcheng

.Tongling

22-33
Zongyang
.Anqing
22-24

22-17

22-23
.Guichi
22-25

Jingxian
22-09

Guangdze
29-11

22-08
.Susong

29-25
.Taiping

Shuxian
29-26

22. Anhui Province (LRC-22)   Collected Number: 37

No.	Name of LRC	Location	Number	Remarks
22-01	Wuhu Prison	Wuhu C.	2,000	
22-02	Taihe LRD	Taihe Co.	D	
22-03	Fuyang Nanfangji LRD	Fuyang Co.	D	
22-04	Yingshang construction brigade	Yingshang Co.	D	
22-05	Huaibei LRD (coal mine)	Huaibei C.	D	
22-06	Huaibei RTL	Huaibei C.	C	
22-07	Xinsheng Farm	Mengcheng Co.	C	
22-08	Susong Farm	Susong Co.	C	
22-09	Chengcun Construction General Brigade	Jingxian Co.	A	
22-10	Chaohu Automobile Factory	Chaoxian Co.	Unknown	
22-11	Hefei Water Conservancy Construction Brigade	Hefei C.	D	
22-12	Sanshan Coal Mine	Fanchang Co.	D	
22-13	Xinanhuai Coal Mine	Huaiyuan Co.	C	
22-14	Provincial No. 2 Prison	Unknown	Unknown	
22-15	Bengbu Rubber plant	Bengbu C.	4,000	
22-16	Provincial No. 1 LRD	Unknown	Unknown	
22-17	Pujiwei Farm (RTL+LRD)	Longshan T. Zongyang Co.	20,000	
22-18	Danshan LRD	Unknown	Unknown	
22-19	Linbi LRD	Linbi Co.	Unknown	
22-20	Guzhen Construction Detachment	Guzhen Co.	Unknown	
22-21	Sixian Farm	Sixian Co.	D	
22-22	Ma'anshan RTL	Ma'anshan C.	B	
22-23	Tongling LRD	Tongling C.	Unknown	
22-24	Anqing RTL	Anqing C.	B	
22-25	Guichi LRD	Guichi Co.	D	
22-26	Huainan LRD (coal mine)	Huainan C.	D	
22-27	Chuxian LRD	Chuzhou Co.	D	
22-28	Conservancy Construction General Brigade in Harnessing Huaihe River	General Ministry in Bengbu C.	D	Included 6 Detachments. Amount of members is as high as 200,000. Taking part in harnessing Huaihe river project: Fuziling reservoir, Meishan reservoir, Xiangshuikou reservoir, Hualiangting reservoir, Chuxian reservoir, Dingyuan reservoir, Fengyang reservoir.
22-29	Provincial No. 3 LRD	Unknown	Unknown	
22-30	Provincial No. 6 LRD	Unknown	Unknown	
22-31	No. 1 LR Independent Detachment	Suxian Co.	Unknown	
22-32	Provincial No. 2 LRD	Unknown	Unknown	
22-33	Baihu Farm	Tongcheng Co.	D	General output value of industry and agriculture was 40,210,000 yuan/ 1985.
22-34	Chaohu Farm	Chaoxian Co.	D	Farming and breeding fish.
22-35	Tianchang Farm	Tianchang Co.	A	
22-36	Dangshan Orchard Farm	Dangshan Co.	D	
22-37	Jianghuai Automobile Factory	Hefei C.	A	

Code No: LRC-23
LRC Distribution of Jiangsu Province
Code No: LRC-29
LRC Distribution of Shanghai

23. Jiangsu Province (LRC-23)

No.	Name of LRC	Location	Number	Remarks
23-01	Provincial No. 1 Prison	Nanjing C.	1,000[W]	Female inmates produced knitting gloves; male inmates produced machine tools, high quality, exported to Hong Kong.
23-02	Gaoyou Farm	Gaoyou Co.	D	
23-03	Nanyang Farm	Yancheng Co.	D	
23-04	Dalianshan RTL	Unknown	Unknown	
23-05	Sheyang LRD	Sheyang Co.	D	
23-06	Nantong Farm	Nantong Co.	D	
23-07	Dongtai RTL	Dongtai Co.	A	
23-08	Qidong LRD	Qidong Co.	D	
23-09	Suzhou Prison	Suzhou C.	Unknown	
23-10	Provincial No. 2 Prison	Unknown	Unknown	
23-11	Liuhe LRD	Liuhe Co.	D	
23-12	Judong RTL	Jurong Co.	Unknown [W]	Attached embroidery shop, portion of products exported.
23-13	Shuyang Prison	Shuyang Co.	A	
23-14	Danyang LRD	Danyang Co.	D	
23-15	Wujin LRD	Wujin Co.	C	
23-16	Wuxi RTL	Wuxi C.	A	
23-17	Yixing LRD	Yixing C.	Unknown	
23-18	Liyang LRD	Liyang Co.	C	
23-19	Yangzhou Prison	Yangzhou C.	B	
23-20	Jinling Machinery Factory (Provincial No. 1 LRD)	Unknown	Unknown	
23-21	Lianyungang RTL	Lianyungang C.	Unknown	
23-22	Xuzhou RTL	Xuzhou C.	Unknown	
23-23	Qingjiang LRD	Qingjiang C.	Unknown	
23-24	Taizhou Farm	Taizhou C.	D	
23-25	Provincial No. 22 LRD	Unknown	Unknown	
23-26	Hongzhe Farm	Huaiyin Co.	D	
23-27	Provincial No. 3 Prison	Suzhou C.	D	
23-28	Provincial No. 2 LRD	Unknown	Unknown	Included farm, sewing factory, and casting plant.
23-29	Provincial No. 4 Prison	Unknown	Unknown	
23-30	Provincial No. 6 LRD	Unknown	C	
23-31	Provincial No. 13 Prison	Wuxi C.	5,000	
23-32	Zhuze Coal Mine	Unknown	5,000	
23-33	Provincial No. 9 LRD	Unknown	Unknown	Included cement plant. General output value 18 million yuan; profits 5.2 million yuan in 1984.
23-34	Taihu RTL	Unknown	Unknown	Exploited stone.
23-35	Provincial No. 19 LRD	Yancheng Co.	Unknown	
23-36	Sihong Farm	Unknown	Unknown	
23-37	Dazhong Farm	Unknown	Unknown	
23-38	Xuzhou Forging Machine Tool Factory	Xuzhou C.	Unknown	The second class of national enterprise.

29. Shanghai Municipality (LRC-29)

No.	Name of LRC	Location	Number	Remarks
29-01	Laodong Glassworks (FJP)	Nanhui Co.	1,200	
29-02	Jiangwan Prison	Jiangwan D.	Unknown	
29-03	Huishan Prison	Nanhui Co.	2,000	
29-04	Dachang Prison	Dachang T.	2,000	
29-05	Tilanqiao prison (Shanghai printing factory, Shanghai stationery factory)	Tilanqiao D.	B	Produced teaching aids.
29-06	Pudong Prison	Pudong D.	2,200	
29-07	Huadong Electric Welder Plant (FJP)	Shanghai C.	2,000	Output value was 32.24 million yuan and profits 14.56 million yuan during January to November 1985.
29-08	Huadong Farm	Hejin D., Shanghai C.	Unknown	
29-09	Shanghai No. 3 RTL	Shanghai C.	Unknown	
29-10	Chongming Farm	Chongming Co.	D	
29-11	Baimaoling Farm (Shanghai No. 2 LR General Brigade)	Guangde Co. in Anhui province	D[W]	Included Laodong Valve Factory and Brickyard. The kiln workshop has 200 members and profits of 170,000 yuan. The Laodong Valve Factory profits 9.02 million yuan and made 1.6 million foreign exchange. The output value is 30 million yuan yearly in 1980s. Included a women's RTL battalion, produced woolen fabrics.
29-12	Dafeng Farm	Yancheng Pr. in Jiangsu province	D	
29-13	Qingdong Farm	Qingpu Co., Shanghai C.	5,000	
29-14	Shanghai JOD	Shanghai C.	B	
29-15	Shanghai No. 3 LR General Brigade	Shanghai C.	Unknown	
29-16	No. 8 battalion of Shanghai Prison	Shanghai C.	Unknown	
29-17	Shanghai No. 2 RTL	Shanghai C.	C	Farming. Produced beans, wheat, barley, and rape.
29-18	Laodong Steel Pipe Plant (Shanghai No. 7 LRD)	Beixinjin D. in Shanghai C.	2,000	The second class of national enterprise.
29-19	Jiangxi Farm	Shangrao Pr. in Jiangxi province	Unknown	
29-20	Laodong Tool Factory (Shanghai No. 1 LRD)	Yangpu D. Shanghai C.	1,500	The tool with Laodong trademark is famous in the country and internationally.
29-21	Xinsheng Construction Co. (Shanghai No. 9 LRD)	Xuhui D. Shanghai C.	1,000	
29-22	No. 1 Detention Center	Nanshi D. Shanghai C.	Unknown	Most are political convicts.

29-23	No. 2 Detention Center in Shanghai	Sinan street, Shanghai C.	Unknown	Zheng nian, the author of *Life and Death in Shanghai*, was imprisoned here.
29-24	Xinsheng Auto-Parts Plant	Yingao street, Shanghai C.	Unknown	Produced auto body of Daxiang trademark.
29-25	Huangshan Tea & Tree Farm	Taiping Co. in Anhui province	D	Most are FJP.
29-26	Nenjiang Farm	Shexian Co. in Anhui Province	Unknown	Farming and stock raising.
29-27	Fanchang Mining Co.	Fanchang Co. in Anhui province	20,000	Included Yangshan mine, Shunfengshan mines.

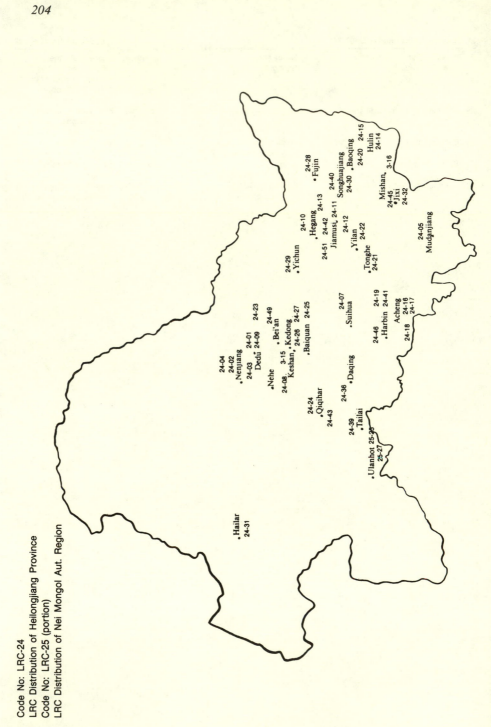

204

Code No: LRC-24
LRC Distribution of Heilongjiang Province
Code No: LRC-25 (portion)
LRC Distribution of Nei Mongol Aut. Region

24. Heilongjiang Province (LRC-24)

No.	Name of LRC	Location	Number	Remarks
24-01	Qixingpao LRD	Nenjiang C.	C	
24-02	Jiatoushan LRD	Nenjiang C.	C	
24-03	No. 7 branch of Nenjiang Farm (Nenjiang LRD)	Nenjiang C.	5,000	
24-04	Shanhe LRD	Nenjiang C.	3,000	
24-05	Mudanjiang RTL	Mudanjiang C.	Unknown	Profits 8.5 million yuan/1988.
24-06	Yong'an LRD	Unknown	Unknown	
24-07	Suihua Prison	Suihua Co.	Unknown	
24-08	Lehe LRD	Nehe Co.	D	
24-09	Longzhen Farm	Dedu Co.	D	
24-10	Hegang Coal Mine	Hegang C.	D	
24-11	Heli LRD	Jiamusi C.	D	
24-12	Jiamusi Farm	Jiamusi C.	D	
24-13	Wutonghe Farm (RTL+LRD)	Hegang C.	30,000	Area: 400 sq. km. growing rice, beans, corn, grapes, and cabbage.
24-14	Mishan Farm	Mishan Co.	25,000	
24-15	Hulin Farm	Hulin Co.	32,000	
24-16	No. 1 Battalion	Yuccheng T. Acheng Co.	D	
24-17	No. 2 Battalion	Daqingshan, Acheng Co.	Unknown	
24-18	No. 3 Battalion	Wanggang, Harbin C.	A	
24-19	No. 4 Battalion	Chongfang, Harbin C.	A	
24-20	Yanwodao LRD	Baoqing Co.	D	
24-21	Tonghe LRD	Tonghe Co.	Unknown	
24-22	Yilan Farm	Yilan Co.	D	
24-23	Shuanghe Farm	Dedu Co.	D	There are several hundred ha. cultivated land
24-24	Qiqihar RTL	Qiqihar C.	Unknown	
24-25	Baiquan Farm	Baiquan Co.	D	
24-26	Keshan Farm	Keshan Co.	D	
24-27	Kedong Farm	Kedong Co.	C	
24-28	Fujin Farm	Fujin Co.	50,000	
24-29	Cuiluan Tree Farm	Yichun Co.	5,000	
24-30	X X Coal Mine	Shuangyashan C.	3,000	
24-31	Hake LRD	Hailar C.	D	
24-32	X X Coal Mine	Jixi C.	B	
24-33	Bijiashan LRD	Unknown	D	
24-34	Xinzhao Prison	Unknown	Unknown	
24-35	Gezhi Prison	Unknown	Unknown	
24-36	Daqing Prison	Daqing C.	A	
24-37	Fenghuangshan LRD	Unknown	Unknown	
24-38	Lianjiangkkou LRD	Unknown	Unknown	
24-39	Tailai LRD	Tailai Co.	C	
24-40	Yuquan LRD	Along Songhuajiang River, Songhuajiang Pr.	D	
24-41	Wanjia RTL	Harbin C.	B	Sewing shop.
24-42	Fulitun RTL	Jiamusi C.	5,000	
24-43	Fularji RTL	Fularji C.	D	
24-44	Huayuan RTL	Unknown	Unknown	
24-45	Jixi LRD	Jixi C.	Unknown	
24-46	Harbin Prison	Harbin C.	Unknown	
24-47	Provincial No. 1 Prison	Unknown	Unknown	
24-48	Huashan LRD	Unknown	Unknown	
24-49	Bei'an Farm	Bei'an Co.	Unknown	
24-50	Yangyuan Farm	Unknown	Unknown	
24-51	Lianjiangkou Farm	Jiamusi C.	Unknown	
24-52	Fenghuangshan LRD	Unknown	Unknown	

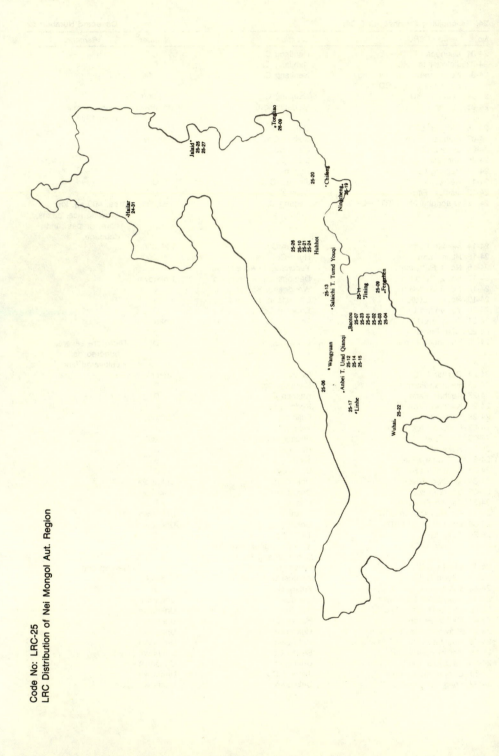

Code No: LRC-25
LRC Distribution of Nei Mongol Aut. Region

25. Nei Mongol (Inner Mongolia) Autonomous Region (LRC-25) **Collected Number: 27**

No.	Name of LRC	Location	Number	Remarks
25-01	X X coal mine	Baotou C.	D	
25-02	X X Construction General Brigade	Baotou C.	D	
25-03	Auto. region No. 6 LRD	Baotou C.	D	
25-04	Auto. region No. 7 LRD	Baotou C.	D	
25-05	Dongtucheng RTL	Unknown	B	
25-06	Langshan LRD	Wangyuan Co.	B	
25-07	Baiyun'ebo Iron Mine	Baiyun'ebo, n. of Baotou C.	D	
25-08	Auto. region No. 1-5 LRD	Unknown	Unknown	
25-09	Fengzhen RTL	Fengzhen Co.	Unknown	
25-10	Xinsheng Brickyard	Huhhot C.	B	
25-11	Jining RTL	Jining C.	B	
25-12	Xinsheng Farm	Anbei T. Urad Qianqi	D	
25-13	Saxian Farm	Salaichi T. Tumd Youqi	Unknown	
25-14	Laomushan Farm	Anbei T. Urad Qianqi	Unknown	
25-15	Anbei Farm	Anbei T. Urad Qianqi	Unknown	
25-16	Delong LRD	Unknown	D	
25-17	Xinhua Farm	Linhe	D	
25-18	Beidahuang LRD	Unknown	D	
25-19	Tumuji RTL	Ningcheng Co.	Unknown	
25-20	Chifeng LRD	Chifeng C.	B	
25-21	Huhhot RTL	Huhhot C.	B	
25-22	Wuhai RTL	Wuhai C.	A	
25-23	Baotou RTL	Baotou C.	B	
25-24	Xinsheng Machinery Factory	Huhhot C.	B	
25-25	Bao'anzhao Farm	Jalaid B., Ulanhot C.	13,000[W]	Area: 22,000 ha. Cultivated land.
25-26	Nei Mongol Prison (Clothing factory)	Southern suburbs of Huhhot C.	Unknown	
25-27	Bao'anzhao JOD	Jalaid B., Ulanhot C.	Unknown	

208

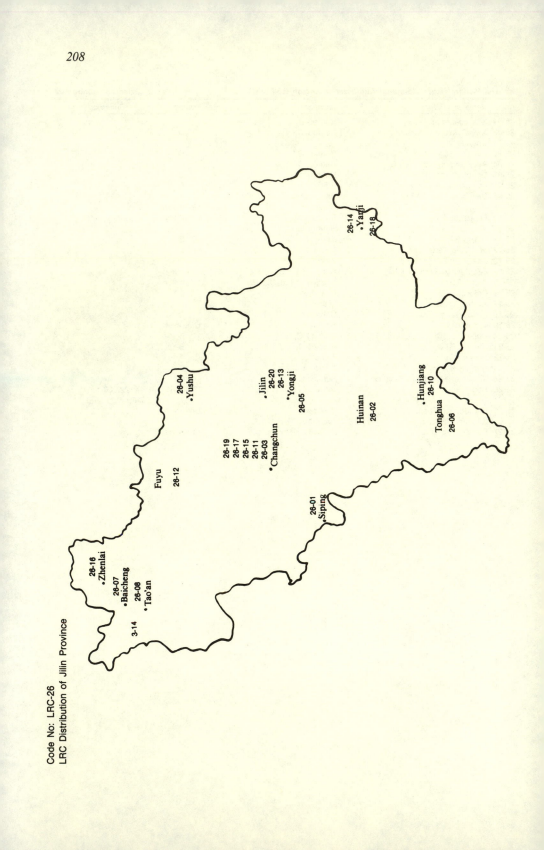

Code No: LRC-26
LRC Distribution of Jilin Province

26. Jilin Province (LRC-26)   **Collected Number: 22**

No.	Name of LRC	Location	Number	Remarks
26-01	Siping LRD	Siping C.	D	
26-02	Huinan LRD	Huinan C.	D	
26-03	Heizhuizi RTL	Changchun C.	Unknown	
26-04	Yushu Farm	Yushu Co.	D	
26-05	Liugang LRD	Yongji Co.	C	
26-06	Tonghua LRD	Shiling, Tonghua Co.	D	
26-07	Baicheng Farm	Baicheng C.	80,000	
26-08	Taohe Farm	Tao'an Co.	75,000	
26-09	Tongliao LRD	Tongliao C.	D	
26-10	Daojiang LRD	Hunjiang C.	D	
26-11	Changchun LRD	Changchun C.	D	
26-12	Fuyu Farm	Fuyu Co.	B	
26-13	Jilin RTL	Jilin C.	B	
26-14	Yanji RTL	Yanji C.	Unknown	
26-15	Tiebei LRD	Changchun C.	B	Produced machinery.
26-16	Zhenlai LR General brigade	Zhenlai Co.	D	Cultivated land: 10,000 ha. Farming and stock raising.
26-17	Changchun RTL	Changchun C.	B	
26-18	Yanbian Chaoxian Auto. Pr. RTL	Yanji C.	A	
26-19	Changchun Prison	Changchun C.	Unknown	Produced shoes.
26-20	Jilin LRD	Jilin C.	Unknown	Produced TWY1-12 automatic electric controller.
26-21	Zhunhua Prison	Unknown	Unknown	
26-22	Changchun Women RTL	Unknown	Unknown	

Code No: LRC-27
LRC Distribution of Liaoning Province

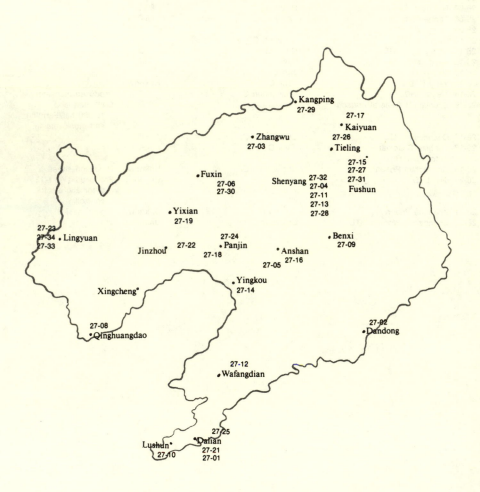

Kangping
27-29

27-17
• Kaiyuan

• Zhangwu   27-26
27-03   • Tieling

27-15
• Fuxin   27-27
27-06   Shenyang 27-32 27-31
27-30   27-04 Fushun
                    27-11
• Yixian   27-13
27-19   27-28

27-23
27-34 • Lingyuan   27-24   • Benxi
27-33   27-22 • Panjin   27-09
        Jinzhou   27-18
                        • Anshan
                    27-05 27-16

Xingcheng•   • Yingkou
                    27-14

27-08   27-02
• Qinghuangdao   • Dandong

            27-12
          • Wafangdian

                27-25
Lushun• •Dalian
27-10   27-21
        27-01

27. Liaoning Province (LRC-27)   Collected Number: 35

No.	Name of LRC	Location	Number	Remarks
27-01	Nanguanling RTL	Dalian C.	Unknown	
27-02	Andong LRD	Dandong C.	A	
27-03	Zhangwu LRD	Zhangwu Co.	Unknown	
27-04	Shenyang RTL	Shenyang C.	B	
27-05	Zhangling Iron Mine	Anshan C.	D	
27-06	X X Coal Mine	Fuxin C.	D	
27-07	Zhaziyao LRD	Unknown	D	
27-08	Qinghuangdao RTL	Qinghuangdao C.	B	
27-09	Benxi RTL (mine)	Benxi C.	4,000	
27-10	Taiyanggou LRD	Lushun C.	B	Hebei Province
27-11	Provincial No. 1 Prison	Shenyang C.	Unknown	
27-12	Wafangdian LRD (Wafangdian Machine Tool Factory)	Wafangdian Co.	2,000	Established in 1952. Output value 2.73 million yuan and profits 7.06 million yuan. The second class of national enterprise. Casting iron plate; Model CJK5112A machine tool exported to Far East. Produced China's first intercontinental ballistic missile's launch plate.
27-13	Masanjia RTL	W. of Shenyang C.	Unknown	
27-14	Yingkou LR General Brigade	Yingkou C.	6,000	Farm.
27-15	X X Coal Mine	Fushun C.	D	
27-16	Anshan Construction Brigade	Anshan C.	A	
27-17	Qinghe Farm	Kaiyuan Co.	A	
27-18	Gaoshanzi Stone-material Mine	Panjin Co.	B	
27-19	Yushu Farm	Yixian Co.	D	
27-20	Xinglongqing LRD	Unknown	Unknown	
27-21	Dalian LRD	Dalian C.	Unknown	
27-22	Jinzhou Prison	Jinzhou C.	3,000	Included zinc-plating factory, 6 battalions.
27-23	Lingyuan Automobile Factory (Lingyuan No. 1 LRD)	Lingyuan Co.	3,000	Established in 1958. Produced automobile parts and automobile instruments. Produced 10,000 "Linghe" trucks in 1989. Permanent capital is 100 million yuan, which is three times as much as Shenyang Auto Factory and same as the Nanjing Auto Factory.
27-24	Panjin LR General Brigade (RTL+LRD+FJP)	Panjin Co.	100,000	
27-25	Dalian RTL	Dalian C.	Unknown	
27-26	Tieling RTL	Tieling C.	A	
27-27	Fushun Prison	Fushun C.	B	
27-28	Longshan RTL	Shenyang C.	A	
27-29	Kangping Farm	Kangping Co.	Unknown	
27-30	Fuxin LRD	Fuxin C.	Unknown	
27-31	Fushun RTL	Fushun C.	Unknown	
27-32	Xinsheng Chemical Plant	Shenyang C.	Unknown	The second class of national enterprise.
27-33	Lingyuan No. 3 LRD	Lingyuan Co.	Unknown	
27-34	Lingyuan No. 2 LRD	Lingyuan Co.	Unknown	
27-35	Dalian Marble Plant	Dalian C.	Unknown	Produced stone plate.

Code No: LRC-28
LRC Distribution of Henan Province

28-24
Anyang

28-29
Puyang

28-11
28-36
Xinxiang

Jiyuan Jiaozuo
28-07 28-15
28-28
Qinyang

28-42
Mianchi 28-23 Zhengzhou Kaifeng
Shanmenxia 28-17 28-38 28-12 28-13
28-22 Luoyang Shenqiu
Linbao 28-14
28-30 Xinzheng 28-08

Taikang
Xuchang 28-09 Yongcheng
28-27 28-25 28-34
Huaiyang
Lushan 28-16 28-26 Shangshui
28-18 Pingdingshan 28-41 Luohe Shangqiu
28-20 28-10
28-21 Shangcai
Runan
Nanyang 28-19
28-05
28-06 Queshan
28-03
Zhengyang
Xixian
28-31 28-04
Xinyang
28-02

28. Henan Province (LRC-28) Collected Number: 43

No.	Name of LRC	Location	Number	Remarks
28-01	Provincial No. 1 Prison	Unknown	4,000	Making paper; sewing; producing electric instruments.
28-02	Xinyang RTL	Xinyang C.	B	
28-03	Queshan Farm	Queshan Co.	D	
28-04	Xiazhuang Farm	Xixian Co.	D	
28-05	Nanyang RTL	Nanyang C.	C	
28-06	Xindian Farm	Nanyang C.	D	
28-07	Hongwuyue Farm	Qinyang Co.	25,000	
28-08	Shangqiu LRD	Shangqiu C.	D	
28-09	Taikang LRD	Taikang Co.	D	
28-10	Shenqiu LRD	Shenqiu Co.	D	
28-11	Xinxiang LRD	Xinxiang C.	D	
28-12	Qiliyan RTL	Zhengzhou C.	B	
28-13	Kaifeng RTL	Kaifeng C.	B	
28-14	Xinzheng LRD	Xinzheng Co.	D	
28-15	X X Coal Mine	Jiaozuo C.	D	
28-16	Pingdingshan Coal Mine (RTL)	Pingdingshan C.	D	
28-17	Mianchi Farm	Mianchi Co.	D	
28-18	Lushan LRD	Lushan Co.	D	
28-19	Runan LRD	Runan Co.	Unknown	
28-20	Luohe RTL	Luohe C.	Unknown	
28-21	Taqiao Farm	Shangcai Co.	Unknown	
28-22	Shanmenxia RTL	Shanmenxia C.	A	
28-23	Luoyang Construction Brigade	Luoyang C.	3,000	
28-24	Anyang LRD	Anyang C.	B	
28-25	Huaiyang LRD	Huaiyang Co.	D	
28-26	Shangshui LRD	Shangshui Co.	D	
28-27	Xuchang Construction Brigade	Xuchang C.	C	
28-28	Jiyuan Farm	Jiyuan Co.	D	
28-29	Puyang LRD	Puyang Co.	D	
28-30	Linbao LRD	Linbao Co.	C	
28-31	Henan Wushan Farm	Zhengyang Co.	Unknown	Hulou company had 200 ha. cultivated land and handed in more than 300,000 yuan profits in 1985.
28-32	Xinxiang RTL	Unknown	Unknown	
28-33	Provincial No. 1 LRD	Unknown	Unknown	
28-34	Mangshan Stone-material Plant	Yongcheng, Shangqiu C.	B	
28-35	Provincial No. 5 Prison	Unknown	Unknown	Most prisoners are women.
28-36	Provincial No. 2 Prison	Xinxiang C.	Unknown	Produced Huanghe X195 diesel engine and won national silver prize.
28-37	Provincial No. 3 LRD	Unknown	Unknown	Farming.
28-38	Provincial No. 5 LRD	Luoyang C.	Unknown	Produced glass.
28-39	Henan Wu'er Farm (RTL)	Unknown	Unknown	
28-40	Provincial No. 6 LRD	Unknown	Unknown	
28-41	Bailou RTL	Pingdingshan C.	Unknown	Established in 1981.
28-42	Xinsheng Brickyard	Mianchi Co.	Unknown	
28-43	Luoyang RTL	Luoyang C.	B	

Appendix 2: Commodities of the Labor Reform Camps of the People's Republic of China as of March 1990

The following list is compiled from official statistics of the U.S. Department of Commerce, "List of Commodities Imported from the People's Republic of China," February 21, 1990. Code numbers of camps are given as LRC-01-07 (see Table A1.1).

01: *Live animals.* Most of the labor reform farms produced; ex. LRC-08-28, LRC-03-11

02: *Meat and edible meat offal.* Most of the labor reform farms produced.

03: *Fish, crustaceans, and aquatic invertebrates.* Most of labor reform farms produced; ex. LRC-03-12, LRC-06-04, LRC-16-07, LRC-22-34.

04: *Dairy Prods; birds eggs; honey; edible animal products; nesoi.* Most of the labor reform farms produced. ex. LRC-03-12.

05: *Products of animal origin, nesoi.* Most of the labor reform farms produced.

06: *Live trees, plants, bulbs etc.; cut flowers, etc.* Most of the Labor Reform Farms produced. ex. LRC-02-103

07: *Edible vegetables and certain roots and tubers.* Most of the labor reform farms produced.

08: *Edible fruit and nuts; citrus fruit or melon peel.* Many labor reform farms produced.

09: *Coffee, tea, maté and spices.* ex. LRC-02-120, LRC-02-132, LRC-02-130, LRC-10-38, LRC-11-31, LRC-11-63, LRC-18-08, LRC-19-03, LRC-29-22

10: *Cereals.* Most of the labor reform farms produced.

11: *Milling products; malt; starch; inulin; wheat gluten.* None found.

12: *Oil seeds, etc.; misc. grain, seed, fruit, plant etc.* Many labor reform farms produced.

13: *Lac; gums, resins and other vegetable sap and extract.* None found.

14: *Vegetable plaiting materials and products nesoi.* None found.

15: *Animal or vegetable fats, oils, etc. and waxes.* Some labor reform farms produced.

16: *Edible preparations of meat, fish, crustaceans, etc.* Many labor reform farms produced.

17: *Sugars and sugar confectionary.* ex. LRC-02-15, LRC-02-116, LRC-02-119, LRC-07-16, LRC-07-27, LRC-11-35, LRC-11-44, LRC-11-63

18: *Cocoa and cocoa preparations.* ex. LRC-11-31, LRC-11-63.

19: *Prepared cereal, flour, starch, or milk; bakers wares.* Many labor reform farms produced.

20: *Prepared vegetables, fruit, nuts, or other plant parts.* Many labor reform farms produced.

21: *Miscellaneous edible preparations.* None found.

22: *Beverages, spirits, and vinegar.* ex. LRC-03-11, LRC-03-12, LRC-11-31, LRC-11-35.

23: *Food industry residues and waste; prepared animal feed.* Some labor reform farms produced.

24: *Tobacco and manufactured tobacco substitutes.* Most of the labor reform farms in northern China produced, ex. Henan, Shandong, and Hebei province.

25: *Salt; sulfur; earth and stone; lime and cement plaster.* ex. LRC-02-27, LRC-02-48, LRC-02-88, LRC-02-90, LRC-02-113, LRC-02-121, LRC-02-123, LRC-05-27, LRC-07-17, LRC-08-03, LRC-10-07, LRC-11-40, LRC-19-03, LRC-27-18

26: *Ores, slag, and ash.* ex. LRC-02-05, LRC-02-27, LRC-03-18, LRC-03-19, LRC-07-18

27: *Mineral fuel, oil, etc.; bitumin substances; mineral wax.* ex. LRC-16-20

28: *Inorganic chemicals; precious and rare-earth metals and radioactive compounds.* ex. LRC-03-02, LRC-03-25, LRC-05-28, LRC-10-05, LRC-10-06, LRC-11-32, LRC-16-25, LRC-27-33

29: *Organic chemicals.* ex. LRC-03-02, LRC-03-25

30: *Pharmaceutical products.* ex. LRC-09-09, LRC-11-11

31: *Fertilizers.* ex. LRC-06-21, LRC-11-04

32: *Tanning and dye ext. etc.; dye, paint, putty, etc.; inks.* None found.

33: *Essential oils, etc.; perfumery, cosmetics etc., preparations.* ex. LRC-01-14

34: *Soap, etc.; waxes, polish, etc.; candles; dental preparations.* ex. LRC-01-14

35: *Albuminoidal substabces; modified starch; glue; enzymes.* None found.

36: *Explosives; pyrotechnics; matches; pyro alloys, etc.* ex. LRC-01-11

37: *Photographic or cinematographic goods.* None found.

38: *Miscellaneous chemical products.* None found.

39: *Plastics and articles thereof.* ex. LRC-03-09, LRC-05-28, LRC-10-07, LRC-19-23

40: *Rubber and articles thereof.* ex. LRC-11-29, LRC-11-63, LRC-26-19

41: *Raw hides and skins (no furskins) and leather.* ex. LRC-16-12

42: *Leather articles; saddlery, etc.; handbags, etc.; gut articles.* None found.

43: *Furskins and artificial fur; manufactures thereof.* None found.

44: *Wood and articles of wood; wood charcoal.* Some labor reform farms produced.

45: *Cork and articles of cork.* None found.

46: *Straw goods, esparto, etc.; basketware and wickerwork.* Some labor reform farms in Shandong Province.

47: *Pulp of wood, etc.; waste, etc. of paper and paperboard.* None found.

48: *Paper and paperboard articles (including paper pulp products).* ex. LRC-07-18, LRC-11-35, LRC-28-01

49: *Printed books, newspaper, etc.; manuscripts, etc.* ex. LRC-03-08, LRC-05-28, LRC-29-05

50: *Silk, including yarns and woven fabric thereof.* ex. LRC-19-25

51: *Wool and animal hair, including yarns and woven fabric.* ex. LRC-05-28

52: *Cotton, including yarn and woven fabric thereof.* Most of the labor reform farms in northern China produced.

53: *Vegetable textile fibers nesoi; vegetable fiber and paper yarns and woven fabrics.* ex. LRC-11-07

54: *Artifical filaments, including yarns and woven fabrics.* ex. LRC-19-03

55: *Artifical staple fibers, including yarns and woven fabrics.* None found.

56: *Wadding, felt, etc.; spun yarn; twine, rope, etc.* None found.

57: *Carpets and other textile floor coverings.* None found.

58: *Specialty woven fabrics; tufted fabrics; lace; tapestries, etc.* None found.

59: *Impregnated, etc. textile fabrics; textile articles for industry.* ex. LRC-01-12, LRC-02-26, LRC-02-112, LRC-05-18, LRC-09-01, LRC-19-03, LRC-19-25

60: *Knitted or crocheted fabrics.* ex. LRC-03-09, LRC-23-01

61: *Apparel articles and accessories, knit or crocheted.* ex. LRC-25-26, LRC-27-13, LRC-28-01

62: *Apparel articles and accessoories, not knit, etc.* ex. LRC-02-110, LRC-14-01, LRC-16-12, LRC-23-28, LRC-24-41

63: *Textile art nesoi; needlecraft sets; textile clothing.* None found.

64: *Footware, gaiters, etc., and parts thereof.* ex. LRC-02-95, LRC-03-09, LRC-10-10, LRC-14-01, LRC-26-19

65: *Headgear and parts thereof.* None found.

66: *Umbrellas, walking sticks, riding crops, etc. parts.* None found.

67: *Prepared feathers, down, etc.; artificial flowers; hair articles.* None found.

68: *Articles of stone, plaster, cement, asbestos, mica, etc.* None found.

69: *Ceramic products.* ex. LRC-01-09, LRC-01-23, LRC-02-13, LRC-02-90, LRC-02-95, LRC-02-91, LRC-02-111, LRC-07-18, LRC-07-20, LRC-07-29, LRC-10-38, LRC-11-31, LRC-11-38, LRC-11-51, LRC-11-54, LRC-18-11, LRC-18-19, LRC-19-23

70: *Glass and glassware.* ex. LRC-05-27, LRC-19-23, LRC-28-38, LRC-29-01

71: *Natural pearls, precious and semiprecious stones, precious metals, etc.; coins.* None found.

72: *Iron and steel.* ex. LRC-02-26, LRC-02-121, LRC-07-05, LRC-11-53, LRC-11-54, LRC-11-66, LRC-25-27

73: *Articles of iron or steel.* ex. LRC-09-08, LRC-03-20, LRC-16-07, LRC-29-19

74: *Copper and articles thereof.* ex. LRC-01-37, LRC-17-11, LRC-18-22

75: *Nickel and articles thereof.* None found.

76: *Aluminum and articles thereof.* ex. LRC-11-23

78: *Lead and articles thereof.* ex. LRC-06-09, LRC-11-37, LRC-11-38, LRC-11-61, LRC-18-23

79: *Zinc and articles thereof.* ex. LRC-18-23

80: *Tin and articles thereof.* ex. LRC-02-11, LRC-07-10, LRC-07-11

81: *Base metals nesoi; cermets; articles thereof.* ex. LRC-02-03, LRC-02-07, LRC-02-52, LRC-07-04, LRC-08-15, LRC-09-03, LRC-15-13, LRC-16-27, LRC-18-36

82: *Tools, cutlery, etc. of base metals and parts thereof.* ex. LRC-03-01, LRC-23-01, LRC-23-28, LRC-23-31, LRC-29-22

83: *Miscellaneous articles of base metals.* None found.

84: *Nuclear reactors, boilers, machinery, etc.; parts.* ex. LRC-01-17, LRC-01-35, LRC-03-04, LRC-03-05, LRC-10-05, LRC-11-09, LRC-11-06, LRC-11-34, LRC-12-12, LRC-12-13, LRC-14-01, LRC-15-21, LRC-16-12, LRC-17-14, LRC-18-12, LRC-18-13, LRC-18-25, LRC-19-03, LRC-19-27, LRC-19-28, LRC-20-25, LRC-20-26, LRC-21-23, LRC-21-39, LRC-22-17, LRC-23-38, LRC-25-24, LRC-26-15, LRC-27-12, LRC-29-7, LRC-29-11

85: *Electric machinery, etc.; sound equipment; tv equipment; parts.* ex. LRC-05-01, LRC-08-08, LRC-02-82, LRC-03-12, LRC-11-44, LRC-14-06, LRC-21-42, LRC-26-20, LRC-28-01, LRC-28-36

86: *Railway or tramway stock etc; traffic signal equipment.* None found.

87: *Vehicles, except railway or tramway, and parts etc.* ex. LRC-01-07, LRC-08-02, LRC-08-24, LRC-11-34, LRC-18-34, LRC-21-05, LRC-22-10, LRC-11-37, LRC-27-23, LRC-29-26

88: *Aircraft, spacecraft, and parts thereof.* None found.

89: *Ships, boats, and floating structures.* None found.

90: *Optic, photo, etc., medical or surgical instruments, etc.* ex. LRC-03-03

91: *Clocks and watches and parts thereof.* None found.

92: *Musical instruments; parts and accessories thereof.* None found.

93: *Arms and ammunition; parts and accessories thereof.* None found.

94: *Furniture; bedding, etc.; lamps nesoi etc. prefab. bedding.* None found.

95: *Toys, games, and sports equipment; parts and accessories.* None found.

96: *Miscellaneous manufactured articles.* ex. LRC-29-05

97: *Works of art, collectors' pieces and antiques.* None found.

98: *Special classification provisions.* None found.

99: *Special import provisions, including low value est.* None found.

Appendix 3: Three Sample *Laogaidui*

1. Qinghe Farm

- Public name: State Operated Qinghe Farm of Beijing.
- Internal name: No.1 Labor Reform Camp Detachment of Beijing

The author served at this camp twice, first from June 1961–June 1962 and then from August 1968–December 1969.

Location

Qinghe Farm is located in Ninghe county, Tianjin Municipality, approximately 120 km southeast of Beijing and 30 km northeast of Tianjin city. The farm is about 20 km long and 15 km wide, oriented east to west, and the Chaobei River, Jingzhong River, and Jiyun River all flow through it. It is situated at 117°65' east latitude and 39°28' north longitude.

Brief History

Before 1949, the Japanese occupation forces had set up a detention center west of the Chadian Railway Station (on the line from Beijing to Shenyang). After the Japanese surrendered, the Chinese government used these buildings as a prison, but for only a few hundred prisoners. It was a large piece of marshlands beside the railway.

In 1949, when the CCP took control, Qinghe Farm started a period of great development, divided into four phases.

First Phase (1955–1957). In 1950, several tens of thousands of landlord class elements and military officers and officials of the Kuomintang government from Beijing and Tianjin were escorted as counter-revolutionaries to the farm for forced labor. Under armed guard, sunk knee-deep in the marshland mud, they were forced to dig channels and build roads, brick walls, and jails for their shelter as well as to plant the rice for their food. These counter-revolutionaries were the "founding members" of Qinghe Farm. In less than ten years, most of them had died. In 1955–1956, another two groups were added, some who had been arrested in 1956 in the Eliminate Counter-revolutionaries Movement, some who were purged from the government and transferred to the farm. So, before 1958, about

Headquarters of Qinghe Farm, located at center of the farm. The signboard on right reads "Beijing No. 1 LRD"; the one in the middle reads "Beijing Qinghe Farm."

This is a reduction of a satellite photograph focused on Qinghe Farm. (Purchased from Earth Observation Satellite Company, Maryland, USA, in August 1989.) The photograph size is 4 feet × 6 feet; the area covered is 60 kilometers × 60 kilometers. (UL CNR NO393802/E1171341; UR CNR NO391812/E1173053; LL CNR NO390650/E1170152; UR CNR NO385811/E1174841) Lutai Farm (LRC-05-27) also shows in this photo. It is about 20 kilometers north of Qinghe Farm.

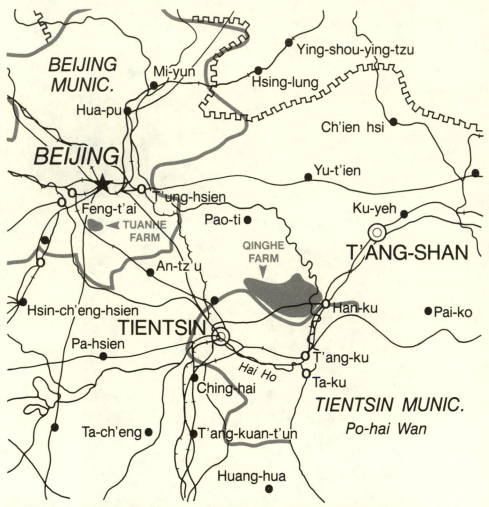

MAP A3.1 Location of Qinghe Farm and Tuanhe Farm in Beijing-Tianjin Area

80–90 percent of the prisoners in Qinghe Farm were political counter-revolutionaries.

Second Phase (1957–1965). In 1957, the CCP introduced the policy of reeducation through labor and launched the Anti-Rightist Movement. Thousands of
people were arrested, including several thousand rightists from Beijing. The farm
expanded to the west, creating a new area—the "west wasteland." This was the
second major expansion of Qinghe Farm.

In 1958, in coordination with the nationwide Great Leap Forward Movement,
Qinghe Farm was given over to labor production, and the number of prisoners
increased greatly.

From 1959–1961, because of nationwide starvation, the continued rule of the
CCP was in peril; to maintain the regime, the CCP rulers arrested thousands and
thousands of people as "thought reactionaries" and "active counter-revolutionaries" and removed them to Qinghe farm. At that time, all sections of the Farm
were full of prisoners, totaling more than one hundred thousand. This was the
"golden age" of Qinghe Farm.

Third Phase (1966–1978). During the Cultural Revolution, when the whole of
mainland Chinese society was experiencing the "red terror," the Red Guards and
the CCP arranged for a system of detention centers where prisoners could be
detained without the need for any sort of legal procedure. This obviated the need
for the LRC. Therefore, Qinghe Farm's population stagnated.

In 1969, on the orders of Lin Biao, Qinghe Farm was quiet for a time. A
number of policemen and prisoners were transferred to other camps. In the next
year, 1970, when Lin died, the order was canceled and the policemen returned,
but the prisoners remained in the new camps to which they had been transferred,
most of which were located in other provinces. Before long, however, new prisoners
began refilling Qinghe Farm.

Fourth Phase (1978–1988). When Deng came to power, Qinghe Farm entered
a new period, its second "golden age."

Because Deng's four cardinal principles are based on the *laogaidui* system,
since 1978 Qinghe Farm has developed significantly both in economic production
and in number of prisoners.

Organization

The farm includes five different groups of people, as follows:

1. Convicted labor reform (*laogai*): Approximately 20,000 are housed in
   several sections in the eastern area of the farm.
2. Reeducation Through Labor prisoners (*laojiao*): Approximately 20,000 are
   housed in several sections in the western area of the farm.
3. Forced job placement personnel (*jiuye*): approximately 25,000 are distributed throughout all sections of the farm.
4. The families of the FJP personnel: approximately 15,000. *Jiuye* are also
   called "ex-prisoners." Although they will never be permitted to live anywhere but the *laogaidui,* they are now given certain minimal privileges.
   Since the late 1950s, the authorities of the farm have allowed some women

family members to live on the farm as ordinary workers. Their children then grow up and become workers on the farm. Because they are offspring of prisoners, these children constitute on entire group of second-class citizens.

5. The policemen and their families: approximately 15,000–20,000 people. Most members of police families work as accountants, engineers, jailers, clerks of banks or shops, salesmen, truck drivers, managers, teachers, etc.

The Farm is divided into more than twenty-five sections, as follows:

- No. 1 section (He-dong No. 1 battalion)
- No. 2 section (Nan-chang No. 2 battalion)
- No. 3 section (Bei-chang No. 3 battalion)
- No. 4 section (Cha-dian Dong-cun)
- No. 5 section (Cha-dian Xi-cun)
- No. 6 section (Qian-jin Bei-chang)
- No. 7 section (Qian-jin Nan-chang)
- No. 8 section (Yu-jia-lin Dong-cun)
- No. 9 section (Yu-jia-lin Xi-cun)
- No. 10 section (He-xi No. 1 battalion)
- No. 581 section (western wasteland)
- No. 582 section (western wasteland)
- No. 583 section (western wasteland)
- No. 584 section (western wasteland)
- No. 585 section (western wasteland)
- Qinghe Mechanical Factory
- Qinghe Paper Mill
- Qinghe Knitting Mill
- Qinghe Grain Mill
- Qinghe Brick Factory
- Qinghe Ceramic Plant
- Qinghe Construction Company
- Qinghe Dairy Products Factory

After forty years, the marshland has been developed into a system of agricultural lands with its own reservoirs, channels, irrigation and drainage network, road, forest belt, orchards, fish ponds, and about a hundred thousand *mu* of farmland. In order to increase profits, many industrial factories have also been built, with a total production value per year of more than a hundred million *yuan*. The forced labor products from Qinghe Farm Enterprises not only sell to the domestic market but some products such as grapes, ceramics, and knitwear are sold on the international market.

Wu ke is the center of Qinghe Farm. There are many buildings: administrative offices, headquarters, a post office, a school, a department store, a cinema, a restaurant, and a hospital. *Wu ke* resembles the downtown district of a city.

The rear view of No. 585 section of Qinghe Farm, recently named the Beijing Qinghe Cultivated Shrimp Yard.

Each section of the labor camp has a prison compound surrounded by a high brick wall topped with electric wire. The CLR and RTL prisoners are locked in the compound barracks. During the day they are escorted by the policemen out to labor. The FJP live outside the brick wall in a compound dormitory. Beside the prison, there is a building complex for the policemen and their families. In the police complex is a school, a small department store, clinic, and public bath.

2. Tuanhe Farm

- Public name: Local State-operated Tuanhe Farm of Beijing.
- Internal name: Beijing Reeducation Through Labor Camp.

Location

Daxing County, in the vicinity of Huang Cun, Beijing. Approximately 7,000 *mu* of tilled land, 39°40′ north, 116°25′ east.

Brief History

The farm was started in the 1950s. At first it was principally for CLR prisoners. In the first half of the 1960s it contained five units:

The author shown at Tuanhe Road, which runs east-west across Tuanhe Farm (Beijing RTL Camp).

- No. 1 Battalion: CLR prisoners, approximately 2,500 people
- No. 2 Battalion: FJP and RTL prisoners (rightists), approximately 3,000 people
- No. 3 Battalion: Juvenile offenders, approximately 2,000 people
- Chicken farm: FJP personnel and female prisoners, approximately 500 people
- Agricultural Equipment Factory: Predominantly FJP personnel, approximately 500 people.
- Recently, it contained seven RTL battalions and one detention center.

Because of its proximity to Beijing, the farm does not have a complete system of social services and education. Battalion No. 2 specializes in growing grapes, pears, strawberries, and apples, and in breeding milk cows and muskrats (for their pelts). Some of these products are sold on the international market. For instance, in 1965, 40 million kg of grapes were exported to Hong Kong and Japan. Now the grapes are used to make Dynasty wine.

Battalions No. 1 and No. 3 specialize in planting rice paddies and also maintain many fish ponds as well as cattle, pigs, chickens, and ducks. The rice is grown to supply high-level cadres and for export.

At one time Tuanhe Farm had a section for police dog training for the Beijing Public Security Department. Tuanhe Farm contains a resort for high-level cadres from the Beijing Public Security System. Attached to the farm is a base for cadres who have been demoted ("sent down"). Before the Cultural Revolution, a large group of members of the Kuomintang and public security cadres with "unstable thought" were sent there. In the Cultural Revolution, the labor reform prisoners, rightists, and juvenile delinquents were moved to make room for detainees.

Tuanhe Farm is state-operated, and in 1958 it was selected by the State Council of the PRC as one of forty model "progressive red banner units." The reasons given were: The farm was well planned; labor production was effective; production administration had been perfected; high profits were submitted to the government; it had high-yield crops; etc. Units selected as red banner units usually have some model workers recorded in government documents or in the newspaper. But because the Tuanhe Farm was made up completely of prisoners, this red banner unit only had a few model administrators and no model workers.

3. Wangzhuang Coal Mine

- Public name: Local State-operated Wangzhuang Coal Mine of Shanxi province
- Internal name: No. 4 Independent Labor Reform Detachment of Shanxi Province.

Location

Linfen prefecture in Shanxi Province, in Huoxian County on the Nandong bu railway (Taiyuan to Fanglindu) four kilometers east of the Wangzhuang station, 36°32′ north, 111°45′ east.

Historical Development

The mine was started in 1958. Before 1969, it was composed of approximately 2,500–4,000 labor reform prisoners. On the side it developed high-quality soft coal and smelting. In its highest year of production it produced 400,000 tons of coal. It makes use of tunnels and inclined shafts. The mine developed from manual transport to half-mechanized production. Wangzhuang also constructed a large group of factory buildings, supervisory buildings, and residential halls.

In 1969, except for FJP personnel, all labor reform prisoners were transferred. In 1969, 1,000 FJP personnel were transferred in from the Qinghe Farm of Beijing. Approximately 2,000 FJP personnel were then formed into a labor reform independent detachment to continue mining coal. Its annual production was approximately 250,000 tons.

After 1975, because the shallow "two meters of coal" had already been dug out, the mine was converted to a local, state-operated electrical machinery factory. However, because of its limited technological capacity (only one technician from the Kuomintang period and one college graduate prisoner), in addition to the poor quality of its products and equipment, there were many difficulties. Later, in 1978, because a number of people were "rehabilitated" and left the labor reform unit, the situation became even more difficult and production of electrical machinery was halted.

Since 1980, when a large group of prisoners were transferred in and capital was provided for the development of deep "six meters of coal" mines, annual production returned to 400,000 tons.

Labor conditions were extremely poor. Work-related injuries occurred periodically. Silicosis was common. The mines lacked water and what water there was was of poor quality.

At present, the mine is made up of 500 CLR prisoners. Three hundred FJP personnel have also been assigned to the mine to continue the excavation of coal.

In the 1970s, nine squadrons of FJP personnel—approximately 2,000 people—came under the jurisdiction of this independent detachment. They are organized as follows:

- Company 1: Responsible for coal transport in the mines
- Company 2: Responsible for digging in the mines
- Company 3: Responsible for machinery and electrical equipment in the mines
- Company 4: Responsible for trails, ventilation, and safety in the mines
- Company 5: Responsible for development in the mines
- Company 6: Responsible for excavation of coal
- Company 7: Machine repair factory
- Company 8: Construction and brick manufacturing
- Company 9: Responsible for loading coal onto trains and maintaining the vegetable gardens—fifty female FJP personnel.

Appendix 4: Volvo-Chinter Case

On July 8, 1989, the Brussels-based company Chinter-Belgium wrote a letter to Sweden's Volvo automobile corporation, announcing, "We are representing Chinese Reform of Criminals bureaus of all the provinces along the coast of China. We heard [sic] that your esteemed firm has intention to establish factories in Asia. All the bureau can provide many existing factories for your choice on rent basis. They have also many lands to rent. Besides they can provide large numbers of criminals who received already basic technical training as very cheap labors on lease basis. The number of labors and the security are fully guaranteed. We are ready to show you all the relative information." The president of this company is Charles Chi, who is of Chinese extraction. Regardless of the background of this company or Mr. Chi, this letter illustrates the following very clearly:

1. The CCP's LRP system is economically and technologically very developed and has a central place in the socialist economy of the PRC. This is an achievement that no other system of forced labor or concentration camps has been able to achieve.
2. Under the influence of Deng Xiaoping's economic reforms, the LRCs are entering the international market.
3. The CCP is seemingly indifferent to international public opinion concerning human rights.

The *Hong Kong Standard* of August 11, 1989, reported on the specific conditions that Mr. Chi offered Volvo:

The prisoners would be paid around one-third of the going Chinese labor rate. The average Chinese worker makes about US $40 (HK $312) a month. Security guards would patrol the factory to ensure discipline and safety, he said. But he did not think pro-democracy campaigners jailed after the Tiananmen Square massacre on June 4 would find their way onto Western-style production lines, as "priority has to be given to those who have been inside longer." He said the prisoners would get the most out of the scheme. "Sooner or later they must be returned to society. They will do so not only with money but a skill." . . . Mr. Chi said . . . China is also proposing to cut investor's potential costs by letting them redevelop vacant factory space rather than obliging them to build from scratch.

Volvo rejected the offer, although the deal would have cost them only one-fifth of what a plant in Europe would cost. The main reason given was that Volvo is concerned about "human rights" and is not willing to "borrow" prison laborers.

Was Chinter's offer merely a lot of hot air? According to the author's research, the CCP's LRCs definitely have the ability to produce automobiles on a large scale; the LRCs listed below are only the few that the author is aware of:

- Shanxi Province's Fenhe Automotive Factory (Provincial No. 3 Prison, LRC-01-07), which produces the Liberation brand truck
- Hunan Province's Heavy Truck Factory (Provincial No. 2 Prison, LRC-08-02), which in 1987 produced 3,000 of the HN150 model 8-ton capacity trucks
- Hunan Province's Xinmin Automotive Parts Factory (LRC-08-24), which produces automobile parts
- Szechuan Province's Pengan No. 91 Factory (Pengan Prison, LRC-18-34), which produces high-quality automotive parts
- Linyuan Automotive Factory (Liaoning Province No. 1 Labor Reform Branch, LRC-27-26), which produces the Linyuanhe brand 4-ton capacity truck as well as automotive instruments and parts. It has already assembled 500 automobiles for the Japanese company Isuzu
- Shanghai's Xinsheng Automotive Parts Factory (Shanghai Municipality, LRC-29-24), which specializes in producing auto bodies.
- Chaohu Automobile Factory (Anhui Province, LRC-22-10)
- Jianghuai Automobile Factory (Anhui Province, LRC-22-37)
- Lanzhou Bus Plant (Gansu Province, LRC-12-11)

Appendix 5: A List of Nine Industrial Labor Reform Enterprises That Have Attained the Standard of National Second-Level Enterprises

Laogaidui Name	Code # Population	Location	Remarks
Xingsheng Chemical Factory *laogai + jiuye*	LRC-27-32 unknown	Shengyang City, Liaoning prov.	Chemical products.
Wafangdian Machine Tool *laogai + jiuye*	LRC-27-12 2,000	Fuxian County, Liaoning prov.	Established 1952. Products: cast iron plate; CJK112A lathe; set-off plate of 1st intercontinental missile. Output value 27.23 million/1986, profits 7.06 million.
Shengjian Graphite Factory Provincial No. 1 RTL camp	LRC-21-06 unknown	Beishu, Jinan City, Shandong prov.	Products: silicon; carbon bar; graphite moderated reactor; hardened fireclay (exported to Japan and Pakistan).
Shengjian Basan Machinery Factory Provincial No. 3 Prison	LRC-21-39 3,000	Waifang City, Shandong prov.	Products: air compressors; chemical fertilizer equip., spinning and weaving equip. (exported).
Laodong Steel Pipe Plant No. 7 LRD	LRC-29-19 2,000	Beixinjin, Shanghai City	Products: special steel pipe (exported).
Xuzhou Forging Machine Tool Factory	LRC-23-38 unknown	Xuzhou City, Jiangsu prov.	Products: machine tools.
Wuyi Machinery Factory	LRC-20-26 unknown	Zhejiang prov.	Products: unknown.
Wulin Machinery Factory *laogai + jiuye*	LRC-20-25 unknown	Hangzhou City, Zhejiang prov.	Products: unknown.
Daizhuang Coal Mine *laogai + jiuye*	LRC-21-44 3,000	Weishang Co., Shandong prov.	Established 1984. Coal: 70,000 T/1985; 311,000 T/1988; profits 4.8 million.

According to official CCP information as of 1988, a total of twenty-four Labor Reform Enterprises should have attained the standard of national second-level enterprises.

About the Author

Ted Slingerland

Hongda Harry Wu was born in Shanghai in 1937, one of eight children of a local bank manager, and grew up in Shanghai's international settlement. He was baptized as a Catholic at age thirteen and attended a Catholic high school, St. Francis College, which was later closed down by the CCP as part of its efforts to force Chinese Catholics to break ties with the Vatican.

Accepted by Beijing College of Geology in 1955, despite his bourgeois background, Mr. Wu excelled at baseball and generally avoided politics. At this time the CCP began its Let a Hundred Flowers Bloom and a Hundred Schools of Thought Contend Movement, which encouraged the people to offer helpful criticisms of the Party without fear of reprisal; Mr. Wu was urged by a female Party secretary to voice his suggestions. Reluctant at first, Mr. Wu finally offered a few criticisms, including his opinion that the Soviet invasion of Hungary in 1956 was true to socialist internationalism but in violation of international law; that the CCP had been responsible for the deaths of many innocent people during the political movement of 1955; and that the Communist Party at times treated people as second- or third-class citizens.

Once people overcame the natural fear of voicing personal opinions, the criticisms and comments being published in state organ publications grew into a flood as people gave vent to resentments built up over many years. As this tide of resentment grew and became increasingly vocal, the CCP began to feel the Hundred Flowers Movement had gone too far, and a backlash resulted. Thousands of intellectuals were denounced as counter-revolutionary rightists. Mr. Wu's innocent remarks put him in this category, which included as many as one million people. As this huge number of people could not all be imprisoned at once, only high-level rightists were incarcerated immediately; others, like Mr. Wu, were merely placed under investigation.

In 1957, during the Anti-Rightist Campaign, Mr. Wu was formally given a "rightist cap," mainly because he refused to acknowledge his guilt, insisting that the Party had invited him to speak out and that he was only following Party wishes. His rightist label caused Mr. Wu to be socially ostracized. In 1958 his father was also labeled a rightist, his salary was reduced, and the family possessions were gradually sold off to pay basic living expenses.

At this time Mr. Wu already had made the decision to try to escape from the PRC, but on April 27, 1960, he was arrested as a rightist and sentenced to life due to his "poor attitude" (i.e., refusal to admit guilt).

He was first sentenced to Bei Yuan Chemical Factory, a dangerous factory lacking the safety devices a regular plant provides its workers. Acid baths had no splash guards, so workers' clothing was ragged and their bodies always burned. Workers' hands were seared as they had to scoop out spent acid without a pail. The work schedule was divided into two shifts of twelve hours each.

In September of 1960, after many accidents, Mr. Wu was expelled from the plant and sent back to study class to await another assignment. This was in the midst of the Three Years of Natural Disasters, 1959–1961. Millions across the nation were starving, reduced to eating insects, snakes, rodents, tree bark, roots, and grass. Prisoners were packed together like sardines, each allotted only a sixty-centimeter-wide space in which to lie down, stand, or sit. Rations consisted of two steamed corn buns a day. During this period Mr. Wu suffered severe weight loss and mental and emotional depression but at the same time learned how to survive in prison—how to fight, how to steal.

On October 23, 1960, Mr. Wu was assigned to Yingmen Iron Mine, north of Beijing, where he endured severe cold and survived on coarse cornmeal buns and whatever raw cabbage he could steal. This was a very difficult period of time all over the PRC; there was little food even for the guards, and the mines were not worked as everyone was too weak from hunger. The situation was much the same at Xihongshan Iron Mine, where Mr. Wu was subsequently transferred. Finally, in May 1961 he was transferred to Qinghe Farm.

Qinghe Farm was enormous, a veritable county unto itself consisting mainly of reclaimed marshland along the railway from Tianjin to the northeast. Formerly wasteland, Qinghe was developed by convict labor into a vast agricultural complex that produced fruit, pigs, livestock, milk, and wine and possessed maintenance shops, a TV-part factory, a battery-powered car factory, a ceramics factory, and a paper mill. When Mr. Wu first arrived at Qinghe the country was still in the midst of the great famine of 1959–1961; although prison authorities tried to provide the prisoners with food to keep them from revolting, many of Mr. Wu's fellow convicts died of starvation, and he himself came very close to death. He managed to survive by digging up small bits of carrots left in a frozen field.

In June of 1962 Mr. Wu was transferred to Tuanhe Farm in Taxin County, Beijing. There he got into trouble for being the leader of a small group of prisoners who managed to secretly mail a letter to Chairman Mao protesting the conditions in the LRC. Put into solitary confinement for eleven days in a 6 foot × 3 foot × 3 foot bare cement cell for refusing to reveal the names of those in his group, he came very close to starving to death, kept alive only by his captors' force-feeding him through a plastic tube inserted in his nose.

Mr. Wu was interned at Tuanhe Farm for four years, then transferred back to Qinghe Farm and then to Wangzhung Coal Mine in Shanxi Province. He weathered the insanity of the Cultural Revolution and eventually had his "rightist cap" removed. In his new classification as an FJP worker he remained at the Shanxi Labor Reform Coal Mine for nine years, from 1969 to 1979.

With Deng Xiaoping's assumption of power a wave of reform began; in 1979 it was announced that the 1957 Anti-Rightist Movement had been "necessary" but perhaps a bit exaggerated. In this year, nineteen years after he was first confined to the *laogaidui,* Mr. Wu was released.

Accepted to a post as a university lecturer, he found himself working side by side with Party members who had denounced him as a rightist nineteen years earlier. In his own words, "I tried to tuck my tail tightly between my legs and start my university teacher's life," but this was not to be. The death of his brother in 1981 at the hands of the Beijing Police Department hardened his resolve to follow his elderly father's wishes and go to the United States where his older sister lived. His application for a passport for study in the United States was long denied because of a suit he had brought against the Beijing government in connection with his brother's death. In 1985, however, he managed to obtain a passport and came to the United States as a visiting scholar with a J-1 visa at the invitation of the University of California at Berkeley's Department of Civil Engineering.

Since this time Mr. Wu has been focusing all of his energy on fulfilling a promise he made to himself in an oxcart leaving #586, the mass graveyard stretching across the fields behind Qinghe Farm—to reveal to the world the true nature of China's *laogaidui* system in the hope that one day it will take its place in history beside Treblinka and Dachau.

About the Book

In this original and evocative work, Hongda Harry Wu reveals the hidden world of the *laogaidui*—the PRC's labor reform camps—to the Western reader. Wu, himself a survivor of nineteen years in the camps, takes the reader through the harsh landscape found there. He thoroughly explains their ideological origins, complex structure, and living conditions—which the author claims are approached only by the Nazi concentration camps and the Soviet Gulag. What makes the PRC's *laogaidui* unique, according to Wu, is the essential contribution to China's GNP of the commodities produced by the prisoners and the concomitant indispensability to the nation's economic health. The author bolsters the text with a rich compilation of photographs, charts, and maps that reflect his exhaustive research and personal history in the camps. This book provides a comprehensive view of the grim reality of the labor camps, presenting a rare glimpse into the inner workings of the PRC.

Index